# First World War
## and Army of Occupation
# War Diary
## France, Belgium and Germany

63 (ROYAL NAVAL) DIVISION
188 Infantry Brigade
Anson Battalion
1 June 1916 - 30 April 1919

WO95/3111/1

The Naval & Military Press Ltd
www.nmarchive.com
**Published in association with The National Archives**

Published by

The Naval & Military Press Ltd

Unit 10 Ridgewood Industrial Park,

Uckfield, East Sussex,

TN22 5QE England

Tel: +44 (0) 1825 749494

www.naval-military-press.com

www.nmarchive.com

*This diary has been reprinted in facsimile from the original. Any imperfections are inevitably reproduced and the quality may fall short of modern type and cartographic standards.*

# Contents

| Document type | Place/Title | Date From | Date To |
|---|---|---|---|
| Heading | WO95/3111 (1) | | |
| Heading | Anson Bn R.N. Divn. Jun 1916-Apr 1919. | | |
| Heading | War Diary-Volume III Of Anson Battn. From 1st August To 31st August (incl) | | |
| Heading | War Diary Of 1st Anson Battn R.N. Divn. From 1st June 1916 To 30th June 1916. | | |
| War Diary | Airaines | 01/06/1916 | 01/06/1916 |
| War Diary | Barlin | 02/06/1916 | 11/06/1916 |
| War Diary | Lorette Spur | 12/06/1916 | 12/06/1916 |
| War Diary | Barlin | 13/06/1916 | 13/06/1916 |
| War Diary | La Comte | 14/06/1916 | 19/06/1916 |
| War Diary | Estree-Cauchie | 19/06/1916 | 30/06/1916 |
| Miscellaneous | Appendix A 1st June 1916 Officers of 1st Anson for RND | 01/06/1916 | 01/06/1916 |
| Heading | War Diary Of Anson Battn From 1st July 1916 To 31st July 1916 Volume 2 | | |
| War Diary | Estree-Cauchie | 01/07/1916 | 13/07/1916 |
| War Diary | Hersin | 14/07/1916 | 14/07/1916 |
| War Diary | Angres Section | 14/07/1916 | 21/07/1916 |
| War Diary | Angres 1 | 21/07/1916 | 26/07/1916 |
| War Diary | Angres Section | 27/07/1916 | 28/07/1916 |
| War Diary | Angres | 29/07/1916 | 31/07/1916 |
| War Diary | Angres 1. | 31/07/1916 | 01/08/1916 |
| Operation(al) Order(s) | Operation Order No 1 By Lieut. Col. F.J. Saunders D.S.O. R.M.L.I. Commanding Anson Battn Appendix A | 18/07/1916 | 18/07/1916 |
| Operation(al) Order(s) | Operation Order No 2., By Lieut Colonel F.J. Saunders D.S.O. R.M.L.I. Commanding Anson Bn R.N.D. Appendix B. | 19/07/1916 | 19/07/1916 |
| Miscellaneous | No. 4 Lieut. Col. F.J. Saunders D.S.O., R.M.L.I. Commanding Anson Bn. 1. Appendix C | 24/07/1916 | 24/07/1916 |
| Operation(al) Order(s) | Operation Order No. 5 By Lieut. Col. F.J. Saunders, D.S.O., R.M.L.I. Commanding Anson Bn. Appendix D | 28/07/1916 | 28/07/1916 |
| Operation(al) Order(s) | Operation Order No. 6. By Lieut Col. F.J. Saunders, D.S.O., R.M.L.I. Commanding Anson Bn 63rd (R.N.) Div. Appendix E. | 28/07/1916 | 28/07/1916 |
| Operation(al) Order(s) | Operation Order No 8 By Lieut Col. F.J. Saunders D.S.O. Commanding Anson Batt. | 30/07/1916 | 30/07/1916 |
| Operation(al) Order(s) | Operation Order No 7. By Lieut Col. F.J. Saunders D.S.O. R.M.L.I. Commanding Anson Bn. Appendix F | 29/07/1919 | 29/07/1919 |
| War Diary | Angres 1 | 01/08/1919 | 02/08/1919 |
| War Diary | Bully-Grenay | 02/08/1919 | 05/08/1919 |
| War Diary | Angres 1 | 06/08/1919 | 10/08/1919 |
| War Diary | Bully Grenay | 10/08/1919 | 13/08/1919 |
| War Diary | Angres 1 | 14/08/1919 | 18/08/1919 |
| War Diary | Fosse 10 | 18/08/1919 | 22/08/1919 |
| War Diary | Angres 1 | 22/08/1919 | 26/08/1919 |
| War Diary | Reserve | 26/08/1919 | 30/08/1919 |
| War Diary | Angres 1 | 30/08/1919 | 31/08/1919 |

| | | | |
|---|---|---|---|
| Operation(al) Order(s) | Operation Order No 9 By Lieut Col. F.J. Saunders D.S.O., R.M.L.I. Commanding Anson Bn. 63rd (R.N.) Divn | 01/08/1916 | 01/08/1916 |
| Operation(al) Order(s) | Operation Order No 10. By Lieut Colonel F.J. Saunders D.S.O. R.M.L.I. Commanding Anson Bn. | 04/08/1916 | 04/08/1916 |
| Miscellaneous | C.O. | | |
| Operation(al) Order(s) | Operation Order No. 11. By Lieut: Colonel, F.J. Saunders D.S.O. R.M.L.I. Commanding Anson Bn. | 05/08/1916 | 05/08/1916 |
| Operation(al) Order(s) | Operation Order No 12 By Lieut Colonel F.J. Saunders D.S.O. R.M.L.I. Commanding Anson Bn. | 09/08/1916 | 09/08/1916 |
| Miscellaneous | C.O. | | |
| Operation(al) Order(s) | Operation Order No 13 Lieut. Col. F.J. Saunders D.S.O. R.M.L.I. Commanding Anson Batt. | 13/08/1916 | 13/08/1916 |
| Miscellaneous | C.O. | | |
| Operation(al) Order(s) | Operation Order No. 14. By Lieut. Colonel F.J. Saunders D.S.O. R.M.L.I. Commanding Anson Bn. | 15/08/1916 | 15/08/1916 |
| Operation(al) Order(s) | Operation Order No. 14(2). By Lieut Col. F.J. Saunders D.S.O. R.M.L.I. Commanding Anson Bn. | 15/08/1916 | 15/08/1916 |
| Operation(al) Order(s) | Operation Order No 15 By. Lieut Col. F.J. Saunders D.S.O. R.M.L.I. | 16/08/1916 | 16/08/1916 |
| Operation(al) Order(s) | Operation Orders No 16 By Lieut Col. F.J. Saunders D.S.O. R.M.L.I. Commanding Anson. Bn. 63rd (R.N.) Div. | 17/08/1916 | 17/08/1916 |
| Operation(al) Order(s) | Operation Order No. 17 Lieut Col. F.J. Saunders D.S.O. R.M.L.I. Commanding Anson Bn. | 21/08/1916 | 21/08/1916 |
| Operation(al) Order(s) | Operation Order No. 18 Lieut Col. F.J. Saunders D.S.O. R.M.L.I. Commanding Anson Bn. | 22/08/1916 | 22/08/1916 |
| Operation(al) Order(s) | Operation Orders No. 19 By Lieut Col. F.J. Saunders D.S.O. R.M.L.I. Commanding Anson Bn. | 25/08/1916 | 25/08/1916 |
| Miscellaneous | C.O. | | |
| Operation(al) Order(s) | Operation Orders No. 20 Lieut Col. F.J. Saunders D.S.O. R.M.L.I. Commanding Anson Bn. | 29/08/1916 | 29/08/1916 |
| Heading | Original Copy War Diary Vol IV Anson Battn From 1st September 1916 To 30th September 1916 (Inch) | | |
| War Diary | Angres 1. | 01/09/1916 | 02/09/1916 |
| War Diary | Bully Grenay (Support) | 03/09/1916 | 03/09/1916 |
| War Diary | Support | 04/09/1916 | 06/09/1916 |
| War Diary | Angres 1 | 07/09/1916 | 10/09/1916 |
| War Diary | Support | 11/09/1916 | 14/09/1916 |
| War Diary | Angres 1 | 15/09/1916 | 19/09/1916 |
| War Diary | Coupigny | 20/09/1916 | 20/09/1916 |
| War Diary | Dieval | 20/09/1916 | 30/09/1916 |
| Operation(al) Order(s) | Operation Order No 21 By Lieut Col. F.J. Saunders DSO R.M.L.I. Commanding Anson Bn. | 02/09/1916 | 02/09/1916 |
| Operation(al) Order(s) | Operation Order No. 22 By Lieut Col. F.J. Saunders DSO R.M.L.I. Commanding Anson Bn. | 06/09/1916 | 06/09/1916 |
| Miscellaneous | | | |
| Operation(al) Order(s) | Operation Order No. 23. By Lieut Colonel F.J. Saunders D.S.O. R.M.L.I. Commanding Anson Bn. | 10/09/1916 | 10/09/1916 |
| Miscellaneous | C.O. | | |
| Operation(al) Order(s) | Operation Order No. 24. By Lieut. Colonel F.J. Saunders, D.S.O., RMLI. Commanding Anson Battalion. | 09/09/1916 | 09/09/1916 |
| Miscellaneous | C Form (Duplicate). Messages And Signals. | 11/09/1916 | 11/09/1916 |
| Operation(al) Order(s) | Operation Order No. 25 By Lieut. Col. F.J. Saunders D.S.O. R.M.L.I. Commanding Anson Bn. | 14/09/1916 | 14/09/1916 |

| | | | |
|---|---|---|---|
| Operation(al) Order(s) | Operation Order No. 26 By Lieut. Col. F.J. Saunders D.S.O. R.M.L.I. Commanding Anson Battalion | 18/09/1916 | 18/09/1916 |
| Operation(al) Order(s) | Operation Order No. 27 By Lieut. Col F.J. Saunders D.S.O. R.M.L.I. Commanding Anson Bn. | 19/09/1916 | 19/09/1916 |
| Miscellaneous | C.O. | | |
| Heading | War Diary Anson Battn. From 1st October 1916 (Inch) To 31st October 1916. (Inch) Vol V | | |
| War Diary | Dieval | 01/10/1916 | 04/10/1916 |
| War Diary | Marquay | 04/10/1916 | 04/10/1916 |
| War Diary | Mailly-Maillet | 05/10/1916 | 08/10/1916 |
| War Diary | Hedauville | 08/10/1916 | 19/10/1916 |
| War Diary | Englebelmer | 20/10/1916 | 30/10/1916 |
| War Diary | Hedauville | 31/10/1916 | 31/10/1916 |
| Operation(al) Order(s) | Operation Order No. 28 By Lieut Col. F.J. Saunders D.S.O. R.M.L.I. Commanding Anson Bn. | 03/10/1916 | 03/10/1916 |
| Miscellaneous | | | |
| Operation(al) Order(s) | Operation Order No. 29 By Lieut. Col. F.J. Saunders D.S.O. R.M.L.I. Commanding Anson Batt. | 07/10/1916 | 07/10/1916 |
| Operation(al) Order(s) | Operation Order No. 30 By Lieut Col. F.J. Saunders DSO R.M.L.I. Commanding Anson Bn. | 20/10/1916 | 20/10/1916 |
| Operation(al) Order(s) | Operation Order No. 29. By Lieut Col. F.J. Saunders D.S.O. R.M.L.I. Commanding Anson Bn. | 20/10/1916 | 20/10/1916 |
| Operation(al) Order(s) | Operation Order No. 31 By Lieut Col. F.J. Saunders D.S.O. R.M.L.I. Commanding Anson Bn. | 29/10/1916 | 29/10/1916 |
| Operation(al) Order(s) | Operation Order No. 32 By Lieut Col. F.J. Saunders D.S.O. R.M.L.I. Commanding Anson Bn. | 30/10/1916 | 30/10/1916 |
| Operation(al) Order(s) | Operation Order No. 33. By Lieut Col. F.J. Saunders D.S.O. R.M.L.I. Commanding Anson Bn. | 04/11/1916 | 04/11/1916 |
| Miscellaneous | Training Programme For Week Ending | 02/12/1916 | 02/12/1916 |
| Operation(al) Order(s) | Operation Order No. 35.A. By Lieut Col. F.J. Saunders D.S.O. R.M.L.I. Commanding Anson Bn. | 24/10/1916 | 24/10/1916 |
| Operation(al) Order(s) | Operation Order No. 36 Lieut Col. F.J. Saunders D.S.O. R.M.L.I. Commanding Anson Battn. | 12/11/1916 | 12/11/1916 |
| Heading | War Diary Of Anson Battalion 63rd Division From 1st November To 30th November 1916 | | |
| War Diary | Hedauville | 01/11/1916 | 04/11/1916 |
| War Diary | Move To Puchevillers | 05/11/1916 | 05/11/1916 |
| War Diary | Move To Hedauville | 06/11/1916 | 06/11/1916 |
| War Diary | Hedauville | 06/11/1916 | 06/11/1916 |
| War Diary | Move To Englebelmer | 07/11/1916 | 07/11/1916 |
| War Diary | Englebelmer | 08/11/1916 | 12/11/1916 |
| War Diary | Assembly Positions | 12/11/1916 | 12/11/1916 |
| War Diary | Trenches | 13/11/1916 | 13/11/1916 |
| War Diary | Battle Of The Ancre | 13/11/1916 | 13/11/1916 |
| War Diary | Ancre | 13/11/1916 | 13/11/1916 |
| War Diary | Battle Of Ancre | 13/11/1916 | 14/11/1916 |
| War Diary | Battle Of The Ancre | 14/11/1916 | 15/11/1916 |
| War Diary | Hedauville | 15/11/1916 | 16/11/1916 |
| War Diary | Puchevillers | 16/11/1916 | 18/11/1916 |
| War Diary | Beaumetz | 19/11/1916 | 21/11/1916 |
| War Diary | Coulenvillers | 22/11/1916 | 22/11/1916 |
| War Diary | Domvast | 23/11/1916 | 23/11/1916 |
| War Diary | Nouvions | 24/11/1916 | 24/11/1916 |
| War Diary | Noyelles | 25/11/1916 | 26/11/1916 |
| War Diary | Lannoy | 27/11/1916 | 30/11/1916 |

| | | | |
|---|---|---|---|
| Operation(al) Order(s) | Operation Order No 34 By Lieut Col. F.J. Saunders D.S.O. R.M.L.I. Commanding Anson Battn | 06/11/1916 | 06/11/1916 |
| Operation(al) Order(s) | Operation Order No 35 By Lieut Col. F.J. Saunders D.S.O. R.M.L.I. Commanding Anson Bn. | 06/11/1916 | 06/11/1916 |
| Operation(al) Order(s) | Operation Order No. 37 By Lieut Commdr B.H. Ellis Commanding Anson Bn. | 15/11/1916 | 15/11/1916 |
| Operation(al) Order(s) | Operation Order No 38 By Lieut. Commdr. B.H. Ellis R.N.V.P. Com'd Anson Bn. | 16/11/1916 | 16/11/1916 |
| Operation(al) Order(s) | Operation Order 39. By Lieut. Commdr B.H. Ellis R.N.V.R. Commanding Anson Bn. | 17/11/1916 | 17/11/1916 |
| Operation(al) Order(s) | Operation Order No 40 By Lieut Commdr B.H. Ellis Commanding Anson Bn. | 20/11/1916 | 20/11/1916 |
| Operation(al) Order(s) | Operation Order 41 By Lieut Commdr B.H. Ellis R.N.V.R. Commanding Anson Bn. | 21/11/1916 | 21/11/1916 |
| Miscellaneous | | | |
| Operation(al) Order(s) | Operation Order No 42 By Lieut-Commdr B.H. Ellis R.N.V.R. Commanding Anson Bn. | 22/11/1916 | 22/11/1916 |
| Operation(al) Order(s) | Operation Order No 43 By Lieut Commander B.H. Ellis R.N.V.R. Commanding Anson Batt. | 23/11/1916 | 23/11/1916 |
| Operation(al) Order(s) | Operation Order No 44 By Lieut. Commdr B.H. Ellis R.N.V.R. Commanding Anson Bn. | 25/11/1916 | 25/11/1916 |
| Miscellaneous | C.O. | | |
| Miscellaneous | Anson Battn. | | |
| Miscellaneous | Notice | 25/11/1916 | 25/11/1916 |
| Miscellaneous | C.O. | | |
| Miscellaneous | 63rd (R.N.) Div. Ancre Attack. | | |
| Miscellaneous | Training Programme For Week Ending | 02/12/1916 | 02/12/1916 |
| Heading | War Diary Of Anson Battalion From 1st Dec 1916 To 31st Dec 1916 | | |
| Map | | | |
| War Diary | Lannoy | 01/12/1916 | 11/12/1916 |
| War Diary | Lannoy Villers | 12/12/1916 | 18/12/1916 |
| War Diary | Villers | 18/12/1916 | 13/01/1917 |
| War Diary | Nouvion | 14/01/1917 | 14/01/1917 |
| War Diary | Marcheville | 15/01/1917 | 15/01/1917 |
| War Diary | Heuzecourt | 16/01/1917 | 17/01/1917 |
| War Diary | Terramesnil | 18/01/1917 | 20/01/1917 |
| War Diary | Englebelmer | 21/01/1917 | 24/01/1917 |
| War Diary | Trenches Opposite Grandcourt | 25/01/1917 | 31/01/1917 |
| War Diary | Englebelmer | 31/01/1917 | 06/02/1917 |
| War Diary | Thiepval | 06/02/1917 | 07/02/1917 |
| War Diary | Trenches South Of Grandcourt | 08/02/1917 | 09/02/1917 |
| War Diary | Englebelmer | 10/02/1917 | 14/02/1917 |
| War Diary | Puisieux Trench R.8.b.6.6 | 15/02/1917 | 21/02/1917 |
| War Diary | McKenzie Huts W.10.C.3.8. | 22/02/1917 | 28/02/1917 |
| War Diary | McKenzie Huts at Martinsart | 01/03/1917 | 18/03/1917 |
| War Diary | McKenzie Huts | 19/03/1917 | 19/03/1917 |
| War Diary | Herissart | 19/03/1917 | 20/03/1917 |
| War Diary | Longuevillette | 20/03/1917 | 21/03/1917 |
| War Diary | Fortel | 22/03/1917 | 22/03/1917 |
| War Diary | Croix | 23/03/1917 | 24/03/1917 |
| War Diary | Fiefs | 24/03/1917 | 25/03/1917 |
| War Diary | Ecquedecques | 26/03/1917 | 26/03/1917 |
| War Diary | Quentin | 27/03/1917 | 27/03/1917 |
| War Diary | Noeux Les Mines | 27/03/1917 | 31/03/1917 |
| Miscellaneous | A.G. Base G.H.Q. | 06/05/1917 | 06/05/1917 |

| | | | |
|---|---|---|---|
| War Diary | Noeux Les Mines | 01/04/1917 | 14/04/1917 |
| War Diary | Ohlain Camp | 14/04/1917 | 15/04/1917 |
| War Diary | Maroeuil | 16/04/1917 | 20/04/1917 |
| War Diary | St Catherines | 21/04/1917 | 22/04/1917 |
| War Diary | Trenches At La Bois De La Maison Blanche | 23/04/1917 | 23/04/1917 |
| War Diary | Point Du Tours | 24/04/1917 | 26/04/1917 |
| War Diary | Gavrelle | 27/04/1917 | 29/04/1917 |
| War Diary | Roclincourt | 30/04/1917 | 30/04/1917 |
| War Diary | Bray | 30/04/1917 | 01/05/1917 |
| War Diary | Villers Brulin | 02/05/1917 | 04/05/1917 |
| War Diary | Hermin | 05/05/1917 | 08/05/1917 |
| War Diary | Mont St Eloy | 09/05/1917 | 09/05/1917 |
| War Diary | C 10 B 5.4 | 10/05/1917 | 11/05/1917 |
| War Diary | Pontefract Camp | 12/05/1917 | 19/05/1917 |
| War Diary | Trenches | 20/05/1917 | 20/05/1917 |
| War Diary | Bois De La Maison Blanche | 21/05/1917 | 22/05/1917 |
| War Diary | Cavrelle | 23/05/1917 | 28/05/1917 |
| War Diary | Trenches At Bois De La Maison Blanche | 29/05/1917 | 10/06/1917 |
| War Diary | Mont St Eloi | 11/06/1917 | 14/06/1917 |
| War Diary | St Aubin | 15/06/1917 | 16/06/1917 |
| War Diary | Maroeul | 17/06/1917 | 22/06/1917 |
| War Diary | Rollincourt | 23/06/1917 | 09/07/1917 |
| War Diary | Cavrelle | 10/07/1917 | 31/07/1917 |
| War Diary | Aubrey Camp | 01/08/1917 | 01/08/1917 |
| War Diary | Roclincourt | 02/08/1917 | 07/08/1917 |
| War Diary | Cavrelle | 08/08/1917 | 11/08/1917 |
| War Diary | Black Line | 12/08/1917 | 14/08/1917 |
| War Diary | Cavrelle | 15/08/1917 | 23/08/1917 |
| War Diary | Aubrey Camp | 24/08/1917 | 31/08/1917 |
| War Diary | Cavrelle | 01/09/1917 | 15/09/1917 |
| War Diary | Roundhay Camp | 16/09/1917 | 16/09/1917 |
| War Diary | Roclincort | 17/09/1917 | 30/09/1917 |
| Miscellaneous | Battalion Order By Lieut Colonel H.F. Kirkpatrick Commanding Anson Battalion. Appendix A. | | |
| Miscellaneous | Reference Map: Special 1/10,000 Gavrelle "B" Ed 6. | 02/09/1917 | 02/09/1917 |
| Miscellaneous | | 08/09/1917 | 08/09/1917 |
| War Diary | Nouveau Monde | 23/10/1917 | 23/10/1917 |
| War Diary | Ypres | 24/10/1917 | 24/10/1917 |
| War Diary | S Of Poelcapelle | 25/10/1917 | 26/10/1917 |
| War Diary | Dambre Camp | 27/10/1917 | 31/10/1917 |
| War Diary | Dambre Camp Near Brielen | 01/11/1917 | 08/11/1917 |
| War Diary | School Camp | 09/11/1917 | 12/11/1917 |
| War Diary | Arneke | 13/11/1917 | 22/11/1917 |
| War Diary | Murat Camp | 23/11/1917 | 01/12/1917 |
| War Diary | Ypres | 02/12/1917 | 05/12/1917 |
| War Diary | School Camp | 06/12/1917 | 10/12/1917 |
| War Diary | Beaulencort | 11/12/1917 | 13/12/1917 |
| War Diary | Rocquigny | 14/12/1917 | 14/12/1917 |
| War Diary | Etricourt | 15/12/1917 | 16/12/1917 |
| War Diary | Metz | 17/12/1917 | 21/12/1917 |
| War Diary | In The Line | 22/12/1917 | 31/12/1917 |
| War Diary | Villers-Plouich | 01/01/1918 | 04/01/1918 |
| War Diary | Metz | 05/01/1918 | 07/01/1918 |
| War Diary | Line | 08/01/1918 | 11/01/1918 |
| War Diary | Villers-Plouich | 12/01/1918 | 13/01/1918 |
| War Diary | Line | 14/01/1918 | 17/01/1918 |

| | | | |
|---|---|---|---|
| War Diary | Villers-Plouich | 18/01/1918 | 19/01/1918 |
| War Diary | Metz | 20/01/1918 | 22/01/1918 |
| War Diary | Equancourt | 23/01/1918 | 25/01/1918 |
| War Diary | Beaulencourt | 26/01/1918 | 13/02/1918 |
| War Diary | Lechelle | 14/02/1918 | 17/02/1918 |
| War Diary | Line | 18/02/1918 | 20/02/1918 |
| War Diary | Lechelle | 21/02/1918 | 22/02/1918 |
| War Diary | Line (Support) | 23/02/1918 | 26/02/1918 |
| War Diary | Front Line | 27/02/1918 | 28/02/1918 |
| Heading | 188th Brigade. 63rd Division "Anson" Battalion March 1918 | | |
| War Diary | Front Line | 01/03/1918 | 02/03/1918 |
| War Diary | Havrincourt Wood | 03/03/1918 | 06/03/1918 |
| War Diary | Support Line | 07/03/1918 | 10/03/1918 |
| War Diary | Front Line | 11/03/1918 | 14/03/1918 |
| War Diary | Eastwood Camp | 15/03/1918 | 24/03/1918 |
| War Diary | Martinpouich | 25/03/1918 | 25/03/1918 |
| War Diary | Thiepval | 26/03/1918 | 26/03/1918 |
| War Diary | Martinsart | 27/03/1918 | 27/03/1918 |
| War Diary | Forceville | 28/03/1918 | 31/03/1918 |
| Heading | Anson Battalion. April 1918 | | |
| War Diary | Forceville | 01/04/1918 | 01/04/1918 |
| War Diary | Toutencourt | 02/04/1918 | 02/04/1918 |
| War Diary | Englebelmer | 03/04/1918 | 05/04/1918 |
| War Diary | Aveluy Wood | 06/04/1918 | 08/04/1918 |
| War Diary | Englebelmer | 09/04/1918 | 11/04/1918 |
| War Diary | Forceville | 12/04/1918 | 13/04/1918 |
| War Diary | Arqueves | 14/04/1918 | 06/05/1918 |
| War Diary | Line | 07/05/1918 | 11/05/1918 |
| War Diary | Front Line "Hamel Left" Sector | 12/05/1918 | 12/05/1918 |
| War Diary | Reserve Line. | 13/05/1918 | 18/05/1918 |
| War Diary | Support Line. | 19/05/1918 | 22/05/1918 |
| War Diary | Front Line. | 23/05/1918 | 24/05/1918 |
| War Diary | Reserve | 25/05/1918 | 31/05/1918 |
| War Diary | Line | 01/06/1918 | 06/06/1918 |
| War Diary | Herrissart | 07/06/1918 | 22/06/1918 |
| War Diary | Achieux Wood | 23/06/1918 | 30/06/1918 |
| Miscellaneous | Special Order Of The Day. | 08/06/1918 | 08/06/1918 |
| War Diary | Acheux | 01/07/1918 | 05/07/1918 |
| War Diary | Mailly-Maillet | 06/07/1918 | 20/07/1918 |
| War Diary | Front Line | 21/07/1918 | 23/07/1918 |
| War Diary | Lealvillers | 24/07/1918 | 24/07/1918 |
| War Diary | Arqueves | 25/07/1918 | 28/07/1918 |
| War Diary | Authie | 29/07/1918 | 31/07/1918 |
| War Diary | | 01/08/1918 | 31/08/1918 |
| War Diary | Boiry-Ste Rictrude | 01/09/1918 | 30/09/1918 |
| War Diary | Cambrai Sector | 01/10/1918 | 08/10/1918 |
| War Diary | Niergnies | 08/10/1918 | 09/10/1918 |
| War Diary | Morchies | 10/10/1918 | 17/10/1918 |
| War Diary | Hernicourt | 17/10/1918 | 22/10/1918 |
| War Diary | Maizieres | 23/10/1918 | 31/10/1918 |
| Miscellaneous | Honours & Awards Gained By Men Of Anson Battalion During Operations 21st Aug. To 2nd. Sept. | | |
| War Diary | Maiziers | 01/11/1918 | 01/11/1918 |
| War Diary | Evin Malmaison | 02/11/1918 | 05/11/1918 |
| War Diary | Hulchin | 06/11/1918 | 06/11/1918 |

| | | | |
|---|---|---|---|
| War Diary | Aulnoy | 07/11/1918 | 07/11/1918 |
| War Diary | Sebourquain | 08/11/1918 | 08/11/1918 |
| War Diary | Andregnies | 09/11/1918 | 09/11/1918 |
| War Diary | Sars La Bruyere | 10/11/1918 | 10/11/1918 |
| War Diary | Villers-St-Ghislain | 11/11/1918 | 11/11/1918 |
| War Diary | Villers-St-Ghislain | 11/11/1918 | 14/11/1918 |
| War Diary | Villers-St-Ghislain | 15/11/1918 | 27/11/1918 |
| War Diary | Sars-La-Bruyere | 28/11/1918 | 30/11/1918 |
| Miscellaneous | 188th. Infantry Brigade (Warning) Order No. 241. App 1. | 03/11/1918 | 03/11/1918 |
| Miscellaneous | Anson Battalion. | | |
| War Diary | Sars-La-Bruyere | 01/12/1918 | 10/12/1918 |
| War Diary | Wasmes | 11/12/1918 | 28/02/1919 |
| Miscellaneous | O In C. Records, 63rd (R.N.) Divn A.G's Office At Base. | 01/04/1919 | 01/04/1919 |
| War Diary | Wasmes | 01/03/1919 | 31/03/1919 |
| Miscellaneous | Memorandum. | 08/05/1919 | 08/05/1919 |
| War Diary | Wasmes | 01/04/1919 | 30/04/1919 |

63RD DIVISION

188TH INFY BDE

~~1ST~~ ANSON BN R.N.DIVN.

JUN 1916-APR 1919.

1st & 2nd BNS AMALGAMATED

1916 JUNE

Confidential

Anson

WO

Headquarters
Anson Battn
1st September 1916

War Diary - Volume III
of
Anson Battn
from
1st August
to
31st August (incl)

[illegible] Saunders
Lieut Col
Comdg Anson Battn

To The A G's Office
3rd Echelon

1st Anson Bn June Vol 1

Confidential

Hd Qrs 1st Anson Battn
30th June 1916

War Diary
of
1st Anson Battn R.N. Divn

from
1st June 1916
to
30th June 1916.



J. Saunders.
Lieut Col. R.M.L.I.
Comdg 1st Anson Battn

To
The A. G's Office
3rd Echelon

Instructions regarding War Diaries and Intelligence Summaries are contained in F. S. Regs., Part II. and the Staff Manual respectively. Title pages will be prepared in manuscript.

# WAR DIARY
or
~~INTELLIGENCE SUMMARY.~~
*(Erase heading not required.)*

Army Form C. 2118.

| Place | Date | Hour | Summary of Events and Information | Remarks and references to Appendices |
|---|---|---|---|---|
| | June | | | |
| AIRAINES | 1 | 8.30am | In accordance with orders received during night of 31 May/1st June, Battalion vacated billets and marched to PONT REMY where it entrained and left at 12.38 pm for BARLIN, arriving at 6.20 pm and went into billets. A fine day. 2 O.R. sent for Cold Shoeing Course. | |
| BARLIN | 2 | | Battalion settled down into billets. Nominal list of Officers on Appendix A attached. | A |
| " | 3 | 2 pm | Battalion paraded and marched to vicinity of MARQUIL (J.36 central), where together with 1st RM it was inspected by G.O.C. 1st Army (Genl Sir Charles Munro K.C.B. KC) | |
| | 4 | [illegible] | Divine Service. | |
| | | | Following Officers and O R were sent to courses of instruction:— | |
| | | | Bomb School 4 Officers + 6 O.R. , [illegible] Gun School 2 Officers + 10 O.R | |
| | | | PT & Trench [illegible] School 2 Officers + 2 O.R | |
| | | | Gas School 2 O.R. | |
| | | | Trench Mortar School 4 Officers + 30 O.R. | |
| | | 5 pm | Two working parties of 100 and 150 were provided to go to ANGRES and SOUCHEZ Sectors respectively. They were taken out in G.S. waggons but owing to a mistake in the orders by which they were taken, did not reach their destinations and eventually marched back arriving early 5th June. | |

T.131. Wt. W708-776. 500000. 4/15. Sir J. C. & S.

Instructions regarding War Diaries and Intelligence Summaries are contained in F. S. Regs., Part II. and the Staff Manual respectively. Title pages will be prepared in manuscript.

# WAR DIARY
*or*
# INTELLIGENCE SUMMARY.
*(Erase heading not required.)*

Army Form C. 2118.

| Place | Date | Hour | Summary of Events and Information | Remarks and references to Appendices |
|---|---|---|---|---|
| | June | | | |
| BARLIN | 5th | 1 pm | B + C Cos marched to Gas School, where they received a lecture on Gas helmets &c and were put through the gas chamber. They then, in accordance with previous arrangements, proceeded to carry out three days training in the trenches in SOUCHEZ Sector. The travelling kitchens proceeded to a rendezvous where the Companies had tea. Lieut Comdr E Jones RNVR (2nd in Command) was in command of this party. C. Co was attached to 11th N.F in SOUCHEZ 1 and B. Co to 12th DLI in SOUCHEZ 2. | |
| | 6th | pm | A + D. Cos marched to Gas School, received lecture and were put through the gas chamber. These two Companies then provided two working parties of 100 and 150 respectively for work at ANGRES + LORETTE SPUR respectively. Owing to their late return from Gas School and insufficiency of time allowed for transport the first party arrived too late for work and marched straight back. The 2nd party worked till 12 midnight and then marched back. | |
| | | | Another party of 50 men under Sub Lieut Allison was also provided from 6 a.m to 5.30 pm and were taken for work in another sector. | |
| | 7th 6 | | Lieut. Comdr GILLILAND and 22 O.R rejoined Battn from leave in ENGLAND. A dull day with some rain. | |
| | 7th | pm | All details not previously sent were marched to Gas School, lectured and put through | |

Instructions regarding War Diaries and Intelligence Summaries are contained in F. S. Regs., Part II. and the Staff Manual respectively. Title pages will be prepared in manuscript.

# WAR DIARY
*or*
# INTELLIGENCE SUMMARY.
*(Erase heading not required.)*

Army Form C. 2118.

| Place | Date | Hour | Summary of Events and Information | Remarks and references to Appendices |
|---|---|---|---|---|
| BARLIN | June 7th | | Gas Chamber | |
| | | | Commanding Officer visited SOUCHEZ 2 and inspected the dispositions there. At about 10.30 p.m. the enemy exploded a camouflet under one of our mines in this sector, and in addition to the casualties to R.E. [illegible] B Co. A.B. J. KIDD who was working there was gassed by the fumes and killed. 2 men wounded by shell fire. A dull day with occasional showers. | |
| | | | Capt. the Hon. L. MONTAGUE R.N. 2nd HOOD BATT^N^ attached temporarily. | |
| | 8th | | C.O. returned [illegible] SOUCHEZ 2 [illegible] SOUCHEZ 1 | |
| | | | A [illegible] D Coys relieved B & C Coys respectively in SOUCHEZ 2 and 1. [illegible] the weather broke and the relief took place in heavy rain. | |
| | 9th | 5 a.m. | B [illegible] C Coys returned to billets. | |
| | | | C.O. visited G.O.C. 69th Brigade to receive instructions to take over LORETTE SPUR. | |
| | | | Capt. the Hon. L. MONTAGUE left for [illegible] to join 2nd HOOD Batt^n^. A dull day. | |
| | 10th | | C.O. visited LORETTE SPUR and inspected the position. | |
| | | | 4 O.R. proceeded to Gas School for a course of instruction. | |
| | | | [illegible] sent on 4th inst to Lewis Gun, P.T. & B.T., Gas and Trench Mortar School returned. A pouring wet day. | |

T2131. Wt. W708–776. 500000. 4/15. Sir J. C. & S.

Instructions regarding War Diaries and Intelligence Summaries are contained in F. S. Regs., Part II. and the Staff Manual respectively. Title pages will be prepared in manuscript.

# WAR DIARY
*or*
# INTELLIGENCE SUMMARY.
*(Erase heading not required.)*

Army Form C. 2118.

| Place | Date | Hour | Summary of Events and Information | Remarks and references to Appendices |
|---|---|---|---|---|
| | | | 2 men wounded by bomb in SOUCHEZ 1. | |
| BARLIN | 11th | p.m. | Headquarters, + B + C Co^s proceeded to LORETTE SPUR, and relieved H.Q^rs + 2 Co^s 8th Yorkshire Reg^t. O.C. 1st ANSON Batt^n assumed command of LORETTE SPUR | |
| | | | Troops disposed as follows:- | |
| | | | Right C^o B C^o 1/ANSON. | |
| | | | Centre C^o C C^o 1/ANSON. | |
| | | | Left C^o C C^o 8/YORKS. | |
| | | | Support C^o B C^o 8/YORKS. | |
| | | | Headquarters in ABLAIN S^T NAZAIRE (map reference X10 b.[illegible]). | |
| | | | Relief took place in heavy rain. | |
| LORETTE SPUR | 12th | | A quiet day no shelling. Troops engaged in work of improvement of trenches and digging deep dugouts. | |
| | | | In SOUCHEZ sector, where there was considerable activity with Rifle Grenades, 'Rum Jars' &c. a 'Whizz bang' entered a dugout and caused 3 casualties in D. C^o as follows:- | |
| | | | A. B. W. WEBB. killed. | |
| | | | A. B. J. W. NELSON wounded and died same day. | |
| | | | A. B. D. MACKAY wounded and died 14th. | |

T.131. Wt. W708-776. 500000. 4/15. Sir J. C. & S.

Instructions regarding War Diaries and Intelligence Summaries are contained in F. S. Regs., Part II. and the Staff Manual respectively. Title pages will be prepared in manuscript.

# WAR DIARY
*or*
# INTELLIGENCE SUMMARY.
*(Erase heading not required.)*

Army Form C. 2118.

| Place | Date | Hour | Summary of Events and Information | Remarks and references to Appendices |
|---|---|---|---|---|
| [illegible] | June 12th | 9 pm | Battn (less A + D Cos) with 2 Cos 8th YORKSHIRE Regt relieved by 8th LONDON Regt (Post Office Rifles). Relief took place in torrential rain and was completed at 11.55 p.m. | |
| BARLIN. | 13th | [illegible] am | Battn returned to billets in BARLIN. A + D Cos having been relieved in [illegible] [illegible]. | |
| " | | [illegible] | Battn vacated billets and marched to LA COMTÉ, arriving at 1.30 p.m. and went into billets. A dull and showery day. | |
| LA COMTE | 14th | | Battalion occupied in training. C.O. proceeded to CAMBLAIN L'ABBÉ to sit on G.C.M. A party of 1 officer + 50 O.R. sent to BOIS DE NIEPPE for work until further orders. [illegible] MACAMPBELL, 2nd Lieut R DONALDSON and 23 O.R. struck off strength and posted to [illegible] L.T.M. Battery [illegible] Division. | |
| | | [illegible] pm | Capt [illegible] E R ELLIS + 110 O.R. proceeded on leave to ENGLAND from 15th to 22nd. | |
| " | 14th/15th | 11 pm | Clocks advanced one hour | |
| | | | Battalion occupied in training | |
| | | | A working party of 1 officer + 100 men provided for construction of Bde Bombing Ground | |
| | | | 15th [illegible] [illegible] 2nd Lieut [illegible] marched to BARLIN to attend the funeral of | |

T. 134. Wt. W703–776. 500000. 4/15. Sir J. C. & S.

Instructions regarding War Diaries and Intelligence Summaries are contained in F. S. Regs., Part II. and the Staff Manual respectively. Title pages will be prepared in manuscript.

# WAR DIARY
or
~~INTELLIGENCE~~ SUMMARY.
(*Erase heading not required.*)

Army Form C. 2118.

| Place | Date | Hour | Summary of Events and Information | Remarks and references to Appendices |
|---|---|---|---|---|
| | June | | | |
| LA COMTÉ | 15th (cont) | | A. B. D MACKAY died from wounds. | |
| | | 3pm | 2 O R proceeded on leave to ENGLAND from 16th – 23rd inst. A dull day. | |
| " " | 16th | | Battalion occupied in training. A dull day. 'Gas Alert' signalled about 6pm | |
| " " | 17th | a m | Training. | |
| | | 8pm | Two parties each of 2 Officers 4 P.Os + 50 men were provided for work at AIX LA NOULETTE and BULLY GRENAY – went away in motor lorries and returned about 3.15 a m 18th. A better day fair amount of sunshine | |
| " " | 18th | 9.0 a m | 2 Officers and 25 O R sent for a course of instruction at Bde Bomb School at CUVIGNY. 4 1 Officer and 2 P.Os sent temporarily as Instructors. | |
| | | 11 a m | Divine Service. | |
| | | 2 pm | The whole Battn was inspected by the Commanding Officer to ascertain the numbers requiring new clothes. Clothes and boots are in a very bad condition, about 90% require renewal. | |
| " " | 19th | a m | {Gas Alert cancelled 8.45 a m} Billets cleared up and 1st and 2nd line transport loaded preparatory to move. | |
| | | 2pm | Battalion paraded and marched to ESTRÉE - CAUCHIE. | |
| ESTRÉE - CAUCHIE | | 4.30pm | Battalion arrived and went into billets. Billets were much crowded and dirty. | |

T.2131. Wt. W708–776. 500000. 4/15. Sir J. C. & S.

Instructions regarding War Diaries and Intelligence Summaries are contained in F. S. Regs., Part II. and the Staff Manual respectively. Title pages will be prepared in manuscript.

# WAR DIARY
*or*
# ~~INTELLIGENCE SUMMARY.~~
*(Erase heading not required.)*

Army Form C. 2118.

| Place | Date | Hour | Summary of Events and Information | Remarks and references to Appendices |
|---|---|---|---|---|
| | June | | | |
| ESTREE CAUCHIE | 19th | | New straw was requisitioned from the 2nd Divn Supply Co, and the men were then able to occupy the billets. | |
| " | " | 4.30pm | 2 Officers + 6 O.R rejoined from 47th Divisional Bomb School. | |
| " | " | " | Lieut H E Barlow attached to 3rd Bde H^o Q^rs to assist Staff. | |
| " | 20th | a.m. | Battalion at training 1 C^o on Rifle Range. Bombers, Lewis Gunners, Signallers Scouts + Snipers working under Officer Instructors | Exceedingly good weather |
| " | " | " | 1 Officer + 2 O.R proceeded to CAMIERS for Course of instruction in Lewis Guns. | |
| " | " | 2.30pm | Major Campbell, 3rd Army, gave a most interesting lecture to all the Officers + P.O^s of the Battalion on Bayonet Fighting. G.O.C.^s R.N. Divn + 3rd Brigade with Staffs present | |
| " | 21st | 9 a.m. | C.O. inspected B C^o. [B C^o inspected by Major for Scabies.] Remainder of Battn occupied in training. Commenced | |
| | | a.m. p.m. | special instruction in wiring under Lieut Douglas. 1 P.O + 26 O.R per C^o | |
| | 22nd | 9 a.m. | C.O inspected D. C^o. Remainder of Battn occupied in training. Commenced special instruction of Officers + P.O^s in Bayonet fighting. | |
| | | 9 p.m. | Duty Bugler, Able Seaman A MOUNTFORD whilst sounding "1st Post" was run over and sustained a broken leg. Sub Lieut OATES + 50 O.R. returned this day from BOIS DE NIEPPE. | |
| | 23 | 6.30a.m. 7.30am | Bayonet fighting, and Physical training | |

T.131. Wt. W708–776. 500000. 4/15. Sir J. C. & S.

Instructions regarding War Diaries and Intelligence Summaries are contained in F. S. Regs., Part II. and the Staff Manual respectively. Title pages will be prepared in manuscript.

# WAR DIARY
*or*
# INTELLIGENCE SUMMARY.
*(Erase heading not required.)*

Army Form C. 2118.

| Place | Date | Hour | Summary of Events and Information | Remarks and references to Appendices |
|---|---|---|---|---|
| | 23rd June | | | |
| ESTRÉE CAUCHIE | ~~24th~~ | 9.30 a.m. | C O inspected A Co. Remainder of Battalion carried out training. | |
| " | " | 10 a.m. | Court of Enquiry as to how Able Seaman A MOUNTFORD sustained injuries. | |
| " | " | p.m. | Inoculation commenced of men who had not been inoculated for over 6 months. | |
| " | 23rd | | 2 Officers + 8 O.R proceeded to AUXI-LE-CHATEAU for a course of instruction in Bayonet fighting. A fine day. 3. O R. proceeded on leave to England. | |
| " | 24th | | A wet morning. G.O.C. 3rd Bde came round and watched Bombers Lewis Gunners &c at training and selected a site for bombers trenches to be dug. | |
| " | | | Inoculation continued making a total of 440 inoculated. Men not inoculated at training | |
| | | a.m. | 1 Officer + 4 P.O. proceeded to PERNES for course of instruction in Bayonet fighting | |
| | | | 1 Officer + 2 P.O " " PERNES " " " " " Trench Warfare | |
| | | | 1 Officer + 25 O.R " " 3rd Bde Bomb School at CUVIGNY for course of bombing. | |
| | | | 2 Officers + 25 O.R. returned from " " " " " , having completed " " " | |
| | | | A wet day. | |
| " | | 6 p.m. | 3 Officers + 25 O.R. A Co. ~~left~~ sent out to reconnoitre road to CARENCY | |
| | | " | 3 " " 25 " B Co " " " " BULLY GRENAY | |

T.131. Wt. W708-776. 500000. 4/15. Sir J. C. & S.

Instructions regarding War Diaries and Intelligence Summaries are contained in F. S. Regs., Part II. and the Staff Manual respectively. Title pages will be prepared in manuscript.

# WAR DIARY
*or*
# INTELLIGENCE SUMMARY.
*(Erase heading not required.)*

Army Form C. 2118.

| Place | Date | Hour | Summary of Events and Information | Remarks and references to Appendices |
|---|---|---|---|---|
| | June | | C Co. | |
| ESTREE CAUCHIE | 24th | 6 pm | 3 Officers + 25 O.R. sent out to reconnoitre road to AIX-NOULETTE | |
| " | " | " | 3 Officers + 25 O.R. D Co. sent out to reconnoitre road to ABLAIN ST NAZAIRE | |
| " | " | | 2 O.R. proceeded on leave to England | |
| " | " | | 2 O.R. left for Base on release for munition work | |
| " | 25th | a.m. | [illegible] A few additional Officers + men re-inoculated making a total of 464. 1 P.O. sent [illegible] as Instructor at Base to re-inforcements for 2 months. Training. Bombing, dug by [illegible] party of 100 men. A fair day. 4 O.R. to Signal School | |
| " | [illegible] | a.m. | A signal [illegible] been received that the Corps Commander would inspect the 3rd Bde [illegible] training between 9 a.m. + 1 p.m. — this Battn between 12 noon + 1 p.m. [illegible] parties [illegible] on their instructional grounds until that hour. [illegible] Companies were ordered to be on the main road in order to be seen by the Corps Commander as he passed in his motor car. Corps Commander did not inspect Battn. Training continued in the afternoon. [illegible] indifferent day — plenty of showers | |
| " | 27th | a.m. | The Battn was disposed as on previous day for inspection by the Corps Commander, except that Companies were not required to be marching on the roads. Inspection | |

F.131. Wt. W708-776. 500000. 4/15. Sir J. C. & S.

Instructions regarding War Diaries and Intelligence Summaries are contained in F. S. Regs., Part II. and the Staff Manual respectively. Title pages will be prepared in manuscript.

# WAR DIARY
*or*
~~INTELLIGENCE~~ SUMMARY.
*(Erase heading not required.)*

Army Form C. 2118.

| Place | Date | Hour | Summary of Events and Information | Remarks and references to Appendices |
|---|---|---|---|---|
| ESTRÉE-CAUCHIE | 27th June (contd) | | again postponed. A very wet day. | |
| | | p.m. | 200 men sent to Bde bath at FRESNICOURT. Training continued as usual | |
| " | 28th | a.m. | Battn again disposed for Corps Commander's inspection which was yet again postponed. Another wet day. | |
| | | | 1 Officer & 2 O.R. returned from Lewis Gun Course at CAMIERS. | |
| | | | 1 Officer sent for course at 47th Divnl Gas School | |
| " | | p.m. | Training continued. Another wet day. | |
| | 29th | a.m. | Battn inspected by Corps Commander, who walked round and watched the different Companies and classes at their training. | |
| | | p.m. | Material having been obtained gallows were erected, and trenches dug for Bayonet fighting. A moderately fine day. | |
| " " | 30th | a.m. | Training continued. Arranged with C.E of 4th Corps for 'Wiring' and 'Deep Dug-out' parties to work on BOUVIGNY LINE instead of doing work for practice only — work to commence next day. | |
| " " | | p.m. | Sentence on D Co. No X B 4156 Able Seaman W.J. HUMPHRIES R.N.V.R, who was tried by F.G.C.M on 27th June was promulgated. He was sentenced to 28 days | |

Instructions regarding War Diaries and Intelligence Summaries are contained in F. S. Regs., Part II. and the Staff Manual respectively. Title pages will be prepared in manuscript.

# WAR DIARY
*or*
# INTELLIGENCE SUMMARY.
*(Erase heading not required.)*

Army Form C. 2118.

| Place | Date | Hour | Summary of Events and Information | Remarks and references to Appendices |
|---|---|---|---|---|
| | June 30 (contd) | | F.P. No 1 for "When on Active Service when acting a Sentinel on 3rd Bde H.Q. at FRESNICOURT was asleep". Sentence confirmed by G.O.C. 3rd Bde. Following is strength of Battn this day. 30 Officers, 1 W.O., 47 C.P.O's + P.O's, 48 Leading Seamen 837 A.B's + Privates. Total all ranks 963. | |
| | | | J. Saunders. Lieut Col. Comdg 1st Anson Batt | |

Appendix A 1st June 1916

Officers of 1st Anson Bn R N D

| | | |
|---|---|---|
| C.O. | Lieut Col. | F. J. Saunders |
| 2nd in C | Lieut Com | E. G. Jones. |
| Adjt. | Sub Lieut. | W. R. Fraser. |
| Q.M. | Hon Lieut | R. Kane |
| M.O. | Surgeon | C H Gow |
| A. O.C. | Lieut. | J. Walsh |
| 2nd in C | | H K Douglas |
| 1st P | Sub Lt. | W C J Williams |
| 3rd | | G J Ridler |
| – | | A J Hobbs |
| 4th | | R Donaldson |
| 2nd | | W. A. M. O'Neill. |
| B. O.C. | Lieut Com. | E.B. Pitt |
| 2nd in C | Sub Lieut. | C. Langston |
| | " | C H Cook |
| 7th P. | 7th | G W A Wanchope |
| 5th / 6th | | N. Browning |
| 8th | | H G. Patterson |
| C. O.C. | Lieut Com. | B H Ellis |
| 2nd in C | Lieut. | F C Mundy |
| 9th Pl. | Sub Lt. | W B Moir |
| – | " | S. M. Mitchell |
| 11th Pl | " | R L Cantle |
| 10th Pl | | J L Oates. |
| D. O.C. | Lieut | H G Barlow |
| 13th Pl. | | [illegible] |
| 14th Pl | Sub Lt | K [illegible] |
| 16th Pl. | | D G Hugh |
| 15th Pl. | | D S [illegible] |
| Attached | Lieut | [illegible] |

1st June Total 31.

15th June 29.

63 Div
Anson Bn
Vol 2

H.Q. [illegible] Batt[n]
1st August 1916

War Diary
of
ANSON BATT[N]
from
1st July 1916
to
31st July 1916

Volume 2

Comd[g] [illegible] Batt[n]

To
[illegible]
63rd Royal Naval Division

Army Form C. 2118.

# WAR DIARY
*or*
# INTELLIGENCE SUMMARY.
*(Erase heading not required.)*

Instructions regarding War Diaries and Intelligence Summaries are contained in F. S. Regs., Part II. and the Staff Manual respectively. Title pages will be prepared in manuscript.

| Place | Date | Hour | Summary of Events and Information | Remarks and references to Appendices |
|---|---|---|---|---|
| ESTREE-CAUCHIE | July 1st | | Battalion at Training. Sub-Lieut Williams returned from Course of Instruction at Gas School | |
| | | | Sub-Lieut Ofield and 4 O R proceeded on Course of Instruction in Lewis Gun | |
| | | | Sub Lieuts Cook + Pugh and 4 O R " " " " Trench Warfare | |
| | | | Lieut Douglas + 4 O.R. returned from " " " " " " | |
| | | | Wire and Dug-out parties commenced work at MESNIL BOUCHÉ. The parties leave daily at 7 a.m, work from 8 a.m to 5 p.m and then return to billets | |
| | | | 10 O R left for Course of Instruction in Light Trench Mortars | |
| | 2nd | a.m | Divine Service. Day of rest. | |
| | | | Lieut Lee and Sub Lieut Oates and 5. O R returned from Bayonet Fighting Course. | |
| | | | Lieut Mundy Sub Lieut Moir and 2. C.P.O's left for General Course at CONDETTE. | |
| | | | Lieut Commdr Gilliland and Sub Lieut Allison ~~left~~ and 6. O R left for Bayonet Fighting Course at PERNES. | |
| | 3rd | | Battalion at training | |
| | | | 4 O.R. left for Lewis Gun Course | |
| | 4th | | Battalion marched to training ground near CUVIGNY. Small Outpost scheme practised. On starting back, heavy thunderstorm came on, and march was made in torrents of rain | |

T.131. Wt. W708–776. 500000. 4/15. Sir J. C. & S.

Army Form C. 2118.

Instructions regarding War Diaries and Intelligence Summaries are contained in F. S. Regs., Part II. and the Staff Manual respectively. Title pages will be prepared in manuscript.

# WAR DIARY
*or*
# INTELLIGENCE SUMMARY.
*(Erase heading not required.)*

| Place | Date | Hour | Summary of Events and Information | Remarks and references to Appendices |
|---|---|---|---|---|
| ESTREE CAUCHIE | July 4th | | Sub-Lieut Browning and 14 O.R. returned from Bombing Course | |
| | | | Sub-Lieut Wauchope left for Course of Signalling at 4th Corps School RANCHICOURT | |
| | 5th | | Battalion at training. | |
| | | | D Co. No Z P 1042 A.B. A.H. COTPEN R.N.V.R. tried by Field General Court Martial. | |
| | | | Lieut Comdr Bell and 10 O.R. went to Bde Bomb School for Course of instruction | |
| | 6th | | Battn at training. | |
| | | | Court of Enquiry Lieut Comdr Jones assembled to enquire into a matter connected with return of Maxim Guns at the railhead at PONT REMY. | |
| | 7th | | Battalion transferred to 1st Brigade R.N. Divn. Sub-Lieut Oates transferred to 1st L.T.M. Battery | |
| | | | Training continued. Half Battn attended Divisional Bath. | |
| | | | A.B. COTPEN tried by F.G.C.M., found guilty of "Committing an Assault on an inhabitant" sentenced to 2 months F.P. No1. Sentence promulgated this day. | |
| | | | 1. O. left for Musketry Instructor's Course. 1 O.R. returned from Course of Cookery | |
| | 8th | | Training Continued. Remainder of Battn, including Wire and Dug Out Parties attended Divisional Bath. | |
| | | | Sub Lieut Langston and 2 O.R. returned from Bayonet fighting Course | |

T. 131. Wt. W708–776. 500000. 4/15. Sir J. C. & S.

Instructions regarding War Diaries and Intelligence Summaries are contained in F. S. Regs., Part II. and the Staff Manual respectively. Title pages will be prepared in manuscript.

# WAR DIARY
*or*
# INTELLIGENCE SUMMARY.
*(Erase heading not required.)*

Army Form C. 2118.

| Place | Date | Hour | Summary of Events and Information | Remarks and references to Appendices |
|---|---|---|---|---|
| ESTREE-CAUCHIE | July 8th (Cont) | | Sub-Lieut Ofield and 4 O.R returned from Lewis Gun Course. | |
| | | | 10 O.R. returned from Light Trench Mortar Course | |
| | | | 2. O.R left for Lewis Gun Course at PERNES. | |
| | | | Sub Lieut Pugh + 4. O.R. returned from Trench Warfare Course. | |
| " | " | 9 pm | Bombers and Wire Parties carried out night practice. Very good work performed. | |
| " | 9th | am | Divine Service Kit Inspection and day of rest. | |
| " | 10th | | Battalion at training 2 O.R. sent on Cookery Course | |
| " | 11th | | Battalion complete less Wire + Dug out parties marched to training ground at CUVIGNY carried out short Battalion drill, small outpost scheme and returned at 4.45 pm Dinners on return. A fine day. | |
| " | | | 1 O.R left for Armourer's Course. | |
| | | | 4 O.R returned from Lewis Gun Course. | |
| | | | Lieut Gilliland, Sub Lieut Allison and 6. O.R. returned from Bayonet fighting Course | |
| " | 12th | | Battn at training | |
| " | " | | Lieut Comdr Watson RNVR rejoined Battn from BLANDFORD and resumed duties | |

Instructions regarding War Diaries and Intelligence Summaries are contained in F. S. Regs., Part II. and the Staff Manual respectively. Title pages will be prepared in manuscript.

# WAR DIARY

*or*

# ~~INTELLIGENCE SUMMARY.~~

*(Erase heading not required.)*

Army Form C. 2118.

| Place | Date | Hour | Summary of Events and Information | Remarks and references to Appendices |
| --- | --- | --- | --- | --- |
|  | July |  |  |  |
| ESTREE-CAUCHIE | 12th (Cont) |  | of Transport Officer |  |
|  |  |  | Inspector of Army Cookery visited Batt and inspected Field Cookers – well pleased |  |
|  |  |  | Lieut Comdt Bell and 10 OR returned from Bombing Course. |  |
| " | 13th | 9 am | Billets cleared up and vacated |  |
|  | " | 2 pm | Battn less wire and Dugout parties marched to HERSIN. |  |
| HERSIN |  | 4.30 pm | Arrived at HERSIN and went into billets |  |
|  | 14th | 12 nn | Battn moved from HERSIN and proceeded to ANGRES section and went into |  |
| ANGRES | " |  | Reserve. Relief of 22nd London Regt completed at 3 pm Bn attached to 47th Divn |  |
| SECTION | " | 3 pm | Battalion disposed as follows:– |  |
|  |  |  | A Co at CORONS D'AIX |  |
|  |  |  | B Co } at BULLY GRENAY |  |
|  |  |  | C Co } |  |
|  |  |  | D Co } at FOSSE 10 |  |
|  |  |  | and Headquarters } Fine weather |  |
|  | 15th |  | In Reserve. Company Officers visited ANGRES Sub Section 1 and 2 |  |
|  | " |  | 2nd Lieut BROWNING and 5 OR left for Course of L. T. Mortars. Working parties provided |  |

T2131. Wt. W708–776. 500000. 4/15. Sir J. C. & S.

Instructions regarding War Diaries and Intelligence Summaries are contained in F. S. Regs., Part II. and the Staff Manual respectively. Title pages will be prepared in manuscript.

# WAR DIARY
*or*
# INTELLIGENCE SUMMARY.
*(Erase heading not required.)*

Army Form C. 2118.

| Place | Date | Hour | Summary of Events and Information | Remarks and references to Appendices |
|---|---|---|---|---|
| ANGRES SECTION | July 16th | | Sunday. Officers reconnoitred trenches in ANGRES I. Working parties provided. | |
| | | p.m | Dug-out and Wiring parties rejoined from ESTREE-CAUCHIE. Working parties provided | |
| | 17th | a.m | C.O. + other officers and O.R. reconnoitred ANGRES I. | |
| | | p.m | 31 O.R. detached for service with 255th Tunnelling Company. Working parties provided. | |
| | 18th | a.m | Officers + O.R. reconnoitred ANGRES I | |
| | | " | 7 P.Os + L.S. left for Course of General Instruction at R.N. Divisional School PERNES | |
| | | " | ~~[illegible]~~ A. Co. withdrawn from CORONS D'AIX to FOSSE 10 | |
| | | p.m | Received orders to relieve HOWE Battn in ANGRES I on 20th inst. Lewis Guns to be relieved in afternoon of 19th. Operation Order No 1. for relief of Lewis Guns attached | Operation Order No 1. Appendix A |
| | | p.m | Working parties provided | |
| | | | Distribution of Battn is now as follows:— | |
| | | | Battn Hd Qrs } A + D Cos } in FOSSE 10 | |
| | | | B + C Cos in BULLY-GRENAY | |

T.131. Wt. W708-776. 500000. 4/15. Sir J. C. & S.

Instructions regarding War Diaries and Intelligence Summaries are contained in F. S. Regs., Part II. and the Staff Manual respectively. Title pages will be prepared in manuscript.

# WAR DIARY

*or*

~~INTELLIGENCE SUMMARY.~~

*(Erase heading not required.)*

Army Form C. 2118.

| Place | Date | Hour | Summary of Events and Information | Remarks and references to Appendices |
|---|---|---|---|---|
| ANGRES SECTION | July 19th | a.m. | Company Commanders and specialist Officers attended Bn. Hd. Qrs. and received instructions as to taking over ANGRES I Sub-Section from HOWE Battn. Operation Orders attached | Operation Order No. 2. Appendix B |
| | | p.m. | Working parties provided | |
| | 20th | 8 a.m. | Battn. fell in and marched by Companies at ¼ hour interval and took over ANGRES I Sub-Section. Relief completed by 1 p.m. Battn. disposed as follows | |
| | | p.m. | Rt. Front Co. B Co. | |
| | | | Left " " C Co. | |
| | | | Support Co. A Co. | |
| | | | Reserve " D Co. | |
| | | | Battn. Hd. Qrs. at junction of FOREST ALLEY and CORONS D'AIX ALLEY | |
| | | | A quiet day. | |
| | | 11 p.m. | Patrols visited NO MAN'S LAND. No enemy encountered, but digging was heard in enemy trenches near M 32 C 2 4 and M 32 C 5 9 | |
| | 20th | a.m. | 10 O.R. went to Bomb School for Course of Instruction | |
| | | | Sub-Lieut. Mitchell commenced a Transport Course at ABBEVILLE | |
| | 21st | | General improvement of trenches continued. Fire slips built in MORROW TRENCH | |

T.131. Wt. W708-776. 500000. 4/15. Sir J. C. & S.

Instructions regarding War Diaries and Intelligence Summaries are contained in F. S. Regs., Part II. and the Staff Manual respectively. Title pages will be prepared in manuscript.

# WAR DIARY
*or*
~~INTELLIGENCE SUMMARY.~~
*(Erase heading not required.)*

Army Form C. 2118.

| Place | Date | Hour | Summary of Events and Information | Remarks and references to Appendices |
|---|---|---|---|---|
| ANGRES I. | July 21st | | A quiet day. A few shell fell in the lines in the afternoon. No Z.T. 6860 Able Seaman James SWEENEY Killed. 1 O.R wounded. | |
| | 21/22 | 11pm–1am | Patrols visited NO MANS LAND, no enemy encountered. During the night enemy M.Gs occasionally swept our parapets and wire. Some new wire laid out in front of left front Co. | |
| " | 22nd | | Improvement of communication trenches and fire trenches continued, some new fire steps being built. Dug-out Platoon engaged on dug-outs. | |
| | | | A few 4.2" and 77 m.m. shrapnel fell to the left of the Reserve Company. | |
| | | | A quiet day. | |
| | 22/23 | 11pm–1am | Patrols visited NO MANS LAND, and inspected wire in vicinity of M 26. C 3 2 and report it badly damaged. Enemy working parties heard in M. 32 b. On return of Patrols Lewis Guns were turned on to this spot, but parties did not cease, and were evidently working inside their trenches. | |
| | 22nd | | Lieut HENRY and 2 O.R left for course of Bayonet Fighting at PERNES | |
| | | | Sub Lieut BROWNING and 5 O.R. returned from L.T.M Course | |
| | | | 3 O.R left for Course of Instruction in L.T.M. | |

Instructions regarding War Diaries and Intelligence Summaries are contained in F. S. Regs., Part II. and the Staff Manual respectively. Title pages will be prepared in manuscript.

# WAR DIARY
*or*
# INTELLIGENCE SUMMARY.
*(Erase heading not required.)*

Army Form C. 2118.

| Place | Date | Hour | Summary of Events and Information | Remarks and references to Appendices |
|---|---|---|---|---|
| [illegible] | 22/12 | – | A quiet day – A few 77 m m 'Universal' and some Rifle Grenades fell in the area, 1 O.R. being wounded | |
| | | | General improvement of front line and communication trenches, some new fire steps being built [illegible] laid out in the night strengthening various spots. Dug out Parties employed with the Engineers | |
| | | | 2nd Lieuts Hulbert, Gee, Walker, Bowden, Jones, Harvey & McLaren joined the Batt[illegible] 2nd Lieuts Hulbert and Gee joining their C[os] in the trenches | |
| | | | Distribution of Batt[n] changed as follows:– | |
| | | | Right Front C° – A C° | |
| | | | Left " " – D " | |
| | | | Support C° – B " | |
| | | | Reserve – C " | |
| | | | [illegible] left for [illegible] Course at 4th Corps School | |
| | | | 2nd Lieut [illegible] returned from [illegible] Course | |
| | 23/12 | | Patrols visited NO MANS LAND, no enemy encountered | |
| | " | | A few small shells and Rifle Grenades fell in the area, but it was a very quiet | |

T.131. Wt. W703–776. 500000. 4/15. Sir J. C. & S.

Instructions regarding War Diaries and Intelligence Summaries are contained in F. S. Regs., Part II. and the Staff Manual respectively. Title pages will be prepared in manuscript.

# WAR DIARY
*or*
# ~~INTELLIGENCE SUMMARY.~~
*(Erase heading not required.)*

Army Form C. 2118.

| Place | Date | Hour | Summary of Events and Information | Remarks and references to Appendices |
|---|---|---|---|---|
| ANGRES I | July 24 | | day. Trenches generally improved, new fire steps and parapets built up. LOVERS LANE deepened. | |
| | | pm | HOWE Batt Lewis Guns relieved our Lewis Guns in the Sub-Section | ~~Operation Order No 5~~ |
| | 24/25 | 11pm | Patrols visited NO MAN'S LAND no enemy encountered, but one patrol when near enemy trench opposite Sap 15 had two bombs thrown at it. | |
| | 25 | am | Relieved by HOWE Batt relief completed by 12.5 p.m. Battn moved into Reserve being disposed – A + D Cos in BULLY GRENAY, B + C Cos and Hd Qrs in FOSSE 10. | Operation Order No 4. App. C |
| | | pm | Working parties provided | |
| | 26th | | In Reserve. All Companies attended the bathing establishment in BULLY GRENAY. Working parties provided. 2 O.R. left for Lewis Gun Course | |
| ANGRES Section | 27th | | In Reserve. Working parties provided. Dug out platoon of 2 Officers and 82 O.R detached for duty under the Divisional Engineers | |
| | 28th | | In Reserve. 700 Suits of Clean Underclothing issued. Co Commanders and Specialist Officers attended Conference at Battn Hd Qrs & received instructions as to relieving HOWE Batt in ANGRES I. (O.O No 6) | Operation Orders Nos 5+6 Appendices D+E |
| | | pm | Lewis Guns relieved HOWE Batt Lewis Guns in front line. (O.O No 5 | |

Instructions regarding War Diaries and Intelligence Summaries are contained in F. S. Regs., Part II. and the Staff Manual respectively. Title pages will be prepared in manuscript.

# WAR DIARY

*or*

# ~~INTELLIGENCE SUMMARY.~~

*(Erase heading not required.)*

Army Form C. 2118.

| Place | Date | Hour | Summary of Events and Information | Remarks and references to Appendices |
|---|---|---|---|---|
| ANGRES | July 29 | 9.30am | Commenced relief of HOWE Battn in ANGRES I. During the relief about 20 Universal Shell were thrown over the area and 3 men were wounded. The wounds to two of these men were directly attributable to the fact that the men had not shrapnel helmets, having to take them over from the Battn relieved. Relief completed at 12.5pm. | Operation Order No 8 Appendix G |
| | | | Battn disposed as follows – | |
| | | | Right Front Co. A Co. — [illegible] HURBERT + 1 OR [illegible] Course of Bayonet fighting | |
| | | | Left " D " | |
| | | | Support " C " — Prepared for Gas Attack which was postponed. | Operation Order No 7 App F |
| | | | Reserve " B " | |
| | | | [illegible] Alley built up where damaged by shellfire | |
| | 29th/30th | 11pm | Patrols went out between 11pm and 1am. No enemy encountered | |
| | 30th | | A quiet day. [illegible] LANE improved near junction with LINK ALLEY. Portion of VASSEAU [illegible] ALLEY and front line trench [illegible] improved, and trenches generally improved | |
| | | | [illegible] and 2 O.R. returned from Bayonet Course. | |
| | | Mid | Patrols [illegible] enemy ~~[illegible]~~ NO MAN'S Land at M 26 [illegible] from M 26 C 31. No enemy encountered. | |

T.131. Wt. W708–776. 500000. 4/15. Sir J. C. & S.

Instructions regarding War Diaries and Intelligence Summaries are contained in F. S. Regs., Part II. and the Staff Manual respectively. Title pages will be prepared in manuscript.

# WAR DIARY
*or*
~~INTELLIGENCE SUMMARY.~~
*(Erase heading not required.)*

Army Form C. 2118.

| Place | Date | Hour | Summary of Events and Information | Remarks and references to Appendices |
|---|---|---|---|---|
| ANGRES I. | July 31st | | A quiet day. A few hostile Field Gun shell fell in the sub sector but did no harm.<br>Companies changed over, and were disposed as follows by 3 p.m.<br>Rt Front Co = B Co<br>Left " " C "<br>Support Co D "<br>Reserve A<br>SOUCHEZ [illegible] Sap taken over from NELSON Battn on our right. Improvement of Sap and front trench [illegible] commenced.<br>Sub Lieut OFIELD, [illegible] and CASTLE commenced a course of General Instruction at PERNES. | |
| | 1st Aug | | Patrols reconnoitred enemy Sap at M 32 b 1 4 which they report occupied, and enemy line in vicinity of M 26 C 2 3. No enemy encountered in NO MANS LAND<br>Fine weather has set in and hot days are now experienced | |

J Saunders
Lieut Col
Comdg Anson Battn

T.131. Wt. W708–776. 500000. 4/15. Sir J. C. & S.

Appendix A

SECRET

Operation Order No 1
by
Lieut. Col. F. J. Saunders D.S.O. R.M.L.I.
Commanding Anson Battn 18th July. 16

Lewis Guns. 1. The Battalion Lewis Guns will relieve Howe B Lewis Guns in ANGRES I to-morrow. Relief to be completed by 5 AM.

2. All coy. Lewis Gun detachments will report to Sub. Lt. Cantle at C. Coy. Hdqrs BULLY GRENAY at 1.30 PM.

Ammunition. 3. Fifteen full and twenty empty magazines will be carried for each gun in the nose bags.

Caps, Packs, Steel Helmets. 4. All caps and packs will be returned to Coy. Q.M.S. by 12 noon. Steel Helmets will be taken over from the Gun Detachments relieved.

Rations. 5. Coy. Commdrs will arrange for the Lewis Gunners rations for Thursday to be made up in bags and turned over to O.C. B. Coy by 6 PM. O.C. B. Coy. will provide the necessary carrying party to take these rations to Howe Bn Hdqrs for distribution.

[illegible]
Sub Lt & Adj.

Secret

Operation Order No 2.
by
[illegible] Colonel F. J. [illegible] D.S.O. [illegible]
Commanding Anson Bn R.N.D.

Appendix B.

19th [illegible]

1. Battalion will relieve [illegible] Bn in ANGRES [illegible] on [illegible] 20th inst; — relief to be completed by 1 p.m.

2. Coys parade in sufficient time to reach entrance to CORONS [illegible] Trench as follows.

B Coy at [illegible] a.m.
A " " [illegible] a.m.
C " " [illegible] a.m.
D " " [illegible] a.m.
Hd Qrs " [illegible] a.m.

One guide per platoon will be provided at entrance to CORONS [illegible] Trench.

Coys will move by Sections at 100 yards distance.

3. B Coy will form the Right Coy in front line extending from SOLFERINO inclusive to [illegible] exclusive. One platoon in [illegible] [illegible].

C Coy will form the Left Coy in front line extending from [illegible] inclusive to VASSAU Trench inclusive. One platoon in [illegible] STREET.

A Coy will be in Support in [illegible] Trench extending from [illegible] [illegible] [illegible] of [illegible] Trench and SIDNEY STREET.

In case of attack this Coy will occupy PYRENEES Trench [illegible] of CORONS [illegible] Trench.

D Coy will be in Reserve in [illegible] Trench from [illegible] ALLEY to CORONS D'AIX Trench.

Hd Qrs Details will be in [illegible] ALLEY N of CORONS D'AIX Trench.

4. [illegible] [illegible] [illegible], all [illegible] [illegible] for Coys [illegible] will proceed in advance to take over [illegible] and [illegible] and will be met at 7 a.m. at entrance to CORONS D'AIX Trench.

5. [illegible] [illegible] [illegible] [illegible] [illegible] [illegible] [illegible] [illegible] [illegible] [illegible] [illegible] [illegible] [illegible]

6. All [illegible] [illegible] [illegible] [illegible] [illegible] [illegible]

7. [illegible] Commanding [illegible] [illegible]

1 C.O. [illegible]
1 [illegible] [illegible]
1 [illegible] [illegible]
1 O.C. B [illegible] [illegible]

Secret

No 4

Appendix C

[illegible]

[illegible] will move into Res[illegible] as follows:

[illegible] C. Coy [illegible] Fosse [illegible]

[illegible]

Appendix I

Secret

Operation Order No. 5
by
Lieut. Col. J. J. Saunders, D.S.O., [illegible]
Commanding Anson Bn.

29th July 1916
in ANGRES I

Relief 1. The Lewis Guns of Anson Bn. will relieve those of Howe Bn. today. Relief to be completed by 3 p.m.

Detail 2. Lewis Gun Crews of each Coy., with 21 magazines per gun, will report to [illegible] at the entrance to CORONS d'AIX Trench at 12.30 p.m. Caps and packs will be turned over to Coy. Q.M.S.

Rations 3. Each Coy. Q.M.S. will send rations for tomorrow for Lewis Gun Crews to Q.M.S. D Coy., who will send them up to the trenches by a small carrying party.

~~By Order~~,
M Kols Fraser.
Sub-Lieut & Adjt.

Operation Orders No. 6 Appendix E

by

Lieut Col. [illegible] DSO, RM

Commanding Anson Bn. 63rd (RN) Div.

Secret

Relief. 1. The Anson Bn. will relieve the Howe Bn. tomorrow [illegible], in [illegible] [illegible]. Relief to be completed by 1 pm

Detail. 2. A Coy. will relieve Right Front Line Coy
C " " " Support Coy.
D " " " Left Front Line Coy
B " " " Reserve Coy.

Coys. will enter [illegible] d'Arc Trench at [illegible]
A Coy. 9.30 am C Coy 9.45 am D Coy. 10.0 am B Coy. 10.15 am
HQrs at 11 [illegible] am

An advance party consisting of 1 Off and 1 NCO per Coy and 1 Signaller for each Coy. and 1 from HQ will arrive at the entrance to [illegible] d'Arc Trench at [illegible] am and proceed to [illegible] Coy HQrs and take over all Trench Stores.

Communication 3. O.C. Coys. will report by telephone when the relief is complete. Code word for "Relief complete" will be "Have you any [illegible]" or words to that effect.

Telephone 4. Telephones of this battalion will not be connected up until Relief is reported complete by Coy Commanders.

Lewis Guns. 5. The Lewis Guns will be [illegible] [illegible] [illegible] [illegible] under the command of [illegible] Hobbs who will [illegible] Sub.Lt [illegible] [illegible]

Duty 6. Officers who are not [illegible] in the [illegible] will report to [illegible] at [illegible] at 10 am tomorrow for duty.

Kit 7. All Officers' Kits, and all packs and [illegible] of [illegible] will be [illegible] in Coy. Groups at [illegible] O.C. Coy. [illegible] [illegible] [illegible] that all the [illegible] [illegible] stores are properly kept together [illegible] [illegible] [illegible] [illegible] [illegible] [illegible].

Issued at pm. [illegible]

[illegible]

Secret

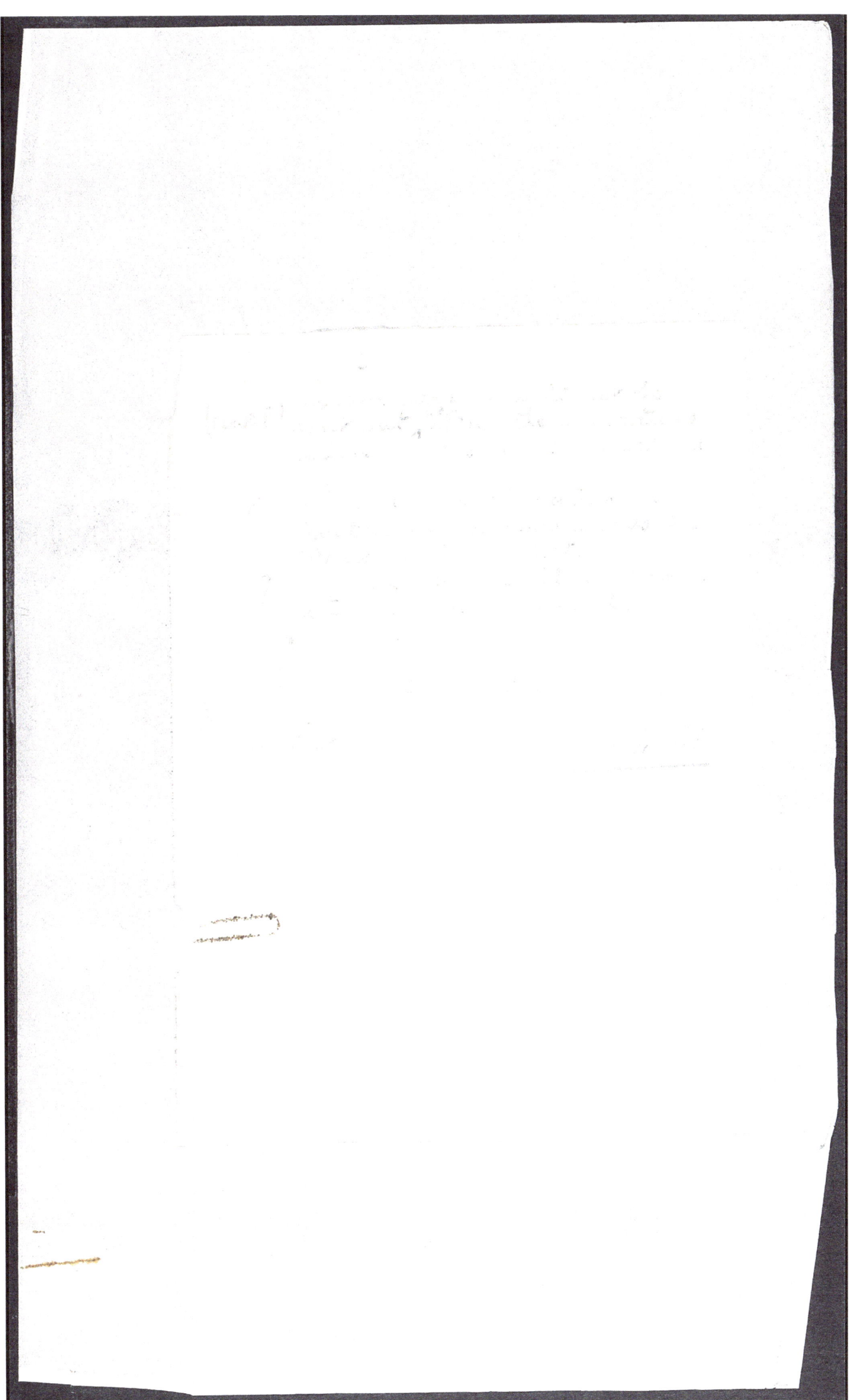

[illegible] Appendix F

Secret

[illegible] Commanding [illegible]

[illegible]

1. A Gas Attack will be made tonight if the wind is suitable. There will be an artillery bombardment but no infantry assault will be made.

2. Bars 3 & 29 [illegible] as [illegible] sub-section and [illegible] under Lieutenant Williams will work under the orders of H Coy [illegible] RE. Each [illegible] [illegible] rifle with bayonet fixed [illegible] [illegible] [illegible] [illegible]
Williams [illegible] Front [illegible] at 6.30 pm.

[illegible] the [illegible] will [illegible] [illegible] [illegible] take [illegible] [illegible] in the [illegible] [illegible] with [illegible] [illegible] [illegible] [illegible]

[illegible] [illegible] [illegible] occupants of
[illegible] [illegible] [illegible] [illegible] [illegible]
quotation [illegible] [illegible] [illegible]
[illegible] [illegible] [illegible]
[illegible] [illegible] [illegible] +40 [illegible]
[illegible] [illegible] [illegible]
[illegible] [illegible] normal [illegible]
[illegible] [illegible] [illegible] by
[illegible] [illegible] [illegible] [illegible]
[illegible] [illegible] [illegible]
[illegible] [illegible] [illegible] 15
[illegible]

Instructions regarding War Diaries and Intelligence Summaries are contained in F. S. Regs., Part II. and the Staff Manual respectively. Title pages will be prepared in manuscript.

# WAR DIARY
*or*
# INTELLIGENCE SUMMARY.
*(Erase heading not required.)*

Army Form C. 2118.

Anson Battn.

| Place | Date | Hour | Summary of Events and Information | Remarks and references to Appendices |
|---|---|---|---|---|
| | Aug. | | | |
| ANGRES I | 1. | | A quiet day in the Sub-section. A few enemy projectiles fell in rear of the Right Co. about 10 p.m but did no damage | |
| | | | Usual work of trench improvement carried | |
| | 1/2 | | Two of our patrols visited NO MANS LAND – no enemy encountered | |
| BULLY – GRENAY | 2nd | 8 am | Moved out of front line on relief by HOWE Battn, and went into Support at BULLY GRENAY. Companies disposed as follows | Operation Order No 9. |
| | | | A + D Coys in BULLY GRENAY | |
| | | | B " in CAP DE PONT | |
| | | | C – in MECHANICS | |
| | | | 1 P.O. left for a Musketry Course | |
| | | | Two Cos and HQ Coy had use of Brigade Bath, and received clean clothes. | |
| | 3rd | | In Support. Working parties provided. Formed a 'raiding party' under Lieut Comdr Ellis with Sub Lieuts Langston and Ridler, for use should occasion arise for a trench raid. | |
| | | | 2. O.R. returned from a Lewis Gun Course at ETAPLES | |
| | | | 8. O.R. returned from Course of Instruction at 63rd (RN) Divl School | |

T2134. Wt. W708–776. 500000. 4/15. Sir J. C. & S.

Instructions regarding War Diaries and Intelligence Summaries are contained in F. S. Regs., Part II. and the Staff Manual respectively. Title pages will be prepared in manuscript.

# WAR DIARY
*or*
# INTELLIGENCE SUMMARY.
*(Erase heading not required.)*

Army Form C. 2118.

Anson Battn

| Place | Date | Hour | Summary of Events and Information | Remarks and references to Appendices |
|---|---|---|---|---|
| | Aug | | | |
| BULLY GRENAY | 4th | | In Support Usual working parties | |
| | | | 6 O.R. left for Course of Instn at 63rd (R.N.) Divn School at PERNES | |
| | | | Remainder of Battn had use of Bath | |
| | | 9pm | Raiding party carried out a rehearsal of a raid | |
| | 5th | | In Support Usual working parties | Operation Order No 10 |
| | | | Lewis Guns under Lieut Henry relieved HOWE Battn Lewis Guns in ANGRES I | |
| ANGRES I | 6th | 6 am | Commenced relief of HOWE Battn in ANGRES I Companies disposed as follows: | O.O. No 11 |
| | | | Rt Front Co A Co | |
| | | | Left " D " | |
| | | | Support B " | |
| | | | Reserve C " | |
| | | | Lieut Lee + 10 O.R returned from Bombing Course. Lieut Gee + 10 O.R. proceeded on Bombing Course | |
| | | | Enemy fired about 30 Light Minenwerfer into vicinity of KELLETT ALLEY | |
| | | | No Z C 336 A.B. G. FLINT wounded and died next day in C.C.S at BARLIN | |
| | | | Usual work of trench repair and improvement continued. | |

T.134. Wt. W703-776. 500000. 4/15. Sir J. C. & S.

Instructions regarding War Diaries and Intelligence Summaries are contained in F. S. Regs., Part II. and the Staff Manual respectively. Title pages will be prepared in manuscript.

# WAR DIARY
*or*
# INTELLIGENCE SUMMARY.
*(Erase heading not required.)*

Army Form C. 2118.

Anson Battn.

| Place | Date | Hour | Summary of Events and Information | Remarks and references to Appendices |
|---|---|---|---|---|
| | Aug | | | |
| ANGRES I | 6/7 | night | Two patrols visited NO MANS LAND and reconnoitred according to instructions. No enemy encountered | |
| | 7 | a.m. | ~~[illegible]~~ Enemy fired about 25 light Minenwerfer into our right area. No casualties. | |
| | | noon | We fired 12 rifle grenades, one of which contained a proclamation and invitation to the enemy to come in and surrender. | |
| | | | Usual trench improvement and working parties provided | |
| | 7/8th | night | ~~[illegible]~~ Usual patrols visited NO MANS LAND | |
| | 8th | a.m. | We fired 24 more rifle grenades, three of which contained proclamations as on previous day but no results. | |
| | | | Enemy threw about 24 L.H.V. into our left area. | |
| | | | No Z.C. 4927 A.B. D.A. CAMERON killed. | |
| | | p.m. | Lieut Mundy, Sub Lieut MOIR and 2 C.P.Os rejoined from Course at 1st Army School at CONDETTE. | |
| | 8/9 | night | Usual patrols in NO MANS LAND. | |

T2131. Wt. W708-776. 500000. 4/15. Sir J. C. & S.

Instructions regarding War Diaries and Intelligence Summaries are contained in F. S. Regs., Part II. and the Staff Manual respectively. Title pages will be prepared in manuscript.

# WAR DIARY
*or*
# INTELLIGENCE SUMMARY.
*(Erase heading not required.)*

Army Form C. 2118.

Anson Battn.

| Place | Date | Hour | Summary of Events and Information | Remarks and references to Appendices |
|---|---|---|---|---|
| | Aug | | | |
| ANGRES I | 9th | | We fired some more Rifle Grenades at enemy trenches | |
| | | | Very little shell fire or Minenwefer from enemy | |
| | | | Our Lewis Guns relieved by Howe Battn | |
| | 9/10 | Night | Usual patrols. | |
| | 9th | 9.6pm | P.O.s Newell and Gray accidentally wounded by a detonator | |
| | 10th | 7am | Howe Battn relieved us and we moved into Support in | OO No 12 |
| BULLY GRENAY | | | BULLY GRENAY. Cos disposed as follows:— | |
| | | | A Co in CAP DE PONT | |
| | | | B " " BULLY GRENAY | |
| | | | C " " " " | |
| | | | D " in MECHANICS. | |
| | | | Slight rain fell in forenoon after continued fine warm days | |
| | | | Headquarters and two Cos bathed in the afternoon and received | |
| | | | clean clothes. | |
| | 11th | | Sub Lieut MITCHELL and 2 OR returned from Transport Course at ABBEVILLE | |
| | | | Usual working parties. A fine day. | |

T2131. Wt. W708-776. 500000. 4/15. Sir J. C. & S.

Instructions regarding War Diaries and Intelligence Summaries are contained in F. S. Regs., Part II. and the Staff Manual respectively. Title pages will be prepared in manuscript.

# WAR DIARY
*or*
# INTELLIGENCE SUMMARY.
*(Erase heading not required.)*

Army Form C. 2118.

Anson Battn

| Place | Date | Hour | Summary of Events and Information | Remarks and references to Appendices |
|---|---|---|---|---|
| | Aug | | | |
| BULLY GRENAY | 12th | | Usual working parties. | |
| | | | Sub Lieut Gee and 10 O.R. returned from Bombing Course. | |
| | | | Sub Lieut Hulbert and 1 O.R returned from Bayonet Fighting Course | |
| | | | Sub Lieut McLaren and 1 O.R. returned from L.T.M. Course | |
| | | | Sub Lieut Walker and 3 O.R. left for L.T.M. Course | |
| | | | In Support. Remainder of Battn had use of Bath and received clean clothes. | |
| | | | C.P.O. High left for Course of Instn at CONDETTE | |
| | | 10 pm | "Raiding Party" carried out a rehearsal on a bombing ground in rear of Town with live bombs. Threw over 90 bombs, a useful and instructive exercise | |
| | 13th | | In Support. Sunday | |
| | | 9.30 am | Divine Service | |
| | | | Lieut J. R. Douglas and 10 O.R. left for Bombing Course | |
| | | | Usual working parties | |

Instructions regarding War Diaries and Intelligence Summaries are contained in F. S. Regs., Part II. and the Staff Manual respectively. Title pages will be prepared in manuscript.

# WAR DIARY

*or*

~~INTELLIGENCE SUMMARY.~~

*(Erase heading not required.)*

Army Form C. 2118.

Anson Batt[n]

| Place | Date | Hour | Summary of Events and Information | Remarks and references to Appendices |
|---|---|---|---|---|
| | August | | | |
| BULLY GRENAY | 13th | 11pm | Lewis Guns under Lieut Henry relieved HOWE Batt Lewis Guns in ANGRES I | |
| ANGRES I | 14th | 8.0am | Relieved HOWE Batt in ANGRES I. Relief completed at 8.0 a.m | |
| | | | Companies disposed as follows - | |
| | | | Right Front - B Co | |
| | | | Left " - C " | |
| | | | Support - A " | |
| | | | Reserve - D " | |
| | | | Enemy were active with Small Minenwerfer and Aerial Torpedoes - The latter are commonly called 'Pineapples' | |
| | | | No Z.2. 3432 Able Seaman J Moon killed and 2 O.R. wounded. | |
| | | | Slight rain in afternoon | |
| | 14/15th | mid | Patrols visited NO MANS LAND but were unable to obtain any information owing to bright moonlight and enemy's vigilance. | |
| | 15th | | Enemy again active with Minenwerfer and 'Pineapples' | |
| | | | No Z.C 6370 Able Seaman J. Frame killed 2 O.R. wounded | |

T.131. Wt. W708-776. 500000, 4/15. Sir J. C. & S.

Instructions regarding War Diaries and Intelligence Summaries are contained in F. S. Regs., Part II. and the Staff Manual respectively. Title pages will be prepared in manuscript.

# WAR DIARY
*or*
~~INTELLIGENCE SUMMARY.~~
*(Erase heading not required.)*

Army Form C. 2118.

Anson Battn

| Place | Date | Hour | Summary of Events and Information | Remarks and references to Appendices |
|---|---|---|---|---|
| ANGRES I | Aug 15th | pm | 31. O.R returned from duty with 255th Tunnelling Co and 1 Officer and 15 O.R. sent to same Tunnelling Co for duty. | |
| | | | A showery day. The usual work of trench improvement being somewhat hampered by the mud. | |
| ANGRES I | 15 | 8 pm | No patrols were sent out – ~~Battn was~~ Front Cos were withdrawn in readiness for a Gas attack to be made. – This attack was however postponed shortly before midnight | O.O. No 14. O.O No 14(2) |
| | 16th | | A quiet day. Enemy rather less active with his Minenwerfer and Pineapples. | |
| | | 6 pm | A 20 minutes bombardment of enemy trenches on our extreme right and in front of the Battn on our right took place. The fire appeared to be very accurate and the trenches must have been very badly damaged. Enemy's reply was very feeble. | |
| | | | A Co 7th Battn Royal Fusiliers arrived in the line and were attached to the Battn 1 Co to each platoon. Sub Lieut. Cook discharged to Hospital. 1 O.R. wounded | O.O. No 15 |
| | 16/17 | mid | Patrols visited NO MANS LAND between 10 p.m and 1 a.m – no enemy encountered | |
| | 17th | | Enemy threw about 30 aerial torpedoes – Pineapples – and about 20. L.H.V. shells into the area. Otherwise very quiet. 1 O.R wounded | |

T.131. Wt. W708–776. 500000. 4/15. Sir J. C. & S.

Instructions regarding War Diaries and Intelligence Summaries are contained in F. S. Regs., Part II. and the Staff Manual respectively. Title pages will be prepared in manuscript.

# WAR DIARY
*or*
~~INTELLIGENCE~~ SUMMARY.
*(Erase heading not required.)*

Army Form C. 2118.

Anson Batt^n

| Place | Date | Hour | Summary of Events and Information | Remarks and references to Appendices |
|---|---|---|---|---|
| ANGRES I | Aug 17th | | Two Officers patrols visited NO MAN'S LAND – No enemy encountered | |
| " | 18th | 7 a.m. | Batt^n relieved by Howe Batt^n relief completed by 3.5 a.m. and moved into reserve as follows:– | O.O. No 15 |
| FOSSE 10. | | | H^d. Q^rs, A + D C^os in FOSSE 10. | |
| | | | B + C C^os in BULLY GRENAY | |
| | | | B+C C^os had use of baths and clean clothes were issued | |
| " | 19th | | in reserve. Fatigues. 1. O.R went to PERNES for Trench Warfare School. | |
| " | 20th | | Lieut Douglas and 10 O.R returned from Course at Brigade Bomb School. | |
| | | | Sub Lieut Harvey + 2 O.R went for Course at Div^l Gas School BOYEFFLES. | |
| | | | 3. O.R returned from Lewis Gun Course at LE TOUQUET. 2 O.R left for course of Lewis Gun Inst^n at LE TOUQUET. | |
| | | | A + D C^os had use of baths and were given clean clothes. | |
| | | | Sub Lieut + 3 O.R returned from L.T.M. Course at PERNES. | |
| " | 21st | a.m. | A draft of 89 O.R arrived from ETAPLES and were distributed amongst the C^os. They were of moderate physique – many should have been in Bantam battalions. Their clothes were in poor condition. Their hair had obviously not | |

Instructions regarding War Diaries and Intelligence Summaries are contained in F. S. Regs., Part II. and the Staff Manual respectively. Title pages will be prepared in manuscript.

# WAR DIARY
*or*
# INTELLIGENCE SUMMARY.
*(Erase heading not required.)*

Army Form C. 2118.

Anson Batt<sup></sup>n

| Place | Date | Hour | Summary of Events and Information | Remarks and references to Appendices |
|---|---|---|---|---|
| FOSSE 10 | Aug 21st | | been cut for about two months and their boots had the appearance of never being blacked or greased. They were turned over to the Co barbers, and indents prepared for new clothing. A most unsatisfactory state of affairs for a draft fresh from the Base. | |
| | | | 6. O.R. returned from Course of General Instruction at Divnl School, PERNES. | |
| | | | Sub Lieuts CANTLE, Wauchope and Ofield returned from Course of Genl Instn, PERNES. | |
| FOSSE 10 | 22nd | 5 a.m | Companies moved out from FOSSE 10 and BULLY GRENAY and relieved HOWE Battn in ANGRES 1. Relief completed by 8.20 a.m. Companies disposed as follows:- | O.O. No 17 |
| ANGRES 1 | " | 8.30 a.m. | Right Front A Co | |
| | | | Left " D " | |
| | | | In Support B " | |
| | | | In Reserve C " | |
| | | | Enemy were active with minenwerfer and aerial torpedoes, about 120 'Pineapples' being put over. Some Artillery activity also: about 15 rounds of 4.2" being sent over of which eight were blinds. | |
| | | | General improvement of ~~trenches~~ to continued | |

T.2131. Wt. W708-776. 500000. 4/15. Sir J. C. & S.

Instructions regarding War Diaries and Intelligence Summaries are contained in F. S. Regs., Part II. and the Staff Manual respectively. Title pages will be prepared in manuscript.

# WAR DIARY
*or*
~~INTELLIGENCE~~ SUMMARY.
*(Erase heading not required.)*

Army Form C. 2118.

Anson Batt^n.

| Place | Date | Hour | Summary of Events and Information | Remarks and references to Appendices |
|---|---|---|---|---|
| AUCHEUL | Aug 22 | | ~~[illegible] killed~~ 4 O.R. wounded. | |
| | | 4.15pm | In the afternoon a quarter of an hour's bombardment by Left Group Divn^l Artillery + 4th Corps Heavy Artillery of the enemy Front + Support Line took place. Trench mortars also took part. The bombardment was very effective and the retaliation was very feeble. | O.O. No. 18 |
| | | [illegible]pm | Patrol visited No Man's Land - no enemy encountered | |
| | | 10.40pm | A heavy rifle and Artillery fire broke out to our N and gradually extended S. and by 11 p.m. a considerable number of shell were falling in the Left Front C^o area and rearwards as far as Batt^n H^d Q^rs. Enemy's signal was a rocket which turned from red to green. All the fire was caused by a Raid which was made by the Btn N of us. Boches evidently are shaky and feared attack all along the line. | |
| | 23^rd | 1.30am | Our Sentries in Long Arm of Sap 13 heard sounds in our wire W of Sap head, but thought it might be men at work. At 2 a.m. Able Seaman SLESSOR came on Sentry and was told of the sounds, and also that one of the previous Sentries had seen a man's head. He expressed disbelief, fired in the direction named, and sprang on to the parapet calling out "Is Anyone there?" He was immediately shot at by two revolvers and fell. | |

T.2131. Wt. W768-776. 500000. 4/15. Sir J. C. & S.

Instructions regarding War Diaries and Intelligence Summaries are contained in F. S. Regs., Part II. and the Staff Manual respectively. Title pages will be prepared in manuscript.

# WAR DIARY
*or*
~~INTELLIGENCE SUMMARY~~.
*(Erase heading not required.)*

Army Form C. 2118.

Anson Batt^n

| Place | Date | Hour | Summary of Events and Information | Remarks and references to Appendices |
|---|---|---|---|---|
| ANGRES I. | Aug 23rd (cont) | 2 30 am | The men in the Sap immediately opened fire, and three or four of the enemy disclosed themselves and ran off. One was seen to fall. Able Seaman WILDE went out and brought in Able Seaman SLESSOR who was then still alive. He then threw two bombs in the direction from which the enemy had appeared, and from which groans could be heard. The Officer on duty, Sub Lieut Ofield then came into the Sap, and a report of the matter having been made to him, made all the men Stand-to with grenades. He then had a Lewis Gun brought in and traversed all the ground with L.G. fire. Groaning continued intermittently and the ground was kept under close | |
| | | 5 am | observation until 5 a.m. when it was growing light. There being no longer danger of a ruse, Sub Lieut Williams and Able Seaman Wilde then went out and found a Bavarian Officer lying wounded in a shell hole about 8^x from our Sap. | |

Prisoner found here

Sap 13

FRONT LINE

T.131. Wt. W708–776. 500000. 4/15. Sir J. C. & S.

Instructions regarding War Diaries and Intelligence Summaries are contained in F. S. Regs., Part II. and the Staff Manual respectively. Title pages will be prepared in manuscript.

# WAR DIARY
*or*
~~INTELLIGENCE~~ SUMMARY.
*(Erase heading not required.)*

Army Form C. 2118.

Anson Batt^n

| Place | Date | Hour | Summary of Events and Information | Remarks and references to Appendices |
|---|---|---|---|---|
| | Aug | | | |
| ANGRES I. | 23rd (Cont) | | Able Seaman Wilde behaved throughout the whole incident with coolness and courage. | |
| | | | Able Seaman SLESSOR unfortunately died, losing his life as the result of a brave but impetuous action | |
| | | | The prisoner captured was Lieut. WILHELM MOHR of 1st Ersatz Batt^n 14th Bavarian Reg^t | |
| | | | The Batt^n received the congratulations of the G.O.C. Brigade on having effected this capture which secured a most important identification | |
| | 23rd | | Sub Lieut Harvey and 2 O.R. returned from Gas Course. 1 O.R. left for a Gas Course | |
| | | | 6 O.R. left for General Course at 63rd Div^l School at PERNES. | |
| | | 2-4 pm | Enemy was very active with Aerial torpedoes throwing over 300 'Pineapples' in addition to about 5 minenwerfer. About 30 shells fell in our lines during the day. | |
| | | 10 pm | An officer's patrol visited NO MANS LAND. No enemy encountered | |
| | | | Casualties for day (in addition to A.B. SLESSOR killed) 4. O.R. wounded | |
| | 24th | | Enemy was active with Minenwerfer and Aerial torpedoes in retaliation for our medium T.M. bombardment. Enemy Artillery inactive | |
| | | | General trench improvement carried out. Patrol visited NO MANS LAND | |

T.131. Wt. W708-776. 500000. 4/15. Sir J. C. & S.

Instructions regarding War Diaries and Intelligence Summaries are contained in F. S. Regs., Part II. and the Staff Manual respectively. Title pages will be prepared in manuscript.

# WAR DIARY
*or*
~~INTELLIGENCE SUMMARY~~.
*(Erase heading not required.)*

Army Form C. 2118.

Anson Battn

| Place | Date | Hour | Summary of Events and Information | Remarks and references to Appendices |
|---|---|---|---|---|
| ANGRES I | Aug 25th | | Enemy again very active with Minenwerfer and Aerial torpedoes as retaliation to our M.T.M. About 600 Pineapples fired at us | |
| | | | 2 Signallers returned from a Course at 4th Corps School. | |
| | | | 7. O.R. (Regtl Q.M.S., 2 C.S.Ms, Transport Sergt, Cook Sergt + 2 others) R.F.R and R.N.R personnel discharged to Base for Sea Service. | |
| | | | Able Seaman (H.G) A Redding killed, 5 O.R. wounded. | |
| " | | 9.58 pm | Enemy suddenly opened with Artillery, Machine Guns and Aerial torpedoes and maintained a heavy fire for two minutes and suddenly ceased | |
| | | | General trench repairs maintained. | |
| " | 26th | 10 am | A fifteen minute bombardment of enemy front and reserve trenches took place by our Artillery. No retaliation beyond 2 H.E which fell near the Support Co | |
| | | 8 am | Relieved by HOWE Battn and moved into Reserve, Battn disposed as follows:– | O.O. No 19 |
| | | | HdQrs, B + C Cos at FOSSE 10. | |
| | | | A + D Cos BULLY GRENAY. | |
| | | | A + D Cos has use of Bath and were issued with clean clothes. | |
| | | | Weather broke – heavy showers fell throughout the day. | |

T.131. Wt. W708–776. 500000. 4/15. Sir J. C. & S.

Instructions regarding War Diaries and Intelligence Summaries are contained in F. S. Regs., Part II. and the Staff Manual respectively. Title pages will be prepared in manuscript.

# WAR DIARY
or
~~INTELLIGENCE SUMMARY.~~
*(Erase heading not required.)*

Army Form C. 2118.

Anson Battn

| Place | Date | Hour | Summary of Events and Information | Remarks and references to Appendices |
|---|---|---|---|---|
| | Aug | | | |
| RESERVE | 26 | 8pm | 400 men employed as carrying parties moving out gas cylinders from front line trenches. | |
| | cont 27 | | | |
| " | 27th | | Divine Service. Fatigues. 480 men employed on carrying as on previous night. Showery day. | |
| | | | 2 O.R. returned from Bayonet Fighting Course at IV Corps School. PERNES | |
| | | | 1 O.R. went for Course at Divisional Gas School. BOYEFFLES. | |
| " | 28th | | Fatigues 480 men employed in carrying as on previous nights | |
| | | | B + C Cos + HdQrs had use of Baths. | |
| " | 29th | | O.C. with G.O.C. 188th Infy Bde left at 7 a.m. and paid a visit to the scene of operations on the SOMME. Heavy thunderstorm in afternoon | |
| | | | Lewis Guns relieved Howe Battn Lewis Guns in ANGRES I. 2 O.R. wounded | |
| | | | 2. O.R. returned from L.G. Course at LE TOUQUET | |
| | | | 1. O.R. left for Musketry Instructor's Course at CAMIERS. | |
| | 30th | 5.a.m | Moved out from Bde Reserve and relieved Howe Battn in ANGRES I. Relief | O.O. No 20 |
| ANGRES I | " | 8.30a.m | completed by 8.30 a.m. Battn ~~was~~ disposed as follows Right front — B Co. | |
| | | | Left " — C " | |
| | | | In Support — D " | |
| | | | Reserve — A " | |

T.131. Wt. W708-776. 500000. 4/15. Sir J. C. & S.

Instructions regarding War Diaries and Intelligence Summaries are contained in F. S. Regs., Part II. and the Staff Manual respectively. Title pages will be prepared in manuscript.

# WAR DIARY
*or*
~~INTELLIGENCE SUMMARY.~~
(*Erase heading not required.*)

Army Form C. 2118.

Anson Battn

| Place | Date | Hour | Summary of Events and Information | Remarks and references to Appendices |
|---|---|---|---|---|
| ANGRES I | Aug 30th | | Rain fell throughout the day, which was very quiet. Enemy threw over about 75 'Pineapples' as retaliation for the two half hour bombardments by our Medium Trench Mortars. | |
| | | | 1 O.R returned from Course at Gas School. | |
| | | | Sub Lieut Hulbert and 2 O.R. left for Lewis Gun Course at PERNES. | |
| | | | Lieut Lee and 1 O.R left for Course of Trench warfare Instruction at IV Corps School, PERNES | |
| " | 31st | | A quiet day. The weather cleared, and troops were occupied clearing up their trenches, and repairing damage caused by rain. M. Trench Mortars carried out two short bombardments, practically no retaliation. 1 O.R. wounded. | |
| | | | Sub Lieut Mitchell left for course of instruction in Medium Trench Mortars at CLARQUES. | |
| | | | Lieut. Comdr Bett + 3 O.R. left for Gas Course at Divl Gas School, BOYEFFLES | |
| " | | 9.30pm | Two Patrols under Officers reconnoitred certain portions of NO MANS LAND. | |

G. Saunders.
Lieut Col.
Comdg Anson Battn

T2131. Wt. W708-776. 500000. 4/15. Sir J. C. & S.

Draft

[illegible] Irishmen [illegible]

[illegible] will be [illegible] in [illegible] Ancient [illegible]

[illegible]

[illegible] Day [illegible]

[illegible] followed [illegible]

[illegible] to the [illegible] of [illegible]

arrangement [illegible]

[illegible] that [illegible]

[illegible] schools [illegible]

[illegible] passing [illegible]

[illegible]

Operation Order No 10,

by

**SECRET.** Lieut Colonel A. J. Saunders, D.S.O., [illegible].

Commanding Anson Bn.

[illegible] August 191[illegible]

Relief 1. The Lewis Guns of Anson Bn, will relieve those of Howe Bn in ANBRES I tomorrow. Relief to be completed by 3. p.m.

Detail 2. Lewis Gun Crews of each Co., with 21 magazines per gun will report to Lieut Henry outside O.R. at 11.30 a.m. Caps and packs will be stacked in square in front of O.R.

Rations 3. Each Co. Q.M.S. will send rations for tomorrow for their Gun Crews to Q.M.S. D Co. who will send them up to the trenches by a ration carrying party.

[illegible] Fraser

Sub Lieut & Adjt.

SECRET.

Operation Order No. 11.
by
Lieut. Colonel F. J. Saunders D.S.O. RMLI.
Commanding Anson Bn.

5th August 1916.

Relief 1. The Anson Bn. will relieve the Howe Bn. tomorrow 6th inst. in ANGRES I. [illegible] to be completed by 9 a.m.

Detail 2. A Coy will relieve Right Front Line Coy B
B " " " Support Coy A
D " " " Left Front Line Coy C
C " " " Reserve Coy D

Coys will enter CORONS D'AIX trench at the following times:– A Coy 5 [illegible] a.m. B Coy 5 [illegible] a.m. D Coy [illegible] a.m.
C Coy 6 15 a.m. HQrs 6 30 a.m.

Communication 3. O.C. Coys will report by telephone when the relief is complete, the code words "Relief Complete" will be [illegible] [illegible] [illegible] [illegible] [illegible] to this effect.

Telephones 4. Telephones of this Bn will not be connected up until relief is reported complete by the [illegible].

Advance Parties 5. An advance party consisting of [illegible] and C.S.M. and 1 [illegible] per each Coy and 1 from H.Q. will rendezvous at the entrance to CORONS D'AIX trench at 5 a.m. and proceed to [illegible] [illegible] and take over all trench stores.

Lewis Guns 6. The Lewis Guns will be used as a Section and will be under command of Lieut. Henry.

Kits 7. All Officers' kits and valises and packs of other ranks will be placed in Coy Dumps at [illegible] a.m. QMS of HQrs and each Coy are responsible that all their Coy kits and stores are properly kept together during transport and on arrival at [illegible].

Duty 8. Officers who are not proceeding to the trenches will report to [illegible] at HERSIN at 10 a.m. tomorrow for duty.

[illegible]
Sec. Lieut. & Adj.

Operation Order No [illegible]

by

[illegible] of [illegible] R.N.A.

Commanding [illegible]

[illegible]

[illegible] 1. [illegible] by [illegible] [illegible] to be completed [illegible] to be returned by [illegible]

[illegible] 2. On [illegible] BULLEY [illegible] A.C. & CORONS D.A. [illegible] and [illegible] ALCHAR [illegible]

[illegible] 3. [illegible] by the following [illegible]
C.D. [illegible] CORONS D.A. ALLEY.
A.B. [illegible] CORNER ALLEY ANGRES ALLEY and ANGRES ROAD TRENCH.
[illegible] authority [illegible] [illegible] ALL [illegible] [illegible] ROAD.

[illegible] [illegible]

[illegible]

<u>SECRET.</u>

Operation Order No. 3
by
Lieut. Col. F. J. Saunders D.S.O. R.M.L.I.
<u>Commanding Anson Batt.</u>

<u>13th August. 1916</u>

<u>Relief</u> 1. The Anson Bn will relieve the Howe Bn to-morrow 14th inst. in ANGRES I. Relief to be completed by 9am

<u>Detail</u> 2.

B. Co will relieve Right Front Line Co.
A. Co " " Support Co.
C. Co " " Left Front Line Co.
D Co " " Reserve Co.

Company will march off in sufficient time to as follows:

B.Co entrance to ANGRES ALLEY at 6am
A Co " " do " " 6.15am
C. Co " " CORONS D'AIX 6 am
D Co " " do MECHANICS at 6.30 am
Hdqrs Co " " CORONS D'AIX at 6.30 am

<u>Communications</u> 3. On Relief being completed Officers will report by telephone. Code words for "Relief Complete" will be sent up [illegible] words.

<u>Telephones</u> 4. Telephones of this Bn will not be connected up until relief is reported complete by Coy Comdrs

<u>Advance Party</u>. 5. An advance party consisting of R.S.M. and C.S.M. and Signaller for each Coy and [illegible] from Hdqrs will arrive at the entrance to CORONS D'AIX at 8 am. and proceed to various Co Hdqrs and take over all trench stores.

W. N. G. [illegible]
Lieut. Lt. & Adjt.

SECRET

Operation Order No 14.
by
Lieut Colonel F. J. Saunders D.S.O. R.M.L.I.
Commanding Anson Bn.

15th Augst 1916.

1. A Gas Attack will be made tonight if the wind is suitable. There will be an Artillery bombardment but no infantry assault will be made.

2. Bays 3 to 29 inclusive in this sub-section will be used. 30 men under Sub Lieut Williams will work under orders of H Coy Special R.E. Each man while so working will place his rifle with bayonet fixed on the parapet of the bay in which he is working. These men will report to Sub Lieut Williams at Junction of PAGE STREET and FRONT LINE at 7.30 p.m.

3. By 8. p.m all bays numbered in the FRONT LINE will be vacated and the one man per bay above mentioned will take up his position in the numbered bays. The garrison will then remain in the unnumbered bays until half an hour before zero, when it will be withdrawn from the FRONT LINE.

4. The occupants will be withdrawn from SAPS three quarters of an hour before zero. The garrison will remain behind FRONT LINE until zero + 40. At that time the garrison will resume its normal position, except as may be directed by the Gas Personnel on the spot, and also except that the portion of the FRONT LINE from SAP 15 to Right flank Boundary (namely B Coy front) which will not be re-occupied until Lieut Beasley, Special R.E. in charge of Right Gas Section, has reported "Gas Clear" to the O.C. Right Coy and Battalion H.Qrs.

5. 2 (Two) Lewis Guns will remain in the FRONT LINE.

6. All troops in the FRONT LINE will wear Gas Helmets down, or box respirators, remainder will wear Gas Helmets rolled up on the head.

7. All watches will be synchronised at 5.30 p.m.

8. No Working or carrying parties will be sent out. Ration parties will not be sent out until after [illegible] when orders will be issued.

9. Should this Operation be postponed the code word "FRESH MILK" will be sent.

10. Zero time will be communicated when received.

[signature] Fraser
Sub Lieut & Adjt

SECRET.

Operation Order No 14(2).
by
Lieut Col. F. J. Saunders D.S.O. RMLI.
Commanding Anson Bn.

15th Augst 1916.

Reference O.O.14. There will be three Zero hours.

First at 9.30 p.m. 15th instant.
Second " 1-0 a.m 16th instant.
Third " 3-0 a.m 16th instant.

Should conditions be favourable the Operation will take place at the first Zero hour without further notice, should they be unfavourable a postponement will be made to the second Zero hour and again to the third Zero hour if necessary. These postponements will only be made if it appears likely that conditions will become unfavourable, otherwise the Operation will be cancelled.

The following codes will be used:—

| Hour to be sent | |
| --- | --- |
| 1st wire before 9-0 p.m | Operation postponed until 1-0 a.m 16th instant. POTSDAM. |
| | Operation postponed until night 16th/17th. BERLIN. |
| 2nd wire at mid-night | Operation postponed until 3-0 a.m 16th instant. SPANDAU |
| | Operation postponed until night 16th/17th. BERLIN. |
| 3rd wire at 2-0 a.m. (if conditions are still unfavourable) | Operation postponed until night 16th/17th. BERLIN. |

In the event of postponement from one Zero time to another the saps should be re-occupied between each postponement.

(Signed) M.R. FRASER.
Sub Lieut & Adjt.

Operation Order No 15
by.
Lieut Col. F.J. Saunders D.S.O. RMLI.

16th Augst 1916

1 A Co. of 7th Battn: Royal Fusiliers will be attached to Battn in ANGRES I for 4 days commencing this afternoon. The Co. will be split up into sections, a section being attached to each platoon of each Front Line Co.

2. The two Lewis Guns of this Co. will be also attached and will be attached to two Front Line guns under direction of Battn: L.G.O.

3. 1 Guide from each platoon of B + C Cos. and 2 Lewis Gun Guides will report to a representative from Bde H Qrs. at BULLY Church at 4 p.m. this day and will lead their sections straight up into the line.

4. Rations for Thursday will be carried by the Co., but rations for following days will be sent up with the usual Ration parties

over.

5. Code word for Sections and Lewis Guns in position "BYSTANDER."

(Sgd) M.R. FRASER.

Sub Lieut & Adj

SECRET

Operation Orders No. 16 17.8.16

[illegible]

Secret

Date 21/8/16.

## Operation Order No 17
by
Lieut Col F. J. Saunders DSO [illegible]
Commanding Anson Bn.

Relief (1) Anson Bn will relieve Howe Bn in ANGRES I tomorrow
Relief to be completed by 9am.

Detail (2) A Co will relieve Right Front Coy.
D " " " Left " "
C " " " support Coy.
B " " " Reserve "
A [illegible] move via ANGRES ALLEY to be at entrance [illegible] ARRAS RD TRENCH at 6 am.
C. Coy will move via ANGRES ALLEY to be at entrance to ARRAS RD TRENCH at 6-15am.
D Coy will enter CORONS D'AIX ALLEY at 6am.
B Coy will enter CORONS D'AIX ALLEY at 6-15am.
HdQs Coy will enter CORONS D'AIX ALLEY at 6-30 am
Usual precautions are to be taken against hostile observation

Advance Party (3) An advance party of C.S.M. and C.P.O.s, 1 Signaller per Coy and one for Hd Qrs will be at entrance to CORONS D'AIX at 5.30 am.

Communication (4) When Cos have taken over [illegible] Commanders will report by telephone to Bn Hd Qrs using the Code Words "[illegible] up" or words to that effect.

Telephones (5) Telephones of the Bn will not be connected up until relief has been reported complete by [illegible].

Attachment (6) A section of [illegible] R.I. will be attached to each platoon [illegible] Anson Bn. for instruction

M. R. J. Fraser
Sublieut & Adj.

SECRET

## Operation Order. No ~~17~~.18

by.

Lieut Col. F J Saunders DSO RMLI

Commanding Anson Bn.

August 22nd 1916.

An artillery bombardment of Front and support Lines in enemy salient M 26 c 4.8 will take place this afternoon from 4-23 pm until 4-38 pm

C. C. D. Co. will clear the Front Line from Sap 17 inclusive to Left Limit inclusive at 4 pm, Garrison will be withdrawn to dugouts in PYRENEES. Front Line will not be reoccupied until ordered., OC Firing Line will communicate with C.O. by telephone at 4.45 pm as to the situation and when all is quiet CO will order "Carry On"

All working Parties will be withdrawn and kept under cover during this period

Deep dugout parties, M.G. Detatchment, TM Battery to be warned.

W K of Fraser.

Sub Lieut & Adjt

Secret

Operation Orders. No 19
of
Lieut Col F. J. Saunders DSO RMLI
Commanding Anson Bn

25/8/16.

Relief. Anson Bn will be relieved by Howe Bn in ANGRES I. to-morrow 26th inst. Relief to be completed by 9 AM.

Move. On relief Battalion will move into reserve & be disposed as follows.

A Company } Bully-Grenay.
D " }

B Company }
C " } FOSSE 10
HQrs " }

Detail. When Coys are relieved they will march out when ordered by the following routes

A Coy. COOKER ALLEY, SPINNEY TRENCH, and CORONS D'AIX.

B Coy. } VIA COOKER ALLEY, ANGRES ALLEY AIX NOULETTE ARRAS ROAD
C " }

D Coy } VIA CORONS D'AIX.
HQrs }

[Comm]unication Coy Commanders will report by telephone when relief is complete using code words HAVE YOU ANY MILK AVAILABLE Code words for moving out will be MILK IS BEING SENT UP or words to that effect

[Hel]mets Steel helmets are to be turned over to relieving Coys to complete relieving Bn to one helmet per man.

[Rep]ort Daily report to be at Bn HQrs by 6 AM tomorrow morning

M. Ross Fraser
Sub Lieut & Adj.

SECRET

G.O.

Secret

Operation Orders No 20 by
Lieut Col. J. Saunders DSO RMLI
Commanding Anson Bn

August 19th 1918

Relief (1) Anson Bn will relieve Howe Bn in [illegible] relief to be completed by 9 am.

Disposition (2) B Coy will relieve Right Front Coy

C " " " Left " "

D " " " Support Coy

A " " " Reserve "

B Coy will move via ANCRES ALLEY to be at entrance to [illegible] ROAD TRENCH at 6 am.

D Coy will move via ANCRES ALLEY to be at entrance to [illegible] ROAD TRENCH at 6 30 am.

C Coy will enter [illegible] ALLEY at [illegible] am.

A Coy will enter [illegible] ALLEY at [illegible]

Advance Party 3 An advance party of Bn. SM and CSM [illegible] one per Coy and one for Headquarters will be at entrance to [illegible] at [illegible] am.

Communications (4) When Coys have taken over Coy Commanders will report by telephone to Bn Hd Qrs. using the code words "Please send up hammer & nails" or words to that effect.

Telephones (5) Telephones of the Bn will not be connected up until relief has been reported complete by Coy Comdrs.

Attachments (6) A section of the [illegible] R.E. [illegible] will be attached to each [illegible] of Anson Bn for instruction.

Steel Helmets (7) Helmets will be taken over from [illegible] Bn [illegible] Coys to one per man.

[illegible] Fraser
[illegible]

Vol IV

Original Copy

War Diary Vol IV.

Anson Batt[illegible]

From 1st [illegible]tember 1916

To 30th September 1916 incl[illegible]

[illegible]

Lieut Col

Commanding Anson [illegible]

[illegible]

Instructions regarding War Diaries and Intelligence Summaries are contained in F. S. Regs., Part II. and the Staff Manual respectively. Title pages will be prepared in manuscript.

# WAR DIARY
or
~~INTELLIGENCE SUMMARY.~~
*(Erase heading not required.)*

Vol IV

Army Form C. 2118.

Anson Battⁿ

| Place | Date | Hour | Summary of Events and Information | Remarks and references to Appendices |
|---|---|---|---|---|
| ANGRES. I. | Sept 1st | | An exceptionally quiet day in the sub-section – only twelve 'Pineapples' and nine Rifle Grenades were counted as having been fired at us. Nº Z C 806 A.B.(H.G.) G HENDRY was killed. | |
| | | | General trench improvement was carried out. Weather was finer | |
| | 1/2 | | Two Officers patrols visited NO MAN'S LAND. No enemy encountered. | |
| " | 2nd | | Another quiet day, – about '20' Pineapples and 20 Rifle Grenades were fired at us. | |
| | | | 1 OR accidentally wounded with a Very's Pistol. Sub Lieut Ridler left for a Sniper's Course. | |
| | | | Two Officers patrols visited NO MAN'S LAND – No enemy encountered | |
| | 3rd | | Relieved by HOWE Battⁿ and moved into Support. Relief completed by 8.23 a.m. | O.O. Nº 21. |
| BULLY GRENAY (Support) | | | Coys in Support disposed as follows:– | |
| | | | Hd Qrs A + D Coys in BULLY GRENAY | |
| " | | | C " " MECHANICS | |
| " | | | B " in CAP DU PONT and CORON D'AIX | |
| | | | Two Coys had use of Baths. | |
| | | | Lieut Comdr Bett +2 OR returned from a Gas Course. | |
| | | | A fine day. | |

T.2131. Wt. W708–776. 500000. 4/15. Sir J. C. & S.

Instructions regarding War Diaries and Intelligence Summaries are contained in F. S. Regs., Part II. and the Staff Manual respectively. Title pages will be prepared in manuscript.

# WAR DIARY
*or*
~~INTELLIGENCE SUMMARY.~~
*(Erase heading not required.)*

Army Form C. 2118.

Anson Batt

| Place | Date | Hour. | Summary of Events and Information | Remarks and references to Appendices |
|---|---|---|---|---|
| SUPPORT | Sept 4th | | Usual fatigues found. | |
| " | 5th | | Usual fatigues. Sub McLAREN and 7 O.R. proceeded on Bombing Course at Brigade Bomb School. | |
| | | | Sub Lieut LANGSTON left for a Lewis Gun Course at LE TOUQUET. | |
| " | 6th | | Usual fatigues found. | |
| ANGRES 1 | 7th | | Relieved Howe Batt in ANGRES 1 – relief completed at 8.15 a.m. – One Co 10th Royal Dublin Fusiliers attached for few days training, and C. Co moved into FOSSE 10. Batt disposed as follows. | |
| | | | Rt Front Co — A. Co | |
| | | | Left " — D " | |
| | | | In Support — B " | |
| | | | " Reserve — C Co & 10th Royal Dublin Fusiliers | |
| | | | A quiet day. – about 50 Pineapples thrown at us & 12 Shrapnel. | |
| | 7/8th | | Two Officers patrols visited NO MAN'S LAND. No enemy encountered. | |
| " | 8th | | A quiet day in the Sub Section about 30 Pineapples being fired at us chiefly in retaliation for medium T.M. bombardments which take place twice daily | |

T. 131. Wt. W708–776. 500000. 4/15. Sir J. C. & S.

Instructions regarding War Diaries and Intelligence Summaries are contained in F. S. Regs., Part II. and the Staff Manual respectively. Title pages will be prepared in manuscript.

# WAR DIARY
*or*
# INTELLIGENCE SUMMARY.
*(Erase heading not required.)*

Army Form C. 2118.

Anson Batt

| Place | Date | Hour | Summary of Events and Information | Remarks and references to Appendices |
|---|---|---|---|---|
| ANGRES I | Sept 7th | a.m. | The following Officers joined the Battalion from the Base Depot at ETAPLES and were posted to Companies as indicated | |
| | | | Sub Lieut W. H. MARTIN } A Co | |
| | | | " " T. B. HARROWER } A Co | |
| | | | " " CEDRIC LEE } B Co | |
| | | | " " G. F. FUNNELL } B Co | |
| | | | " " CECIL HULBERT } C Co | |
| | | | " " H. L. WEBLEY } C Co | |
| | | | " " G. BLACKMORE } C Co | |
| | | | " " J. F. RUSHTON } C Co | |
| | | | " " W. G. MARSHALL } D Co | |
| | | | " " R. H. WAY } D Co | |
| | | | " " F. C. WEAVER } D Co | |
| | | | " " STIMSON } D Co | |

WAR DIARY
*or*
# INTELLIGENCE SUMMARY.
*(Erase heading not required.)*

Instructions regarding War Diaries and Intelligence Summaries are contained in F. S. Regs., Part II. and the Staff Manual respectively. Title pages will be prepared in manuscript.

Army Form C. 2118.

| Place | Date | Hour | Summary of Events and Information | Remarks and references to Appendices |
|---|---|---|---|---|
| ANGRES I | Sept 8th (Cont) 8/9th | | Six (6) P.Os and L.S. returned from a General Course of Military Training at 63rd (R.N.) Divisional School at PERNES. and 4 P.Os & L.S. left for a similar Course. Two Patrols visited NO MAN'S LAND when the following incident took place. A patrol of Lieut F. C. MUNDY and Leading Seamen TURNER and KITCHEN left about 9.30 p.m to reconnoitre the enemy sap and neighbouring wire at M.26.C.2½.4. Whilst lying in a shell crater about 25 or 30 yards from enemy front line, Leading Seaman KITCHEN received a bullet wound in the side of the head from a rifle fired from the enemy trench to their right front. Lieut Mundy and L.S. Turner bandaged Leading Seaman Kitchen who pluckily determined to crawl back. The party then started to return. L.S. Kitchen with great pluck and determination managed to crawl about 25 yards but then collapsed from exhaustion due to his wound. He was dragged into another shell crater where he was violently sick. L.S. Turner then endeavoured to carry L.S. Kitchen on his back but owing to the latter's helpless state this was impossible, so Lieut Mundy and L.S. Turner carried him back between them. This took place within sixty yards of the enemy in bright moonlight and over ground devoid of cover. L.S. Kitchen was carried back in this manner close to our trench where further assistance was obtained. A special | |

T.131. Wt. W708–776. 500000. 4/15. Sir J. C. & S.

Instructions regarding War Diaries and Intelligence Summaries are contained in F. S. Regs., Part II. and the Staff Manual respectively. Title pages will be prepared in manuscript.

# WAR DIARY
*or*
# ~~INTELLIGENCE SUMMARY.~~
*(Erase heading not required.)*

Army Form C. 2118.

Anson Batt<sup></sup>n.

| Place | Date | Hour | Summary of Events and Information | Remarks and references to Appendices |
|---|---|---|---|---|
| ANGRES I | Sept 8/9 | | report on the plucky conduct and determination was forwarded to G.O.C 188th Inf Bde. | |
| | | | The full names of the three concerned are | |
| | | | Lieut FREDERIC CHARLES MUNDY R.N.V.R. | |
| | | | No. K.P. 942 Leading Seaman (H.G) STEPHEN TURNER | |
| | | | No. K.P. 841 " " MARMADUKE KITCHEN — wounded | |
| | 9th | | A quiet day, but about 70 Pineapples were fired at us. | |
| | | | 1. O.R. wounded and Abl Seaman No. Z C 397 J. THOMPSON killed | |
| | | | Sub Lieut C.L. Jones and 1. O.R. proceeded on a Sniper's Course at PERNES | |
| | | | Lieut MARK LEE and 1. O.R. returned from a Trench Warfare course at PERNES (IV Corps School) | |
| | | | 3. O.R. left on a similar course. | |
| | | | Sub Lieut. Stanley Hulbert returned from a Lewis Gun Course at PERNES | |
| | 9/10 | | Two Officers patrols visited NO MANS LAND. No enemy encountered | |
| | 10th | | A quiet day with usual Trench Mortar bombardments and normal number of Pineapples thrown at us. | |
| | | | A complete reconnaissance of the enemy sap at M.26 C.2½.4 having been made on by the patrols that had examined it on 4 nights – two during this period in the trenches | |

T2134. Wt. W708–776. 500000. 4/15. Sir J. C. & S.

Instructions regarding War Diaries and Intelligence Summaries are contained in F. S. Regs., Part II. and the Staff Manual respectively. Title pages will be prepared in manuscript.

# WAR DIARY
*or*
# INTELLIGENCE SUMMARY.
*(Erase heading not required.)*

Army Form C. 2118.

Anson Battn

| Place | Date | Hour | Summary of Events and Information | Remarks and references to Appendices |
|---|---|---|---|---|
| ANGRES I. | 10th | | and line during the previous tour), a raid was planned to be carried out on the evening of this day, and met with entire success.<br>A small party consisting of Lieut F.C. Mundy, Sub Lieut W.B. Moir and 12 O.R. assembled in NO MANS LAND between 9.30 p.m. & 10 p.m. At 10 p.m. our Artillery and Trench Mortars formed a barrage round the selected area and the party moved forward. On approaching the Sap rapid rifle fire was opened on the party by the occupants of the Sap. The wire proving easiest of access at the Sap head it was entered there instead of at the mouth. A bomb was thrown into the Sap head from the parapet by Sub Lieut MOIR and had immediate effect. Two of the enemy ran down the Sap and were chased by Sub Lieut MOIR, but managed to escape up their front line trench.<br>At the same time Lieut Mundy and Leading Seaman LEIGHTON jumped down into the Sap and found another occupant who was slightly wounded. Several others of the party gave chase to others of the party who were seen running away and two or three of the enemy are believed to have been killed. Lieut Mundy received a wound in the chest, believed from our own bomb thrown at very close quarters, but he continued gallantly to lead his party.<br>The remaining occupant of the Sap, who began calling loudly 'KAMERAD', offered no | O.O. No 24 9th Sept. |

T.131. Wt. W708-776. 500000. 4/15. Sir J. C. & S.

Instructions regarding War Diaries and Intelligence Summaries are contained in F. S. Regs., Part II. and the Staff Manual respectively. Title pages will be prepared in manuscript.

# WAR DIARY
*or*
~~INTELLIGENCE SUMMARY.~~
*(Erase heading not required.)*

Army Form C. 2118.

Anson Batt

| Place | Date | Hour | Summary of Events and Information | Remarks and references to Appendices |
|---|---|---|---|---|
| ANGRES I | Sept 10th (Cont) | | resistance, was immediately secured and the whole party withdrew. During the withdrawal from the sap rifle fire was opened on the party from the enemy trench, and Sub Lieut MOIR and L.S. LEIGHTON were both wounded but not severely.<br>Some difficulty was experienced in bringing back the prisoner who either would not or could not walk and owing to his size it took five men to get him along. Fortunately, owing to the splendid support rendered by our Artillery and Trench Mortars the party was not hampered by the enemy fire, and the prisoner was duly brought in.<br>During the operation the enemy artillery fired on our Communication and reserve trenches and four men were slightly wounded by a 5·9".<br>The gallant and determined manner in which LIEUT FREDERIC CHARLES MUNDY, SUB LIEUT WILLIAM BOYD MOIR and Leading Seaman ARCHIBALD A LEIGHTON (R. K.P. 924) behaved was immediately responsible for the success of the operation, but all ranks carried out their duties with dash and gallantry. | |
| ~~Support~~ | Sept 11th | | ~~Relieved by Howe Batt~~ During this day Lieut Mundy, Sub Lieut MOIR and 5 O.R. were wounded. | |

T.131. Wt. W708–776. 500000. 4/15. Sir J. C. & S.

Instructions regarding War Diaries and Intelligence Summaries are contained in F. S. Regs., Part II. and the Staff Manual respectively. Title pages will be prepared in manuscript.

# WAR DIARY
*or*
~~INTELLIGENCE SUMMARY.~~
*(Erase heading not required.)*

Army Form C. 2118.

Anson Batt[n]

| Place | Date | Hour | Summary of Events and Information | Remarks and references to Appendices |
|---|---|---|---|---|
| [illegible] | Sept 11th | 1.30 a m | Relieved by HOWE Batt - relief completed at 7.45 a m - and moved into support. Companies disposed as follows: | O.O. N° 23. |
| | | | N° Q[rs] B & C C[os] in BULLY GRENAY | |
| | | | A C[o] in CAP DU PONT and CORONS D'AIX | |
| | | | D C[o] in MECHANICS | |
| | | | The companies had use of bath - Clean clothes issued. | |
| | | | Following telegrams received during the day. | |
| | | | (1) To Lieut Col. SAUNDERS from G.O.C. 188 Inf Bde | |
| | | | "Best congratulations on the successful issue which reflects very highly on the arrangements you made aaa Please also convey to Lieut Grover and members of patrol appreciation of the way the work was carried out aaa A separate telegram has been sent to Lieut Mundy" | |
| | | | (2) To 188 Inf Bde from 1st Army | |
| | | | The Army Commander desires his congratulations to be conveyed to all concerned for their good and useful work in carrying out the raid last night aaa The identification obtained is of great importance not only to the First Army but to | |

T.131. Wt. W708-776. 500000. 4/15. Sir J. C. & S.

Instructions regarding War Diaries and Intelligence Summaries are contained in F. S. Regs., Part II. and the Staff Manual respectively. Title pages will be prepared in manuscript.

# WAR DIARY
*or*
~~INTELLIGENCE SUMMARY.~~
*(Erase heading not required.)*

Army Form C. 2118.

Anson Battn

| Place | Date | Hour | Summary of Events and Information | Remarks and references to Appendices |
|---|---|---|---|---|
| | Sep | | | |
| SUPPORT | 11th | | allied armies fighting on the Western Front, and the name of the prisoner captured | |
| | (Cont) | | was CURT OEHME, a Pte Soldier of the 103rd SAXON Res Regt, 23rd Res Div, XII Res Corps. | |
| " | 12th | | Usual fatigue parties found. | |
| | | | Sub Lieut WALKER and 6 O.R. left for Bombing Course at Bde Bomb School | |
| | | | Sub Lieut MacLaren and 6 O.R. returned from " " " " | |
| | | | Lieut Comdr BETT discharged to Base for duty there. | |
| | | | Sub Lieut MITCHELL returned from Medium Trench Mortar Course | |
| " | 13th | | Usual fatigue parties found. Two Coys + Hd Qrs had use of baths. | |
| | | | Sub Lieut C. LANGSTON returned from Lewis Gun Course at LE TOUQUET | |
| | | | 4 O.R left for a Lewis Gun Course at LE TOUQUET | |
| | | | Petty Officer H. G. PIDSLEY discharged to Cadet School at G.H.Q. for | |
| | | | Course of instruction prior to receiving a Commission. | |
| " | 14th | | Usual fatigue Parties. 12 O.R. engaged in recent raid were granted 10 days special | |
| | | | leave | |
| ANGRES I | 15th | am | Relieved Howe Battn in Angres I. Relief completed at 7 45 a.m. Battn disposed as follows | 20 M 25 |
| | | | Rt Front – B Co, Left Front – C Co, Support – A Co, Reserve – D Co. | |

T2134. Wt. W708-776. 500000. 4/15. Sir J. C. & S.

Instructions regarding War Diaries and Intelligence Summaries are contained in F. S. Regs., Part II. and the Staff Manual respectively. Title pages will be prepared in manuscript.

# WAR DIARY
*or*
~~INTELLIGENCE SUMMARY.~~
*(Erase heading not required.)*

Army Form C. 2118.

Anson Batt[n]

| Place | Date | Hour | Summary of Events and Information | Remarks and references to Appendices |
|---|---|---|---|---|
| ANGRES I | Sept 15. | a.m. | Sub Lieuts Cecil Hilbert, Mitchell, Kilner and Cedric Lee not required for trenches, attached to 315[th] Bde R.F.A for four days during period in the trenches | |
| | | | Sub Lieut Langston and 3 O.R. left for IV Corps Signal School at RANCHICOURT | |
| | | | Sub Lieut Riddler returned from [illegible] Sniper's Course | |
| | [illegible] | | A quiet day in the Sub-section. The usual two half hour wire cutting bombardments were carried out. The enemy fired a few 'pineapples' during the day. We were active with [illegible] grenades. Our Artillery carried out a practice barrage [illegible] the Southern portion of the enemy salient during the afternoon. The enemy fired three minenwerfer [illegible] right [illegible] - they fell into our lines in rear of fire trench and [illegible] communication [illegible] slightly. Reinforcements of 10 O.R. joined the Batt[n] | |
| | [illegible] | [illegible] | [illegible] patrols [illegible] HOMMES [illegible] but encountered no enemy. One patrol was fired on with rifle fire. | |
| | [illegible] | [illegible] | Our Artillery [illegible] bombarding VIMY to the south of us. This evidently startled the enemy who apparently feared more raids, for they immediately sent up many red and green lights and at 1.40 a.m. heavy artillery fire was opened on to the left [illegible] The parapet was blown in in three places, and the communication | |

T. 134. Wt. W708-776. 500000. 4/15. Sir J. C. & S.

Instructions regarding War Diaries and Intelligence Summaries are contained in F. S. Regs., Part II. and the Staff Manual respectively. Title pages will be prepared in manuscript.

# WAR DIARY
*or*
# INTELLIGENCE SUMMARY.
*(Erase heading not required.)*

Army Form C. 2118.

Anson Batt^n

| Place | Date | Hour | Summary of Events and Information | Remarks and references to Appendices |
|---|---|---|---|---|
| ANGRES 1 | Sept 16th (Cont) | | trenches were damaged. At 2 a.m the bombardment ceased. We had no casualties | |
| | | a.m | 3 O.R proceeded on 10 days leave to England. | |
| | | | Sub Lieut Fraser left for England on transfer to the Machine Gun Corps, and Sub Lieut Williams assumed the duties of Adjutant temporarily. | |
| | | p.m | The day was quiet except for a few 'Rum Jars' (viz heavy Minenwerfer) which came in on our right doing a certain amount of damage, but there were no casualties. | |
| | 16/17 | 9.30 to 12.30 | Two Officers patrols visited NO MANS LAND. No enemy were seen or heard. | |
| | 17th | | There was slight activity on the part of the enemy's Artillery and their Rum Jars were active. They were thrown in about 9 a.m and for about 2 p.m. Each time instant retaliation was obtained from Our Artillery and the Minenwerfer were silenced. | |
| | [illegible] | 9-12 mid | Two Officers patrols visited NOMANS LAND but no enemy were encountered or heard. | |
| | 18th | 3 a.m | A slight drizzle set in which gradually increased. It rained throughout the morning and at 2.30 p.m heavy rain fell. Rain ceased about 6 p.m. The day was most unpleasant and interfered considerably with the work in the trenches, and the comfort of the men. Officers of the 6th Bedford Regt reconnoitred the Sub section | |

T.131. Wt. W708-776. 500000. 4/15. Sir J. C. & S.

Instructions regarding War Diaries and Intelligence Summaries are contained in F. S. Regs., Part II. and the Staff Manual respectively. Title pages will be prepared in manuscript.

# WAR DIARY
*or*
# INTELLIGENCE SUMMARY.
*(Erase heading not required.)*

Army Form C. 2118.

Anson Batt

| Place | Date | Hour | Summary of Events and Information | Remarks and references to Appendices |
|---|---|---|---|---|
| ANCREST [illegible] | Sept 18 | pm | preparatory to relieving the Batt tomorrow | |
| | | | The enemy was very quiet throughout the day. There was no activity of any sort. | |
| | 19 | | [illegible] Battalion [illegible] relieved by [illegible] Batt Bedford Regt – relief completed at 10.30 a m | O.O. N° [illegible] |
| | | | The Battalion [illegible] of the line and marched to COURCELETTE and went into huts [illegible] | |
| | | | [illegible] Platoon and Tunnelling Party rejoined the Batt [illegible] | |
| | [illegible] | | [illegible] Batt [illegible] and marched to [illegible] into billets there [illegible] | |
| | | | [illegible] the road between [illegible] and [illegible] | |
| | | | Capt [illegible] D. [illegible] GORDY DSC [illegible] the Batt and assumed the duties of Adjutant | |
| | [illegible] | | [illegible] day [illegible] clothing and equipment [illegible] 2nd Lieut WAY and 4 O R [illegible] | |
| | | | [illegible] ~~part~~ transfer to Royal Field Artillery | |
| | [illegible] | | [illegible] and the instruction [illegible] | |
| | | | Company [illegible] carried out [illegible] Batt [illegible] the training [illegible] | |
| | | | [illegible] | |
| | [illegible] | | Company [illegible] | |
| | [illegible] | | Batt Training [illegible] attack in open warfare [illegible] a fine day | |
| | | | Sub Lieut [illegible] OR [illegible] England | |

T2134. Wt. W708—776. 500000. 4/15. Sir J. C. & S.

Instructions regarding War Diaries and Intelligence Summaries are contained in F. S. Regs., Part II. and the Staff Manual respectively. Title pages will be prepared in manuscript.

# WAR DIARY
*or*
# INTELLIGENCE SUMMARY.
*(Erase heading not required.)*

Army Form C. 2118.

Anson Batt^n

| Place | Date | Hour | Summary of Events and Information | Remarks and references to Appendices |
|---|---|---|---|---|
| | Sept | | | |
| DIEVAL | 26^th | | Batt^n Training. The attack was again practised, a marked improvement on the previous days work. Another fine day. | |
| | | | 11 O.R. returned from leave from England. | |
| " | 27^th | | Brigade Training. The Brigade attacked from a line of trenches and seized a line of enemy trenches. A showery day. The Batt^n with its [illegible] returned to billets instead of having dinners on the ground. | |
| " | 28^th | | Lieut Com^dr C. G. [illegible] R.N.V.R. discharged to hospital with injuries as result of an accident to his bike during previous day's operation. L^t Com^dr Ellis assumed duties of 2^nd in Command. | |
| | | | Brigade training. The Brigade carried out an attack in open warfare. A fine day. | |
| | | | Sub Lieut Hobbs & 25 O.R. returned from Rest Camp BOULOGNE | |
| | | | Sub Lieut Way returned from English leave | |
| | | | 5 O.R. proceeded on leave to England | |
| | | | Lieut Com^dr WATSON discharged to England | |
| " | 29^th | | Divisional Training. The Division attacked from a line of trenches and seized two lines of enemy trenches. A wet day. Batt^n returned to billets | |

T2134. Wt. W708—776. 500000. 4/15. Sir J. C. & S.

Instructions regarding War Diaries and Intelligence Summaries are contained in F. S. Regs., Part II. and the Staff Manual respectively. Title pages will be prepared in manuscript.

# WAR DIARY
*or*
# INTELLIGENCE SUMMARY.
*(Erase heading not required.)*

Army Form C. 2118.

Anson Batt

| Place | Date | Hour | Summary of Events and Information | Remarks and references to Appendices |
|---|---|---|---|---|
| | Sept. | | | |
| [illegible] | 29 | | [illegible] the conclusion of operation. | |
| | | | Sub Lieut [illegible] [illegible] to Hospital for dental treatment | |
| | [illegible] | | Divisional Training. The Division carried out a route march, billets were vacated and [illegible] [illegible] [illegible] completely and returned at 12 noon. | |
| | | | No work was carried out in the afternoon. | |
| | | | [illegible] [illegible] R [illegible] [illegible] [illegible] [illegible] | |

J. Saunders
Lieut Col
Comdg. Anson Batt

T2134. Wt. W708—776. 500000. 4/15. Sir J. C. & S.

SECRET.

Operation Order No 21 by ~~Sept 1916~~. 2nd Sept 1916

Lieut Col F. J. Saunders DSC RMLI.

Commanding Anson Bn.

Relief. The Anson Bn will be relieved by the Hood Bn in ANGRES I tomorrow Coy will hold themselves in readiness to be relieved from 6.30AM.

Move Bn. when relieved will move into support and be disposed as follows.

| | |
|---|---|
| Hdqrs. A and D Coys | BULLY-GRENAY |
| C. Coy. | MECHANICS |
| B Coy | CAP de PONT. |

Detail. Coys will move by the following routes when relieved

"B and "D" Coys via COOKER ALLEY, ANGRES ALLEY and ARRAS Rd TRENCH

Hqrs. A & C Coys via CORONS D'AIX.

The usual precautions against enemy observation to be observed

Communication When Coys are relieved, Coy Cmdrs. will ring up FOCUS using code words "No candles issued yesterday" Code words for moving out are "Candles are being issued today" or words to that effect. After which telephones will be disconnected

Attached Troops. C Coy of R.E. will move out with Coys to which they are attached. When clear of trenches platoons will proceed independently to Bn Hd Qrs in BULLY GRENAY. When Coy has assembled it will move off under orders of O.C. C Coy of R.E.

W. Ross Fraser.

Sub Lieut & Adjt.

SECRET

Sept. 6 1916

# Operation Order No. [illegible]

by

[illegible] Commanding [illegible]

Communications [illegible]

[illegible] Bn. [illegible] Coy. and [illegible] Coy. [illegible] will [illegible] in [illegible] Tomorrow 7th inst.

[illegible]

[illegible]

[illegible] Coy. will [illegible] at [illegible] am.

[illegible] Coy. will enter CORONS [illegible] at [illegible] am.

A Coy. [illegible] R.E. will enter CORONS [illegible] at 6.15 am.

Advance Party. 3. An advance party [illegible] will be at entrance to CORONS [illegible] at [illegible] am.

Communication. When Coy. has taken over Coy. [illegible] will [illegible] by telephone "[illegible] We are short of rations today."

Telephones. 5. Telephones [illegible]

[illegible] 6. [illegible] of MECHANICS at 5 am and will move to FOSSE 10 and will occupy billets vacated by [illegible] Coy. R.E. This Coy. will be under orders of [illegible] for Tactical & Brigade Fatigue purposes.

M.R. FRASER

Lt. [illegible] Adjt.

11th inst.

S E C R E T.

No 24.

OPERATION ORDER by LIEUT.COLONEL F.J.SAUNDERS, D.S.O.,R.M.L.I.
COMMANDING ANSON BATTALION.

Map reference - Trench file map tracing.

1. A snipers post has been located in enemy's sap at R.26.c.2½.4. A party of one Officer and 12 other ranks from "D" Company will carry out a small raid on this sap, and front line trench immediately adjacent, on Sunday evening 10th. instant, with a view to securing an identification. Lieut.F.C.Mundy RNVR will be in command.

2. The party will be divided into three (3) squads, and two (2) strecher bearers with a strecher. Each squad will consist of 1 P.O. and 3 men (2 bombers and 1 bayonet man).

3. There will be no preliminary bombardment, but during the operation and commencing at Zero hour, the artillery will lay a barrage round the immediate neighbourhood of the operation.
x 10 p.m. At Zero hour* the party which will previously have assembled unobserved along the old road in NOMANS LAND, lying between sap 18 and the point of the objective, will move off in quick time to point of entry Point B. Strecher bearers will remain at Point A. No.1 squad on entering enemy trench will form a block about 20 yards south of point B. No.2 squad will form a corresponding block about 20 yards North of Point B. No.3 squad will bomb up the sap WITH ALL SPEED and secure the sniper.
If the sniper surrenders voluntary and is unwounded or able to move freely he should be secured and brought back with all despatch. Otherwise a tunic complete and any other available identifications should be brought in. Should no identification be obtained in the sap, the trench between blocking points will be thoroughly searched.

4. Not more than five (5) minutes will be spent in enemy trench. After that time, or sooner if identification has been obtained, the Officer in command will order the party to withdraw. The word 'RAG' will be the word used to order the withdrawl. On approach should the wire be found to be impenetrable at all points the party will withdraw at once.
At Zero plus 3, RED lights will be burned at two points in our line to guide the party back. These lights will continue to be burned until the party is in. The cessation will be a signal to the artillery to discontinue fire.

5. Riflemen will carry rifles with bayonet fixed and 50 rounds in bandolier. Bombers and P.O's will carry knobkerries. Everyone will carry 6 bombs and a pair of wire cutters (hand or rifle). Two ladders will be carried. A small piece of rope to secure prisoner will be carried.

6. No letters, brass badges or identifications of any description will be carried by any member of the party.
All the party will be warned that a prisoner captured by the enemy should give no information except his full name and rank.

7. The Battalion will stand to arms at Zero - 15 until conclusion of operation.

8. The Battalion Commander will be at Left Front Company Headquarters during the operation.

Signed F.J.Saunders,
Lieut.Colonel,
O.C.ANSON Battalion.

9th. September 1916.

(In pads of 50 dupls.)

# "C" Form (Duplicate).

## MESSAGES AND SIGNALS.

Army Form C. 2123.

No. of Message ..............

SM AC 64

PB WG 9a

Charges to Pay. £ s. d.

Office Stamp. 11/4/16

Service Instructions. PB

Handed in at PB Office 1.15 m. Received 1.25 m.

TO PAYN

| Sender's Number | Day of Month | In reply to Number | AAA |
|---|---|---|---|
| G 59 | 11th | | |

Following from 1st Corps begins aaa The Army Commander desires his congratulations to be conveyed to all concerned for their good and useful work in carrying out the raid last night aaa The identification obtained is of great importance and adds to the First Army list to allied armies fighting on the Western front aaa ends

FROM Chas

PLACE & TIME

W 15660 M/151. 75,000 Pads. McC. & Co., Ltd., London. 1/16. Forms/C.2123.

Secret

Sept. 11th 1916

Operation Order No. 25
Lieut. Col. F. J. Saunders D.S.O. R.M.L.I.
Commanding Anson Bn.

Relief (1) Anson Bn will relieve Howe Bn in ANGRES to morrow the 15th inst. Relief to be completed by 8 am.

Detail (2)

B Coy will relieve Right Front Coy
C " " " Left "
A " " " Support Coy
D " " " Reserve "

Headquarters will enter CORONS D'AIX ALLEY at 6.15 a.m.

B Coy will move via ANGRES ALLEY to be at entrance to ARRAS ROAD TRENCH at 6 am.

A Coy will move via ANGRES ALLEY to be at entrance to ARRAS ROAD TRENCH at 6.15 am.

C Coy will enter CORONS D'AIX ALLEY at 6 am.
D Coy will move from MECHANICS immediately in rear of C Coy.

Advance Party (3) An advance party of Bn. S.M. and C.S.Ms 1 signaller per Coy and one for Headquarters will be at entrance to CORONS D'AIX at 5.30 a.m.

Communication (4) When Coys have taken over Co. Commanders will report by telephone to Bn. Hd. Qrs. using the Code words "Verey Lights complete" or words to that effect

Telephones (5) Telephones of the Bn will not be connected up until relief has been reported complete by Coy. Cmdrs.

Dress (6) Full Marching Order will be worn

Wm. [illegible] Whitham[?]
Sub Lt. & Adjt.

SECRET

Operation Order No 26
by
Lieut Col. F. J. Saunders D.S.O. R.M.L.I.
Commanding [illegible]on Battalion

18th September

1. The Anson Battalion will be relieved by the 6th Battalion Bedford Regiment to-morrow.
Relief will commence at 8 am.

2. On relief the Battalion will move to COUPIGNY HUTS.
A. B. & D. Coys. will move via ANGRES ALLEY, FOSSE 10. and HERSIN.
Hdqrs. & C. Coy. will move via CORONS D'AIX, BULLY, FOSSE [illegible] and HERSIN.

3. One guide per platoon and one from Lewis Guns will report at Bn. Hdqrs at 5.30 am to meet incoming reliefs at BULLY CHURCH and lead them into the sub-sections.
On reaching FOSSE 10. parties will close [illegible] platoons [illegible] and the companys will move in platoons at 100 yards distance to HERSIN. At HERSIN platoons will form company column of route.

4. Relief of Lewis Guns will commence at 7 am.
On relief, guns crews will move out with their compa[illegible]

5. Breakfast rations only will be sent up to trenches to-night including those for Lewis Gunners.
Field Cookers with dinners will meet the companys at COUPIGNY.

6. Deep Dug Out Platoons, Tunnelling Parties and Staff of Brigade Bomb School will rejoin their coys to-morrow.

7. Greatest care is to be taken to ensure that all Trenches, Dug Outs, and Latrinae are turned over scrupulous[ly] clean.

8. When Companys are relieved they will report "more candles are required" or words to that effect.
Permission to move off will be given by the word "more candles are being sent up".

[signature]
Sub Lieut. & Act. Adj

SECRET

Operation

Movement Order No 27 by
Lieut Col F J Saunders DSO RMLI
Commanding Anson Bn.

19-9-16.

Move. The Battalion will move at 8am tomorrow morning

Reveille Reveille at 5am tomorrow morning
Breakfast at 6am.

Water All bottles will be filled at water carts at 5-30am.

Parade. Coys will fall in on their respective parade grounds at 7am & will afterwards form up on the road.

Lewis Guns. Coy Lewis gunners will move off in rear of their respective Coys.

Rations Dinner will be ready by 11 o'clock & will be served on route.

Off Kit All excess Kit will be handed into QM Stores at 9pm tonight

Mess Cart. will be outside CO's billet No 93 at 7-30am to collect Officers mess gear required on the march. All Officers Kit will be outside C.O's billet at 7am. tomorrow

Billets A billeting Party consisting of Lieut Lee & 1 PO per Coy. & 1 HdQrs & Interpreter will leave OR. at 7am tomorrow morning & will report to Lieut Barlow at DIEVAL 9am at Q8. a 9.4.

W.C.J. WILLIAMS

Sub Lieut & Adjt.

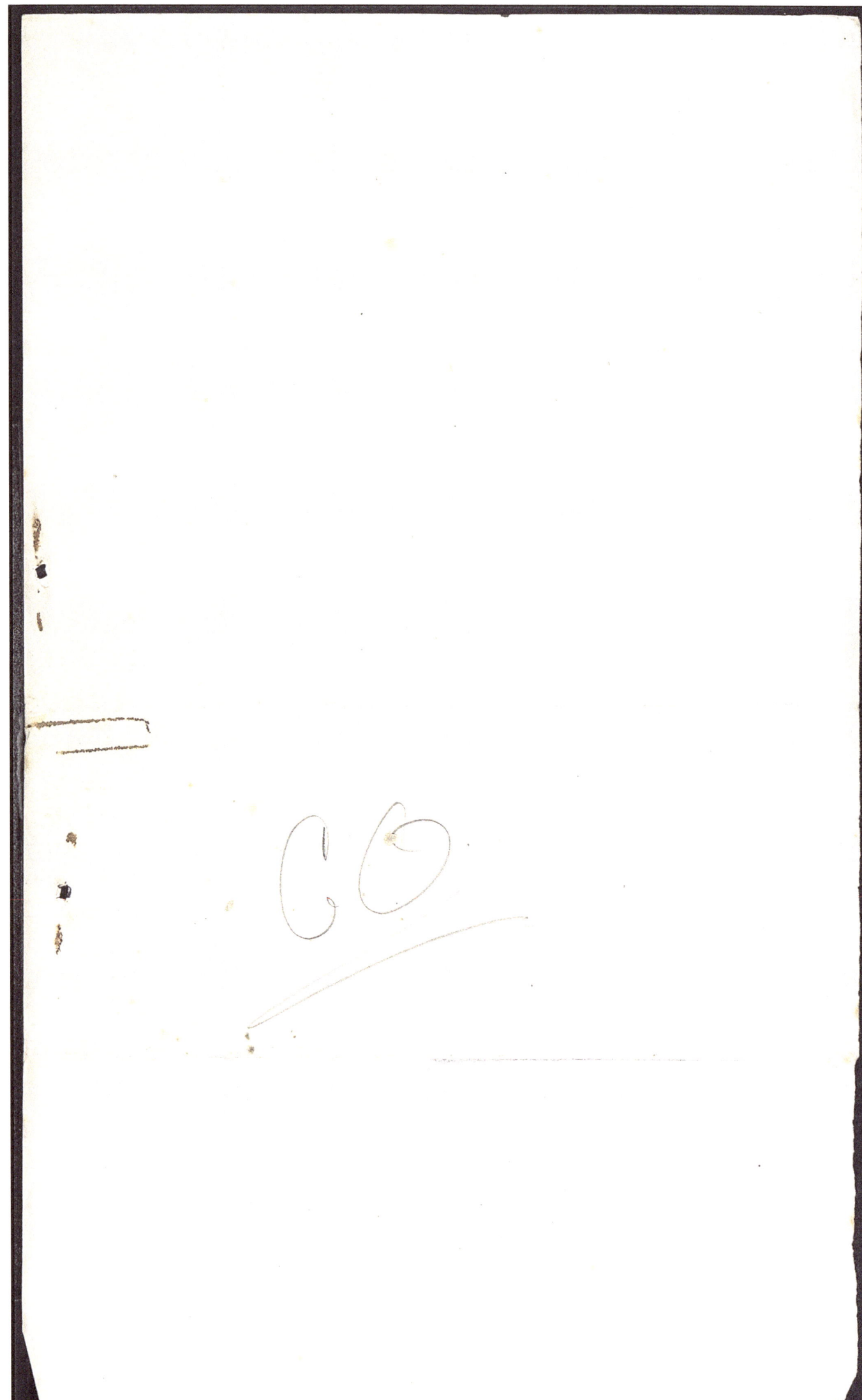

Anson Battn

Secret

War Diary. Vol V

Anson Battn

from

1st October 1916 incl

to

31st October 1916. incl

[illegible] Commdr.
[illegible]
Cmdg Anson Battn

To

The Officer in Charge

A G's Office

Base

Instructions regarding War Diaries and Intelligence Summaries are contained in F. S. Regs., Part II. and the Staff Manual respectively. Title pages will be prepared in manuscript.

# WAR DIARY
*or*
~~INTELLIGENCE SUMMARY.~~
*(Erase heading not required.)*

Army Form C. 2118.

Vol V

Anson Batt

| Hour, Date, Place | | Summary of Events and Information | Remarks and references to Appendices |
|---|---|---|---|
| DIEVAL | 1st Oct 1916 1 am | Sunday. Clock put back one hour, ordinary time resumed. | |
| | 11 am | Divine Service. A quiet day. | |
| | | Sub Lieut MOIR + 1 OR proceeded on leave to England. | |
| | | 4 OR returned from leave in England. | |
| " | 2nd Oct. | Company Training. Cos marched out to training area but rain set in and Cos marched back to billets for dinner. | |
| | | Sub Lieut Weaver sent to hospital. | |
| | 3rd " 6 am | ~~[illegible]~~ No training carried out. Wet day. Battn made preparations to move next day. | |
| | 6 pm | Transport Officer and Transport less Cookers + 1 SAA waggon together with a billeting party for transport proceeded by march route to new area. | |
| | 4th 9.15 am | Battalion paraded complete and marched off at 10.15 am to entrain at LIGNY ST FLOCHEL. On arrival at MARQUAY information was received that a breakdown had occurred on the Railway and that there would be a delay of at least nine hours. It was a wet day but the Battalion found shelter in four farms in the | O.O. No 28 |

Instructions regarding War Diaries and Intelligence Summaries are contained in F. S. Regs., Part II. and the Staff Manual respectively. Title pages will be prepared in manuscript.

# WAR DIARY
*or*
# INTELLIGENCE SUMMARY.
*(Erase heading not required.)*

Army Form C. 2118.

Anson Batt^n

| Hour, Date, Place | Summary of Events and Information | Remarks and references to Appendices |
|---|---|---|
| MANDUAT 4th October | village. Dinner and tea were served from the Cookers during the halt. Batt^n again fell in at 7.15 p.m. marched to LIGNY S^T FLOCHEL, entrained and left at 10.45 p.m. The night was spent in the train, and Batt^n arrived at ACHEUX – Railhead – at 6.30 a.m. | |
| MAILLY MAILLET 5th Oct. | Detrained immediately and marched to MAILLY MAILLET and bivouacked in wood there. Batt^n breakfasted on arrival at 10. a.m. Accommodation – tents and canvas huts and bivouacs. The day was spent in pitching the camp and cleaning up generally. | |
| 6th | Companies carried out training. | |
| 7th | Sub Lieut [illegible] sent to hospital | |
| 7th | Company training and working parties. 2 Officers [illegible] men [illegible] working parties. | |
| 8th | Sub Lieut [illegible] proceeded to England for transfer to M. G. Corps | |
| | Sub Lieut [illegible] and 1 O.R. proceeded on leave to England. | |
| | 2 Officers [illegible] employed on working parties. | |
| [illegible] | [illegible] the Batt^n fell in and marched to HEDAUVILLE [illegible] and arrived at [illegible] p.m. and went into billets | O.O. No 29 |
| | Sub Lieut [illegible] & [illegible] O.R. attached to 252^nd Tunnelling Co. | |
| [illegible] a.m. | Sub Lieut OFIELD and 4 O.R. proceeded on leave to England | |
| | Companies at training. [illegible] reconnoitred [illegible] position | |
| | [illegible] | |

(73989) W4141—463. 400,000. 9/14. H.&J.Ltd. Forms/C. 2118/10.

Instructions regarding War Diaries and Intelligence Summaries are contained in F. S. Regs., Part II. and the Staff Manual respectively. Title pages will be prepared in manuscript.

# WAR DIARY
*or*
~~INTELLIGENCE~~ SUMMARY.
*(Erase heading not required.)*

Army Form C. 2118.

Anson Battn

| Hour, Date, Place | Summary of Events and Information | Remarks and references to Appendices |
|---|---|---|
| HEDAUVILLE 9th October | 2 Officers & 100 O.R. employed on working parties | |
| 10th " | 6 Officers & 400 O.R. employed on working parties. 2nd in Command Adjutant and Co Commanders reconnoitred the line. Remainder of Battn carried out training. Sub Lieut Stimson to hospital | |
| 11th Oct | 5 O.R. detached to Salvage Co and 3 O.R. detached to A.P.M. for traffic control | |
| 11th Oct | Companies carried out training independently. C.O. & Signal Officer reconnoitred line. Lieut Comdr Jones struck off strength on transfer to England with damaged knee | |
| 12th " | Co training. 3 Officers and 150 O R employed on working parties. Sub Lieut Webley sent to hospital. 2nd in Command, Adjt & Company Commanders again reconnoitred the line — also 1 Platoon Officer per Co proceeded by bus for same purpose. | |
| 13th " | 10 officers and 550 O.R. employed on working parties. Those men who were not required until the evening carried out training before dinner. | |

(73989) W4141—463. 400,000. 9/14. H.&J.Ltd. Forms/C. 2118/10.

Instructions regarding War Diaries and Intelligence Summaries are contained in F. S. Regs., Part II. and the Staff Manual respectively. Title pages will be prepared in manuscript.

# WAR DIARY
*or*
~~INTELLIGENCE SUMMARY.~~
*(Erase heading not required.)*

Army Form C. 2118.

Anson Battn

| Hour, Date, Place | Summary of Events and Information | Remarks and references to Appendices |
|---|---|---|
| [illegible]. 14th Feby. | 1. O.R. proceeded to LE TOUQUET for a Lewis Gun Course. Company Training. 6 Officers and 370 O.R. employed on working parties. | |
| " 15th " | No working parties. Day of rest. Divine Service. H^d Q^rs + 3 Companies had use of Baths at ACHEUX. | |
| | Sub Lieut. Weaver rejoined from Hospital | |
| " 15th " | " " Moir " " leave | |
| | " " Funnell + 10. O.R. proceeded to Rest Camp at AULT | |
| | " " / John A McMillan and E A J Harris R.N.V.R. joined the Battalion from Base Depôt at ETAPLES | |
| " 16th " | Training under Company arrangements. 4 Officers + 230 O.R. employed on working parties | |
| " 17th " | Company Training. Two Companies carried out bombing instruction. 3 Officers and 130 O.R. employed on working parties. Lieut W K Douglas R.N.V.R. attached to 189th Brigade as Staff Learner | |
| " 18th " | Company Training. Remainder of Battn. carried out bombing practice. Sub Lieut C. Langston accidentally wounded by a fragment of a bomb. C.O and Co Commanders reconnoitred Front Line in vicinity of MESNIL. | |

(73989) W4141—463. 400,000. 9/14. H.&J.Ltd. Forms/C. 2118/10.

Instructions regarding War Diaries and Intelligence Summaries are contained in F. S. Regs., Part II. and the Staff Manual respectively. Title pages will be prepared in manuscript.

# WAR DIARY
*or*
~~INTELLIGENCE SUMMARY.~~
*(Erase heading not required.)*

Army Form C. 2118.

Anson Batt^n

| Place | Date | Hour | Summary of Events and Information | Remarks and references to Appendices |
|---|---|---|---|---|
| HÉDAUVILLE | Oct 18th | – | 140. O.R employed on working parties. | |
| " | 19th | – | Received orders to move to ~~E~~ a bivouac E of ENGLEBELMER. Pouring wet day, move postponed | |
| | | | Co Commanders visited trenches. | |
| ENGLEBELMER | 20th | 2pm | Moved to ground E of ENGLEBELMER and bivouacked. Cold but fine. | O.O. No. ~~[illegible]~~ 30 |
| | | | 11 Officers and 595 O.R employed on working parties during day and night. | |
| " | 21st | | A bitterly cold night was experienced in the bivouac | |
| | | | 2 Officers and 180 O.R employed on working parties | |
| | | | 5 O.R proceeded on leave to England | |
| " | 22nd | | Another bitterly cold night | |
| | | | Sub Lieut Harrower returned from leave in England. | |
| | | | Sub Lieut Gunnell + 11 O.R returned from AULT Rest Camp | |
| | | | 11 Officers + 520 O.R employed on working parties | |
| " | 23rd | | Milder weather. 4 Officers + 320 O.R employed on working parties | |
| | | | Sub Lieut Mitchell discharged to England for transfer to R.G.A | |
| " | | | Q.M Stores and all Officers (12) ~~Supernumerary~~ in excess of a total of 20 returned to HEDAUVILLE. | |

T2134. Wt. W708–776. 500000. 4/15. Sir J. C. & S.

Instructions regarding War Diaries and Intelligence Summaries are contained in F. S. Regs., Part II. and the Staff Manual respectively. Title pages will be prepared in manuscript.

# WAR DIARY
*or*
# INTELLIGENCE SUMMARY.
*(Erase heading not required.)*

Army Form C. 2118.

Anson Battn

| Place | Date | Hour | Summary of Events and Information | Remarks and references to Appendices |
|---|---|---|---|---|
| ENGLEBELMER | Oct 24 | | A wet day. Bivouac very uncomfortable | |
| | | | 3 Officers and 240 O.R. employed on working parties | |
| | | | 2 O.R. left for leave to England | |
| | 25th | | Another wet day. Sandbags, straw and planks were issued to minimise the discomfort in the shelters | |
| | | | 4 Officers and 240 O.R. employed on working parties | |
| | | | Sub Lieut [illegible] and 62 O.R. returned from duty with 252nd Tunnelling Co | |
| | 26th | | Another wet day | |
| | | | 5 Officers and 310 O.R. employed on working parties. Remainder of Battn carried out training in vicinity of Camp | |
| | | | No [illegible] R.N.V.R. Leading Seaman George Spencer attd 188th L T M Battery awarded the Military Medal for [illegible] | |
| | 27th | | Another wet day. Moved a portion of the bivouac to less muddy ground | |
| | | | 6 Officers and 340 O.R. employed on working parties. | |
| | | | Sub Lieut Ofield [?] returned from leave in England. | |
| | 28th | | Another wet day. 4 Officers + 380 O.R. employed on working parties. | |

T2134. Wt. W708—776. 500000. 4/15. Sir J. C. & S.

Instructions regarding War Diaries and Intelligence Summaries are contained in F. S. Regs., Part II. and the Staff Manual respectively. Title pages will be prepared in manuscript.

# WAR DIARY
*or*
# ~~INTELLIGENCE SUMMARY.~~
*(Erase heading not required.)*

Army Form C. 2118.

Anson Batt

| Place | Date | Hour | Summary of Events and Information | Remarks and references to Appendices |
|---|---|---|---|---|
| ENGLEBELMER | Oct 29th | | Another poor day. 4 Officers and 300 O.R. employed on working parties. During night of 28/29. 3. O.R. were wounded whilst digging in front of the Front Line trenches. No. ZC 1572 Able Seaman John DOCHERTY afterwards died from Shell shock and was buried by the Roman Catholic Chaplain of the Brigade. | |
| " | 30th | | Moved into billets in ENGLEBELMER, being relieved by the 10th Royal Dublin Fusiliers in the trenches. A pouring wet afternoon. Received orders to move again to HEDAUVILLE. 140 O.R. employed on working parties | O.O. No. 31 |
| HEDAUVILLE | 31st | 10.30 a.m. | Moved to HEDAUVILLE and occupied former billets. A fine day. 4 Officers and 200 O.R. employed on working parties. 2. O.R. left for Lewis Gun Course at LE TOUQUET. | O.O. No. 32 |

J. Saunders.
Lieut Col
Comdg Anson Batt

SECRET

Operation Order No 28.
by
Lieut Col. F.J. Saunders D.S.O. RMLI
Commanding Anson Bn.

3. 10. 16.

1. The Battn will move by rail tomorrow entraining at LIGNY ST BLOCHEL (T23 d)
Fall in at 9.30 a.m.

2. Dress Marching Order and Steel helmets will be worn. Caps to be placed inside packs – all grummets to be removed from caps.

3. Blankets are to be tied up tightly in bundles by sections, labelled, and to be taken to QM Store before 7 a.m.

4 All billets are to be vacated by 8.30 a.m, when they will be inspected by Co Comdrs who will report to 2nd in C.

5 Cookers will not accompany the Battn, but rations for tomorrow will be issued at 7.30 a.m by Co Q.M.S. to platoon Sergts and Section Commanders, who will distribute them.
The dinner ration will be issued cooked.

6 The Q.M. will detail 1 P.O. + 1 man from his staff to accompany the blankets.
Batt^n QMS. + Staff and a fatigue party of 1 P.O. and 10 men from B C^o will report at 9. a. m at Orderly Room and will proceed as an advanced party to the entraining Station, to draw rations for 5^th inst;

7. The following will not accompany the Batt^n but will leave billets at 4 30 p.m and arrive at LIGNY S^T FLOCHEL at 6 30 p.m joining up with B^de H^d Qrs. Column at X roads at N 30. a. at about 5 p.m.
1 Limbered wagon with 2 horses and 1 Driver.
4 Cookers with 8 horses and 4 Drivers.

8 The following will accompany Batt^n to Station and will await the arrival of the cookers + limbered wagon and entrain with them.
1 Mess cart with 1 horse + 1 Driver
8 pack horses with 8 men.

[signature]
Capt + adj

[illegible] to [illegible].
[illegible] to [illegible].

Operation Order No 29
by
[illegible]
Commanding [illegible] Batt.

Map Ref. [illegible] 7-[illegible]-16

| | | |
|---|---|---|
| Move. | 1 | Battalion will march to [illegible] at 1 Pm. Dinner at 11am [illegible] |
| Order of March | 2. | [illegible] |
| Dress | 3. | Full Marching order. |
| Striking Camp | 4. | Orders will be issued later. |
| Advance Party | 5. | Sub-Lieut [illegible] and [illegible] will fall in and move off at [illegible] am for billeting duties. |
| Billets, huts etc | 6. | Will be vacated and ready for inspection by [illegible] am |
| Officers Baggage | 7 | Officers Baggage Wagon will be in rear of camp at 10 am. [illegible] at [illegible] by 11 am. |
| Mess Cart | 8. | Will be in rear of camp [illegible] for Officers Mess [illegible] by [illegible] Pm. |
| Transport | 9. | [illegible] |
| Q.M. Store | 10. | A working party [illegible] 1 P.O. with [illegible] men [illegible] at [illegible] am for loading [illegible] |
| [illegible] | 11 | [illegible] |
| [illegible] | 12. | Will be [illegible] and carried on the [illegible] |

[illegible]

SECRET

Operation Order No 30
by
Lieut Col F J Saunders DSO RHLI
Commanding Anson Bn

20 Oct 1916

Move 1. The Bn, less Transport will move into Shelters today at about [illegible]

Parade 2. At 2-0PM Bn to be in position by 2-25PM ready to move at 2-30PM

Order of March 3. B. C. D. A Coys Head of Column to be at + roads

Blankets 4. To be rolled in Sectional bundles, tallied & taken to QM Stores by 11-0AM

Officers Kit 5 Transport to be at Officers Huts at 1-30PM for Officers baggage
Transport to be at Bn HQrs at 1-45pm for HQ Officers & attached Officers baggage

Mess Cart 6. To be at Bn HQrs at 1-45pm

Fatigues 7. A Fatigue party from D Coy consisting of 1 NCO & 12 men to be at QM Stores at 10-45AM

Lewis Guns 8. Lewis Guns will accompany the Coys

Cookers 9. To be filled up

Billets 10. To be cleared up & ready for inspection by 1-30pm. Billeting claims (if any) to be rendered to OR by noon today

[illegible]
Capt & Adjt

Secret.

Operation Order No 29.
by Lieut Col F.J. Saunders DSO RMLI
Commanding Anson Bn
20 Oct 1916

Move. 1 The Bn, less Transport will move into Shelters today at about Q20 central

Parade 2. At 2.0PM. Bn to be in position by 2-25pm ready to move at 2-30pm

Order of March 3 B.C.D.A. Coys. Head of Column to be at + Roads

Blankets. 4. To be rolled in Sectional bundles tallied + taken to QM Stores by 11-0AM

Officers Kit 5 Transport to be at officers huts at 1-30 pm for Officers baggage.
Transport to be at Bn HQrs at 1-45pm for HQrs officers + attached officers baggage.

Mess Cart 6 To be at Bn HQrs at 1-45 pm

Fatigues. 7 A fatigue party from D Coy consisting of 1 NCO + 12 men to be at QM Stores at 10-45 AM

Lewis Guns. 8. LG will accompany the Coys

Cookers 9. To be filled up

Billets 10 To be cleared up + ready for inspection by 1-30pm. Billeting claims (if any) to be rendered to OR by noon today

[illegible signature]
Capt + Adjt

Operation Order No 31

~~Movement Order No 2.~~ 29-10-16.

by:

Lieut Col F J Saunders DSO RMLI.

Commanding Anson Bn.

Move 1 The Bn will move into Billets tomorrow at ENGLEBELMER.

Inspection 2. The Camping Ground at present occupied by the Bn, will be ready for inspection by 9-0 AM.

Tents & Trench Shelters 3 Tents & trench-shelters will be handed over to the incoming Unit. All spare trench-shelters not erected will be returned to OR by 9-0 AM.

Guides 4 Sub Lt H Kilner will report to Town Major's office at 8-40 AM. to conduct Billeting party of 10th Bn Royal Dublin Fus^rs to bivouacs, using route to be used by Battalion

Billeting Parties 5 1 Officer & 1 N.C.O. per Coy, will report at 188th Inf Bde HQrs. ENGLEBELMER at 7-55 AM. to meet representatives of NELSON. BN. This party will report to OR before departure at 7.30 AM. Names of Officers & N.C.Os to be rendered to O.R. tonight

Fatigues. 6. 20 men from D Coy will be detailed to report to Q.M. at Dump at 9-30 AM.

Sgd:-

D.J. COWNEY

Capt & Adjt.

SECRET.

Operation Order No 32

by

Lieut Col T. J. Saunders DSO [illegible]

Commanding Prison Bn.

Move. 1. The Bn will move from ENGLEBELMER to HEDAUVILLE. tomorrow 31st inst.

Billeting Party 2. A Billeting party consisting of 1 Officer & 1 NCO per Coy. will proceed to HEDAUVILLE & will report to Lieut Comdr. Ellis afterwards reporting to the Town Major HEDAUVILLE. The Officers for this party will be detailed by Lt Comdr Ellis from the Officers now at HEDAUVILLE. The NCOs will be detailed from Coys & will report to the OR at 7am. names of NCOs to be rendered to OR forthwith. The NCOs of billeting party will meet incoming Coys at entrance to HEDAUVILLE & will conduct Coys direct to billets.

Transport 3. All available transport is to be at ENGLEBELMER not later than 9am. to move stores etc.

Billets 4. All billets will be cleaned up [illegible] by O.C. Coys by 10.am. reports to be made to OC by 10.5.am.

Blankets 5. Will be made up in [illegible] [illegible], tallied, & handed over by C.Q.M.Ss. to representative of the Q.M. department

Lewis Guns 6. All Lewis Guns. magazines, etc, are to be brought to HdQrs. & handed over to [illegible] [illegible] or [illegible]

Parade. 7. Parade. at 10.15 am. for moving [illegible] ready to move off at [illegible]

[illegible] of March. 8. C.D.A.B. Coys, Head of Column to be at [illegible] facing SOUTH. remaining Coys on road running WEST from [illegible] HdQrs.

Loading Party 9. Party of 16 [illegible] men will be detailed from [illegible] as loaders. They will [illegible] when [illegible] have been loaded. [illegible] [illegible] 9.30.am.

Officers Kit. 10. All Officers baggage to be [illegible] & handed over to QM department [illegible]

Officers Chargers. 11. To be at ENGLEBELMER [illegible]

[illegible]

[illegible]

Operation Order No 33 [illegible]

by Lieut Col. [illegible] Saunders D.S.O. R.M.L.I.

Commanding Anson Bn

Move 1. The Batt. will move by road from [illegible] to [illegible]

Fall in 2. Fall in at 8.30 am ready to move off at 9 am.

Order of March 3. [illegible] D.C.B.A. Coys

Blankets 4. To be rolled in [illegible] rolls [illegible] and taken to Q.M. Stores by 7.30 am.

[illegible] 5. To be collected from [illegible] at 8 am.

[illegible] 6. To be at the H^d Q^rs at 8.30 AM.

[illegible] Will be left at Q.M. Stores under supervision of [illegible] These N.C.O. will be rationed by the [illegible]

[illegible] Will provide a fatigue party of [illegible] These party will report to Q.M. at 7 [illegible]

[illegible] To be [illegible] ready [illegible] by 8 am.

[illegible] to be rendered to O.R. by 8.30 am.

Dress 10. Full marching order. [illegible]

[illegible] 11. [illegible] Parade at 6.30 am.

Billeting Party 12. Billeting Party of 1 Officer & 1 N.C.O. per Coy. and 1 man for Transport are to report to O.R. at 5.30 [illegible] tomorrow. They will report to Town Major at [illegible] at 9 am.

Names of billeting party to be rendered to O.R. by 7.30 pm tonight.

[illegible]

Capt. & Adjt.

No 1.

UNIT Anson Bn. TRAINING PROGRAMME for WEEK ENDING Dec 2nd 1916.

| DATE | COY | PLACE | 9-0 AM to 12 NOON NATURE of TRAINING | | PLACE | 2-0 PM to 3 PM NATURE of TRAINING | |
|---|---|---|---|---|---|---|---|
| 24th Nov | A B C D | LANNOY | Physical training<br>Rifle drill & saluting<br>Close order drill<br>Musketry, firing & aiming positions & rapid loading | 3/4 hour.<br>"<br>"<br>" | LANNOY. | Close order drill<br>Semaphore | 1/2 hour.<br>1/2 " |
| 28 Nov | A B C D | " | Physical training<br>Close order drill<br>Visual training & judging distances<br>Extensions from close order and movement in extended order | 3/4 hour.<br>"<br>"<br>" | " | Bayonet Fighting<br>Rifle drill & Saluting | 1/2 hour.<br>1/2 " |
| 29 Nov | A B C D | " | Physical Training<br>Fire orders & Fire Control<br>Musketry, use of ground & cover, rapid loading<br>Close order drill<br>Bayonet Fighting | 3/4 hour<br>1/2 "<br>1/2 "<br>3/4 "<br>1/2 | " | Rapid extension from all formations<br>Passing Orders. | 1/2 hour<br>1/2 " |

Copy No. 16

SECRET

Operation Order No 35.A. by [illegible]
Lieut Col F J Saunders DSO RMLI
Commanding Anson Bn.

MAP REFERENCE. 1/20,000 Long. Slip Attached

The Reserve Army is to attack the enemy on both sides of the River ANCRE.

The Front of attack of the 63rd (RN) Division will be from RAILWAY ROAD to about [illegible].

Date of attack & zero hour will be notified later.

Tasks of Brigades. The GREEN, YELLOW and [illegible] Lines will be captured by the 188th Infantry and 189th Infantry Brigades, the [illegible] line by the 190th Infantry Brigade.

Objectives. Objectives allotted to Battalions of the Brigade are shown on attached maps.

188th Infantry Brigade will assault with two (2) Battalions in the FRONT LINE, two (2) Support Battalions will be in the second line. Battalions will have four (4) Companies in column of Platoons, the Platoons forming 1st, 2nd, 3rd, & 4th waves respectively. Platoons will be extended to two (2) paces, with 10 yards distance between 1st & 2nd waves & 60 yards between the [illegible] [illegible] Distance between Battalions will [illegible] between Battalions [illegible]

[illegible] of Battalions
LEFT FRONT 1st Royal [illegible]
RIGHT FRONT Howe Battn
LEFT SUPPORT 2nd Royal [illegible]
RIGHT SUPPORT Anson Battalion

After front Battns have [illegible]
0 hour [illegible] minutes [illegible]
passing through [illegible]
The 1st & 2nd waves [illegible]
to the line and [illegible]
The 3rd wave [illegible]
The 4th wave will [illegible]
[illegible]

Lieut Comdr. J M Gilliland will command the 1st wave
Sub Lieut W B Moir " " " 2nd "
Lieut E M Lee " " " 3rd "
Lieut J Walsh " " " 4th "

At 0 hour, 50 minutes 1st Royal Marines & Howe Bn will pass through 2nd Royal Marines & Anson Bn and will capture yellow line

2nd Royal Marines and Anson Bn will close up on the yellow line & at 2 hours 20 minutes will advance & capture the dotted yellow line

At 2 hours 39 minutes 1st Royal Marines & Howe Bn will pass through 2nd Royal Marines & Anson Bn & will capture dotted brown line

The 2nd Royal Marines & Anson Bn will follow & at 3 hours 00 minutes the whole Brigade will advance to & consolidate the BLUE line

Battle Patrols — Battle patrols of 10 men will be sent forward to cover the position whilst the consolidation is taking place

At 3 hours 40 minutes the 190th Infantry Brigade will pass through & capture the Brown line

Strong Points — The Anson Bn will form the following strong points

Dotted BLUE line at Q 12 .c.00. (D Company)
Dotted YELLOW line at R.7. a.3.3. (C Company)

The half Section No2 Company Divisional Engineers attached to this Battn will be used for this purpose.

Lewis Guns — Coy Lewis Guns will advance on the flanks of each leading platoon. One M.G. Sp gun will be attached to A Coy & the other to D. Coy

4 Machine Guns will accompany each front line Battn. Bn HQrs will not advance until the objective have been gained. A representative of Battn HQrs will follow the last wave & select a site for Bn HQrs. When this has been notified to the C.O. HQrs will immediately proceed to the new position. Position of

Bn

DOCKET

# Operation Order No 36

12-11-16

Lieut Col F J Saunders DSO R.M.L.I.
Commanding Anson Battn.

**Move** Battalion will move to the place of assembly this afternoon

**Baggage** All Caps, Packs, Blankets, & Officers Baggage will be returned by 12 NOON today

**Billets** Will be thoroughly cleaned up & inspected by Co Cmdrs: Reports handed in to O.R. by 2-15 P.M.

**Parade** The Coys will parade in fighting order, with all War stores issued for operations, in sufficient time to march off as follows.

| | | |
|---|---|---|
| A. Coy. | move at | 2·45 pm |
| B. " | " | " 3·0 " |
| H.Qrs | " | " 3·15 " |
| D Coy | " | " 3·30 " |
| C " | " | " 3·45 " |
| L.T.M. Carrying party | " | " 4·0 " |
| Bearers, Sub Divisn. | " | " 4·15 " |

**Route** VIA. GABION AVENUE. VICTORIA ST, BEDFORD ST.

**Movement.** On arrival in position, no movement will be permitted, except to visit latrines, which will be dug on flank of each Platoon.

**Lights** Every precaution is to be taken to prevent lights being exposed to view from the front or RIGHT flank.

**Meals.** Tea will be provided shortly after arrival in position, & hot cocoa will be provided at 4 AM. Camp kettles to be returned immediatly after use.

**Great Coats** Will be removed one hour before ZERO, tied into Sectional Bundles as previously arranged, & handed over to the Coy Cooks in GIPSY HILL

**Water Bottles** Will be filled, before leaving Billets, for use tomorrow. Men are to be cautioned that no other water will be available tomorrow

**Bn HQrs** Will be in Dug Out in VICTORIA STREET immediatly at Junction with BEDFORD ST. & will be indicated by a BLUE flag, with RED anchor, & ~~white~~ WHITE A3.

Sgd

D.J. COWNEY.

Captn & Adjt.

CONFIDENTIAL

HEADQUARTERS
ANSON BN
DEC 4th 16

War Diary
of
ANSON BATTALION
63rd DIVISION
from
1st November
to
30th November
1916.

To / The A.G.s Office
3rd ECHELON

[illegible]
Lt Commander.
Commanding Anson Bn

Instructions regarding War Diaries and Intelligence Summaries are contained in F. S. Regs., Part II. and the Staff Manual respectively. Title pages will be prepared in manuscript.

# WAR DIARY or ~~INTELLIGENCE SUMMARY.~~

(*Erase heading not required.*)

188/63

Army Form C. 2118.

Anson Batt<sup></sup>

| Place | Date | Hour | Summary of Events and Information | Remarks and references to Appendices |
|---|---|---|---|---|
| | 1916 Nov | | | |
| HÉDAUVILLE | 1st | 9 a.m. | Companies at Close order drill, and bathing at ACHEUX | |
| | | | Fatigues at forward positions :- 8 officers and 430 O.R. 1 O.R. wounded. | |
| do | 2nd | 9 a.m | Weather very wet. | |
| | | | The Battalion was under orders to move to ENGLEBELMER but owing to the weather this was cancelled. | |
| | | | Company training carried out under Company arrangements | |
| | | | Fatigues 30 other ranks. Sub Lt. [illegible]OFIELD & 9 O.R. to 188 Bde for transport duties | |
| do | 3rd | | Fatigues at forward positions 9 officers & 361 O.R. | |
| | | 9 a.m. | Company training; extended order and; bayonet fighting | |
| do | 4th | | Weather very wet | |
| | | | Fatigues 6 officers and 180 O.R. | |
| | | | Company training carried out under Company arrangements. | |
| [Moved] to PUCHEVILLERS | 5th | 9 a.m. | Battalion marched off to PUCHEVILLERS arriving about 1.10 p.m. | Operation Order No 33. |
| | | | There was heavy rain and the roads via VARENNES and TOUTENCOURT were very rough and heavy. The Battalion went into huts. No stragglers. | |
| Moved to HEDAUVILLE | 6th | 1 p.m. | Battalion fell in for return to HEDAUVILLE. Moved off at 1.30 p.m | O.O. No 34. |

T2134. Wt. W708—776. 500000. 4/15. Sir J. C. & S.

Instructions regarding War Diaries and Intelligence Summaries are contained in F. S. Regs., Part II. and the Staff Manual respectively. Title pages will be prepared in manuscript.

# WAR DIARY
~~or~~
~~INTELLIGENCE SUMMARY.~~
*(Erase heading not required.)*

Army Form C. 2118.

ANSON Batt

| Place | Date | Hour | Summary of Events and Information | Remarks and references to Appendices |
|---|---|---|---|---|
| HEDAUVILLE | 1916 Nov 6 | | via TOUTENCOURT and VARENNES. The weather was again wet and the roads even heavier than before. No one fell out. Arrived 5.10 p.m. and occupied our previous billets. | |
| do | 7th | | Still very wet and cold. | |
| moved to ENGLEBELMER | 7th | am 6.40 | Battalion moved off to ENGLEBELMER arriving there at 9.50 a.m and went into billets. | O.O. No 35 |
| | | | Weather still very wet | |
| ENGLEBELMER | 8th | | Fatigues at forward positions 7 officers 325 O.R. One of these parties sustained casualties O.R. 5 killed 2 wounded and 9 O.R. badly gassed [illegible] by gas shells at KNIGHTSBRIDGE and remainder of party 107 in number were ordered to rest for 24 to 48 hours owing to slight gassing. The 5 killed were buried by Rev W.E.F. [illegible] at KNIGHTSBRIDGE. | |
| do | 9th | | Sub Lieut [illegible] to [illegible] gun course at LE TOUQUET. Fatigues 7 officers 297 O.R. at forward positions. | |
| do | 10th | 9 am | Fatigues 7 " 322 O.R. " " " Remainder of Battalion exercised at close order drill 9 – 12.30 pm and 2 – 3.30 pm. | |

Instructions regarding War Diaries and Intelligence Summaries are contained in F. S. Regs., Part II. and the Staff Manual respectively. Title pages will be prepared in manuscript.

# WAR DIARY

~~or~~

~~INTELLIGENCE SUMMARY.~~

*(Erase heading not required.)*

Army Form C. 2118.

ANSON Batt

| Place | Date | Hour | Summary of Events and Information | Remarks and references to Appendices |
|---|---|---|---|---|
| ENGLEBELMER | 1916 Nov 11th | | Sub Lieut RIDLER wounded whilst in charge of party conveying water and stores to positions of assembly for operations. | |
| | | 10am | Scheme of forthcoming operations explained to Company Commanders in conference, | O.O. No 35A |
| | | 8 30 pm | and to all other officers in conference at 8 30 p.m. | |
| | | | Fatigues 32 O.R. | |
| | | | War stores issued to Companies for the operations. | |
| " | 12th | a.m. | Issue of special war stores completed | |
| | | pm 2.45 | Battalion left ENGLEBELMER to take up positions of assembly for operations | O.O. No 36 |
| Assembly positions | | 4.45 | Hostile shelling of GABION AVENUE in which the Battalion was engaged, with gas shells and H.E. Casualties Lieut-Colonel F.J. SAUNDERS killed Lieut J. WALSH wounded O.R 2 killed 13 wounded and missing. | |
| | | 5.00 – 5.45 | Battalion occupied its assembly positions behind ROBERTS TRENCH | |
| | | 7.45 | Lieut Commdr B.H. ELLIS with Sub Lt W.C.J. WILLIAMS arrived at Battn H.Q. in VICTORIA STREET, the former assuming command of the Battalion the latter to command 4th wave of attack. | |
| | | 8-9 | Tea served to the Battalion in assembly positions. | |

T2134. Wt. W708–776. 500000. 4/15. Sir J. C. & S.

Instructions regarding War Diaries and Intelligence Summaries are contained in F. S. Regs., Part II. and the Staff Manual respectively. Title pages will be prepared in manuscript.

# WAR DIARY

~~or~~

~~INTELLIGENCE SUMMARY.~~

*(Erase heading not required.)*

Army Form C. 2118.

ANSON Battn

| Place | Date | Hour | Summary of Events and Information | Remarks and references to Appendices |
|---|---|---|---|---|
| TRENCHES | 1916 Nov 13 | a.m. 4.0 | Hot cocoa served to all the men. Greatcoats rolled in bundles and dumped at VICTORIA STREET. Weather very misty, visibility very small. | |
| Battle of the ANCRE | | 5.45 | Battalion advanced in four waves as per O.O. 35A following HOWE Battalion and that Battn not having taken the German trenches on the right assisted them in the assault. Considerable casualties were incurred in No Mans land and near the 1st & 2nd German trenches on the right. On the left half of the Battn. front the German trenches were taken and Lieut Commd. GILLILAND with the men left of the 1st & 2nd waves advanced to STATION TRENCH and then to the BEAUCOURT ROAD where he found both flanks in the air and the enemy in force in front and retired on STATION TRENCH | |
| | | 7.45 | In the absence of any definite information as to the position Battn H.Q. was advanced to ROBERTS TRENCH | |
| | | 8.00 | Having ascertained the position of HOWE HQ, Battalion H.Q. was advanced to there in German 2nd line about Q 17 b 23. The German trenches south of Q 17 b 52 and Q 17 b 66 were still untaken. | |
| | | 8.30 | All available Ansons were collected and moved into German 2nd line | |

T2134. Wt. W708—776. 500000. 4/15. Sir J. C. & S.

Instructions regarding War Diaries and Intelligence Summaries are contained in F. S. Regs., Part II. and the Staff Manual respectively. Title pages will be prepared in manuscript.

# WAR DIARY

~~or~~

~~INTELLIGENCE SUMMARY.~~

*(Erase heading not required.)*

Army Form C. 2118.

Anson Batt

| Place | Date | Hour | Summary of Events and Information | Remarks and references to Appendices |
|---|---|---|---|---|
| ANCRE | 1916 Nov 13 | | left of Q 17 b 36. In this trench were H.Q. of 1st and 2nd R.M. Battns with some details of those Battalions. | |
| | | | The bottoms of the trenches were in many places impassible owing to the deep soft mud in which a man could get completely stuck, the trenches were blown in in many places and outside the trenches the shell torn land was nearly as bad and very difficult to cross. | |
| | | a.m. 9.30 | It was decided to advance with the details of Anson, 1st & 2nd R.M. Battns to the GREEN LINE beyond STATION ROAD, a message having been received from the G.O.C. to advance Battalion H.Q. to the YELLOW LINE (BEAUCOURT ROAD) with the information that two Battalions were holding the YELLOW LINE on the right. The weather was still misty but growing clearer. | |
| | | | On the advance being begun it was enfiladed by hostile M.G. fire from the German 3rd line and many casualties occurred. Sub Lt. HARVIE acting as liaison officer was killed here and probably Sub Lt. G.W.A. WAUCHOPE (reported missing) the signal officer. The advance was checked except that the O.C. | |
| | | 11.30 | Battalion got through with one man to STATION TRENCH arriving there about 11.30 a.m. | |

T2134. Wt. W708—776. 500000. 4/15. Sir J. C. & S.

Instructions regarding War Diaries and Intelligence Summaries are contained in F. S. Regs., Part II. and the Staff Manual respectively. Title pages will be prepared in manuscript.

# WAR DIARY
~~or~~
~~INTELLIGENCE SUMMARY~~.
(*Erase heading not required.*)

Army Form C. 2118.

ANSON Batt

| Place | Date | Hour | Summary of Events and Information | Remarks and references to Appendices |
|---|---|---|---|---|
| ANCRE | 1916 Nov 13 | a.m. 11.30 | Lieut Comm^dr^ J. H. GILLILAND and under 200 men of various Battalions of 188^th^ & 190^th^ Bdes were found in STATION TRENCH. He was informed of the situation and ordered to advance to YELLOW LINE | |
| | | 11.55 | L^t^ C^r^ GILLILAND advanced with the force under him. Batt^n^ H.Q remained in STATION TRENCH with 6 men. | |
| | | | Meanwhile the remainder of the details of the Batt^n^ were in German 3^rd^ line where they were subjected to a barrage fire from our own guns for some minutes and had to retire to German 2^nd^ line, reoccupying the 3^rd^ line when the barrage had been stopped. Capt D. G. COWNEY remained in command of these details and engaged the portion of the 3^rd^ line occupied by the enemy, with a Vickers and a Lewis gun, and established blocks in the trench. | |
| | | 12.45 | Not having had any message from L^t^ C^r^ GILLILAND the O.C. Battalion moved forward towards YELLOW LINE to reconnoitre, and observed troops holding the southern portion of that line with their left flank in the air and the enemy holding MUCK TRENCH in force. Coming under fire Batt^n^ H.Q retired under it to STATION TRENCH. During the course of the afternoon many prisoners were | |

T2134. Wt. W708–776. 500000. 4/15. Sir J. C. & S.

Instructions regarding War Diaries and Intelligence Summaries are contained in F. S. Regs., Part II. and the Staff Manual respectively. Title pages will be prepared in manuscript.

# WAR DIARY

~~or~~

~~INTELLIGENCE SUMMARY.~~

*(Erase heading not required.)*

Army Form C. 2118.

ANSON Batt

| Place | Date | Hour | Summary of Events and Information | Remarks and references to Appendices |
|---|---|---|---|---|
| Battle of ANCRE | 1916 Nov 13 | p.m. 1–3 | observed being brought in by our troops from Y. RAVINE. A party of 30 Germans was seen to quit their 3rd line South of Y RAVINE and retire hurriedly via STATION ALLEY. They were fired on, the weather being now much clearer. | |
| | | 4.30 | Our guns fired shrapnel into the WEST end of STATION ALLEY and the GREEN LINE | |
| | | 4.30 to 5pm. | Battn H.Q. retired under cover of dusk and returning mist to German 3rd line and joined details of the Battn under Capt. GOWNEY and the H.Q. of 1st & 2nd R.M. Batts. and informed them of the situation, & that GREEN LINE was not occupied. It was decided to advance them as soon as possible. | |
| | | 5.30 to 6.30 | O.C. Battn returned to the telephone in ROBERTS TRENCH via the Northern tunnel and reported fully to G.O.C. and was directed to remain there for the night, and rejoin HQ of 1 & 2 R/M in the morning. | |
| do | 14th | a.m. 4. | Capt GOWNEY with details of Anson Battn advanced to GREEN LINE left of STATION ALLEY with H.Q. 1st & 2nd R.M. and entrenched 50 yds above the high bank east of STATION ROAD with GORDONS on their left and their right in the air. | |
| | | 5.0 | ANSON Battn HQ advanced from ROBERTS TRENCH to German 3rd line | |

T2134. Wt. W708—776. 500000. 4/15. Sir J. C. & S.

Instructions regarding War Diaries and Intelligence Summaries are contained in F. S. Regs., Part II. and the Staff Manual respectively. Title pages will be prepared in manuscript.

# WAR DIARY ~~or~~ ~~INTELLIGENCE SUMMARY.~~

*(Erase heading not required.)*

Army Form C. 2118.

ANSON Battn.

| Place | Date | Hour | Summary of Events and Information | Remarks and references to Appendices |
|---|---|---|---|---|
| Battle of the Ancre | 1916 Nov 14 | noon | Orders were now received from the G.O.C. not to advance further without higher authority. A good supply of drinking water was found close to STATION ROAD. R.H.Q's. Visual signalling communication was opened with German 3rd line at previous 2nd R.N. H.Q. | |
| | | | A message was sent 11.55 a.m. to O C HOWE Battn informing him that the German 3rd line had not been cleared S.E. of Q 17 b 75 and of where the trench could be entered from the North. | |
| | | pm 3.40 | Message to O.C. HOWE informing him of our position and suggesting he should advance and occupy STATION TRENCH. | |
| | | | A P.O. + 2 men sent round 1st 2nd + 3rd line trenches to collect stragglers. | |
| | | 10 pm | Lieut MARTIN arrived with 80 reinforcements | |
| | | 11 pm | The detachment of 4th BEDFORDS was given permission to retire to HAMEL where they said the remainder of their Battalion was, and our reinforcements took their place in the trench. | |
| | | | Three listening posts were established for the night in front of the trench about 50 yards consisting of an NCO and 6 men each. | |

T2134. Wt. W708–776. 500000. 4/15. Sir J. C. & S.

Instructions regarding War Diaries and Intelligence Summaries are contained in F. S. Regs., Part II. and the Staff Manual respectively. Title pages will be prepared in manuscript.

# WAR DIARY
*or*
~~INTELLIGENCE SUMMARY.~~
*(Erase heading not required.)*

Army Form C. 2118.

ANSON Batt

| Place | Date | Hour | Summary of Events and Information | Remarks and references to Appendices |
|---|---|---|---|---|
| Battle of ANCRE | 1916 Nov 14 | a.m. 5.30 | with some ~~men~~ stragglers from the Battn and found there mixed detachments of 4th Bedfords (190th Bde) R.M.L.I. ANSON and 189th M.G. Coy with 3 guns. A detachment of 10 Dublins was in 2nd line with H.Q. | |
| | | | At daylight the Germans in 3rd line were engaged with M.G. & L.G. fire | |
| | | 9. am | and eventually they were observed to have hoisted a white flag. An officer & 20 men of the Bedfords acting under orders of O.C. ANSON advanced on them and | |
| | | 9.30 | they surrendered 31 prisoners (1 severely wounded) being taken and several men of 188th Bde who had been taken prisoners were released. The Bedfords | |
| | | 10 am | were left to clear up the trench and Anson H.Q. advanced with all available men of various Battns from 3rd line and one Vickers gun to GREEN LINE where they entrenched on the right of the R.M.L.I. with the detachment of Bedfords on their right as far as STATION ALLEY about 40 strong. There were about 50 ~~[illegible]~~ Ansons, 3 Nelsons, 2 Howes, and the M.G. crew ~~under~~ and the detachment of Bedfords under the orders of O.C. Anson Batt. | |
| | | 12 noon | About midday the weather cleared, and on the appearance of an aeroplane flares were lighted. Hostile shelling with 5.9's followed, and some casualties were incurred. | |

Instructions regarding War Diaries and Intelligence Summaries are contained in F. S. Regs., Part II. and the Staff Manual respectively. Title pages will be prepared in manuscript.

# WAR DIARY
~~or~~
~~INTELLIGENCE SUMMARY.~~
*(Erase heading not required.)*

Army Form C. 2118.

ANSON Battn

| Place | Date | Hour | Summary of Events and Information | Remarks and references to Appendices |
|---|---|---|---|---|
| Battle of the ANCRE | 1916 Nov 14 | 11 pm | The night was misty and very cold so that the men got little sleep. | |
| | 15th | 12 midnt | Rations were brought up from the dump on the BEAUCOURT HAMEL road. Shelling of our position continued intermittently during the night, and STATION ROAD valley was shelled with 5.9's in the region of the military road all the forenoon. | |
| | 15th | pm 1.20 | The Battalion moved out of GREEN LINE under orders of G.O.C. and arrangements made by C.O. 2nd R.M. and marched in parties of 20 in single file at 50 yards distance via LONG SAP, VICTORIA ST (where greatcoats were picked up again) overland wounded route and CONSTITUTION HILL to | |
| | | 3.30 | KNIGHTSBRIDGE and thence to ENGLEBELMER arriving there at 3.30. Hot | |
| | | 4.0 | food was served to the men there, and at 4 pm. the Battn proceeded to HEDAUVILLE arriving 5 pm | |
| | | [illegible] | Roll call was held, and the men accommodated temporarily in ~~tents~~ off PIGEON LANE. The strength of the Battn moving out of the line with H.Q was 2 officers and 81 O.R. and 80 reinforcements, making 161 O.R. in all. In addition to this 85 O.R had already arrived at HEDAUVILLE with the HOWE | |

T2134. Wt. W708–776. 500000. 4/15. Sir J. C. & S.

Instructions regarding War Diaries and Intelligence Summaries are contained in F. S. Regs., Part II. and the Staff Manual respectively. Title pages will be prepared in manuscript.

# WAR DIARY
~~or~~
~~INTELLIGENCE SUMMARY.~~
*(Erase heading not required.)*

Army Form C. 2118.

ANSON Batt<sup></sup>n

| Place | Date | Hour | Summary of Events and Information | Remarks and references to Appendices |
|---|---|---|---|---|
| HEDAUVILLE | 1916 Nov 15. | | and other Battalions, and other ~~Batt^ns~~ stragglers joined up later. | |
| | | | The following casualties appear to have been sustained on 13th inst. | |

| OFFICERS | KILLED 7 | WOUNDED 8 | MISSING 3. | SHELL SHOCK 2 |
|---|---|---|---|---|
| | Surg^n C. H. GOW | Lieut E. M. LEE | Sub Lt. W. G. A. WAUCHOPE | Sub Lt. JONES |
| | Sub Lt. W. C. G. WILLIAMS | Lt. C. J. M. GILLILAND | " J. BOWDEN | " S. HULBERT. |
| | " J. MACMILLAN | Sub Lt. McLAREN | " O. J. HOBBS | |
| | " Cedric LEE | " W. S. HARVEY | | |
| | " F. C. WEAVER | " R. J. GEE | | |
| | " E. A. G. HARVIE | " W. B. MOIR | | |
| | " H. KILNER | " R. H. WAY | | |
| | | " G. BLACKMORE | | |

| Place | Date | Hour | Summary of Events and Information | Remarks and references to Appendices |
|---|---|---|---|---|
| | | | Other ranks Killed 15, Wounded 153 Missing 126 Shell Shock 6 | |
| | | | Total Casualties Officers (including 12th Nov) 22 | |
| | | | O. R. ( ditto ) 300 | |
| | 16 | a.m. 2.30 | A detachment of 1 off. & 50 men moved off by lorry to PUCHEVILLERS the remainder of the Batt^n following at different times in other lorries | O. O. No. 37 |

Instructions regarding War Diaries and Intelligence Summaries are contained in F. S. Regs., Part II. and the Staff Manual respectively. Title pages will be prepared in manuscript.

# WAR DIARY
~~or~~
~~INTELLIGENCE SUMMARY.~~
*(Erase heading not required.)*

Army Form C. 2118.

ANSON Batt

| Place | Date | Hour | Summary of Events and Information | Remarks and references to Appendices |
|---|---|---|---|---|
| | 1916 Nov | | | |
| PUCHEVILLERS | 16 | 8 am | The Battn went into billets at PUCHEVILLERS | |
| | | 11 am | Roll Call | |
| | | pm 2–4 | Battn employed cleaning up clothes and all gear, and bathing at the camp bath – no clean clothing available there. | |
| | | 2.30 | Conference of C.Os with G.O.C. | |
| | | | Recommendations for immediate rewards sent in as per appendix | List of recommendations |
| " | 17th | am 10.30 | The Battalion proceeded today to GEZAINCOURT, starting at 10.30 a.m. and marching via BEAUQUESNE. Arrived at 2 p.m. and billetted. Weather very fine for marching and roads good no men fell out. | O.O. No 38 |
| | 18th | 10. am | Battn marched to BEAUMETZ starting 10 a.m. proceeding via CANDAS and FIENVILLERS and arriving at 1.45 p.m. There was a slight fall of snow and the roads became icy the weather being very cold. No men fell out. The Battalion went into billets. Sub Lieut N. Browning left Battn yesterday and commenced Lewis Gun Course today. | O.O. No 39 |
| | | | Sub Lieut G.H. Marshall returned from Lewis Gun course | |
| | ~~17~~ 19th | | 21 O.R reinforcements joined the Battn being specialists (Signallers & Lewis Gunners) | |

T2134. Wt. W708–776. 500000. 4/15. Sir J. C. & S.

Instructions regarding War Diaries and Intelligence Summaries are contained in F. S. Regs., Part II. and the Staff Manual respectively. Title pages will be prepared in manuscript.

# WAR DIARY
~~or~~
~~INTELLIGENCE SUMMARY.~~
(*Erase heading not required.*)

Army Form C. 2118.

ANSON Battn

| Place | Date | Hour | Summary of Events and Information | Remarks and references to Appendices |
|---|---|---|---|---|
| | 1916 Nov | a.m. | | |
| BEAUMETZ | 19 | 10.30 | An inspection of the Battalion arranged by the Brigadier having been cancelled the Battalion was inspected by the C.O in a field at the cross roads East of BEAUMETZ. Remainder of the day spent in cleaning up equipment and in completing indents, and serving out ammunition to make up deficiencies | |
| do | 20 | 8.30 | Battalion fell in in drill order and marched to BERNAVILLE where it formed up with the rest of the Brigade in the Court of the Hotel de Ville at 9 45 The Divisional Commander addressed the Brigade at 10 5 a.m. | |
| | | 10.15 | Battn marched back to billets at BEAUMETZ arriving 11 am. | |
| | | 2 pm | Fatigues 25 men employed by the Maire and 12 men by M Boquet at agricultural work. Remainder of Companies at foot + kit inspections Surgeon Ritchie joined up from 1st Field Ambulance. | |
| do | ~~21st~~ | | Reinforcements 21 O.R received. | |
| | 21st | | Battalion marched to COULENVILLERS starting 10 am, arriving 12 noon and went into billets. 2 O.R were knocked down on the road by a lorry the driver of which was drunk, they were not seriously hurt, the matter was reported. | O.O No 40 |

T2134. Wt. W708—776. 500000. 4/15. Sir J. C. & S.

Instructions regarding War Diaries and Intelligence Summaries are contained in F. S. Regs., Part II. and the Staff Manual respectively. Title pages will be prepared in manuscript.

# WAR DIARY

~~or~~

~~INTELLIGENCE SUMMARY.~~

*(Erase heading not required.)*

Army Form C. 2118.

ANSON Batt<sup></sup>n

| Place | Date | Hour | Summary of Events and Information | Remarks and references to Appendices |
|---|---|---|---|---|
| COLLENVILLERS | 1916 Nov 22 | am 10.0 | Battalion marched to DOMVAST via S^T RIQUIER starting 10 am and arriving 12.50 pm. The men were accommodated in billets by 1.20 pm. Roads dry, no men fell out. On the march another Brigade was crossed. | O O Nº 41 |
| | | 6 pm | Sub Lieut Marshall detached to 2nd R M Batt^n who were short of officers, at BRAILLY. | |
| DOMVAST | 23rd | 9.20 | Battalion marched to NOUVIONS passing the starting point at 9.20 and arriving 12.30 pm. Went into billets after some difficulty in finding enough room. Billeting completed by 1.30 pm. | O O Nº 42 |
| NOUVIONS | 24th | 10 am | Battalion marched to NOYELLES-SUR-MER starting 10 am and arriving 11.30 and went into billets. Roads very good, no man fell out. Sub Lt JONES returned from hospital. | O O Nº 43 |
| NOYELLES | 25 | am | Weather warm and rainy. Companies employed cleaning up and overhauling kits. | |
| | | pm 2.15 | Message received to stand by to move tomorrow. | |
| | | | T O D C S and the Bde Signal Officer called. Conferred with them. | |

T2134. Wt. W708–776. 500000. 4/15. Sir J. C. & S.

Instructions regarding War Diaries and Intelligence Summaries are contained in F. S. Regs., Part II. and the Staff Manual respectively. Title pages will be prepared in manuscript.

# WAR DIARY

~~or~~

~~INTELLIGENCE SUMMARY.~~

(*Erase heading not required.*)

Army Form C. 2118.

ANSON Battn

| Place | Date | Hour | Summary of Events and Information | Remarks and references to Appendices |
|---|---|---|---|---|
| NOYELLES | 1916 Nov 26 | 10 am | A, B, and D Companies and H.Q. marched to LANNOY via PONTHOILE and FOREST MONTIERS starting 10 am and arriving 12.30 | O.O. No 44 |
| | | | C Company proceeded to BECQUERELLE and went into billets there. | |
| | | | Billetting of Transport and H.Q was very difficult; H.Q. was situated on the RUE – ARRY road. Roads very wet; no stragglers. | |
| | | pm 2.30 | Reinforcements 214 O.R. arrived, without food. | |
| LANNOY | 27th | am 9–12 pm 2–3 | Companies at training according to attached programme No 1 | No 1 Training programme |
| | | | Signallers and Lewis gunners to instruction separately | |
| | | 12.15 | Conference with G.O.C. at Battn H.Q. Inspected ground to find rifle range. | |
| " | 28th | am 9–12.30 pm 2–3 | Companies to training as before. | |
| | | | Men to outdoor sports, football, running etc | |
| | | | 1 N.C.O. & 20 men employed constructing 30 yards rifle range North of the RUE – FOREST MONTIERS road. Weather cold and foggy. | |
| " | 29th | am 9–12.30 pm 2–3 | ~~[illegible]~~ Companies to training according to revised programme No 1a | No 1a Training programme |
| | | | Men at outdoor sports and recreations | |
| | | | 1 N.C.O. & 20 men employed completing rifle range. An A.B. of C Coy died at BECQUEREL in the night. Court of Enquiry held at 3 pm. constituted | |

T2134. Wt. W708–776. 500000. 4/15. Sir J. C. & S.

Army Form C. 2118.

# WAR DIARY

or

~~INTELLIGENCE SUMMARY.~~

(*Erase heading not required.*)

Instructions regarding War Diaries and Intelligence Summaries are contained in F. S. Regs., Part II. and the Staff Manual respectively. Title pages will be prepared in manuscript.

ANSON Batt^n

| Place | Date | Hour | Summary of Events and Information | Remarks and references to Appendices |
|---|---|---|---|---|
| LANDOY | 1916 Nov 29 | pm 3 | as follows :- President Sub L^t RUSHTON, members Sub Lieuts PAVLING and JONES. Their report was sent to Brigade H.Q the evidence being that the man died of alcoholic poisoning. | |
| | | | Kits and packs of casualties fetched from NOYELLES | |
| do | 30 | am 9-12.30 | Companies at training per programme. 2-3 pm Recreation & sports | |
| | | 11 am | G.O.C came to Batt^n H.Q. and held a conference with C.O and O.C L.T.Ms G.O.C. approved of existing range, and of the use of the gravel pit near RUE for a range at 30 yards. A Company started firing on the field range. | |
| | | pm | Burial of AB Raine, who died on night 28^th-29^th, at ARRY. | |
| | | | Accident occurred to a Lewis gunner at drill, owing to a round being fired accidentally. | |
| | | 4 pm | Court of enquiry assembled, President Sub L^t W.H.MARTIN members Sub Lieuts HARROWER and FUNNELL | |

T2134. Wt. W708—776. 500000. 4/15. Sir J. C. & S.

Operation Order No 31
by
Lieut Col F J Saunders DSO RMLI
Commanding Anson Battn

6-11-16

Move. Battalion will fall in at 1pm and move off at 1-30pm today

Dress. Full marching order

Blankets To be made up in sectional bundles tallied & taken to QM Stores by 12-45 pm.

Officers Kit To be at QM stores at 12-45 pm

Mess Cart To be at HdQrs mess at 1-00pm

Duty Coy will detail a platoon as rear party for loading stores etc. Report to QM at 12-45 pm

Order of March HdQrs. A. B. C. D Coys.

[illegible]
Capt & Adjt

Operation Order No 35
by
Lieut Col F. J. Saunders DSO RMLI
Commanding Anson Bn
6-11-16

Move 1 Bn will move by road from HEDAUVILLE to ENGLEBELMER tomorrow

Parade 2 Parade 8·15am move at 8·40 am order of march HQ. A B C D Coys

Dress 3 Fighting Order. Spare pair of socks is to be carried in pocket of coat.

Blankets 4 To be at QM Stores at 7am.

Packs & Caps do Officers Baggage.

Details 5 The following will remain at HEDAUVILLE Supernumerary Officers 1 servant per Co, Transport, & QM Stores

War Stores 6 All War stores will accompany Batt<sup></sup>

Billeting 7 Consisting of 1 Officer + 1NCO per Co Parties will leave OR at 7-30am sharp They will report at HQrs, 190th Inf Bde. at ENGLEBELMER at 8·45 am

[illegible]

[illegible]

[illegible]

[illegible]

[illegible]

[illegible]

[illegible]

[illegible]

[illegible]

[illegible]

[illegible]

[illegible]

[illegible]

Move 1. The Battalion will move tomorrow to GEZAINCOURT

Order of March 2. H.Qrs. A, B, C & D Coys. [illegible] H.Qrs will [illegible] at Orderly Room [illegible] Coys [illegible] right side of road.

Dress 3. [illegible] marching Order

Blankets & Officers Baggage 4. To be at Q.M. Store by 8.45 a.m. sharp

Mess Cart 5. To be at Bn. H.Qrs at 9.30 a.m.

Medical Cart 6. [illegible] to M.O. [illegible] at 9.30 a.m.

Officers Chargers 7. To be at Orderly Room at 9.50 a.m.

Parade 8. 10 a.m. sharp, Move 10.15 a.m.

Baggage 9. Two Baggage Lorries will report to Q.M. at 7.30 a.m.

Transport 10. Two Cookers and one water cart will accompany Battn. on the march [illegible] will be brigaded [illegible] in rear of [illegible] under orders of the Bde Transport Officer.

Billeting 11. [illegible] & 1 N.C.O. per Coy with 1 from H.Qrs will report to O.R. at 7.15 a.m.

Loading Party 12. A Coy will provide 1 N.C.O. and 15 men for loading stores, will report to Q.M. at 7.25 a.m.

2.

A.B.
and 1 N.C.O. and 32 men will report to [illegible] Willcox at 9.45 a.m. tomorrow at PUCHEVILLERS CHURCH.

Lewis
Guns. 13. Will be taken in carts under Co arrangements they are NOT to be drawn by horses.

Transport
of
Blankets 14. Will be notified later.

Billets 15 To be inspected by Co Comdr at 9.30 a.m. Written reports to be rendered to O.R. by 9.45 a.m.

[illegible signature]

Capt & Adj

[illegible] Order 29

[illegible]

[illegible]

[illegible]

[illegible]

Operation Order No 40
by Lieut Col BA Clay
Commanding Anson B.

2[illegible] Nov 1916

Move — The Bn will move tomorrow to CRAMONT COULONVILLERS area at 9.45 AM

Billets — Anson Bn will be billeted at COULONVILLERS

Order of March — HQ CDAB Coys. Head of column will be at Orderly Room. Distances of 200 yds between Coys will be maintained throughout march. Same distance will be maintained between rear Coy of Bn & Bn Transport. These distances must be strictly maintained. Troops will halt at 10 mins to the clock hour & move off at the clock hour. All watches to be synchronised by CO's watch.

Loans — 1 NCO & 8 men will be detailed from D Coy & placed at disposal of OC 189th LTMB. They will report at 29 Billet at 9.0 am. 1 NCO & 12 men will report to the QM at Stores at [illegible].

**Stragglers.** 1 officer 1 NCO & 4 men will be detailed from B Coy to march in rear of Bn to pick up stragglers

**Billeting Party** Sub Lt C Hulbert & 1 NCO from each Coy will report at OR at 7-AM & will proceed on cycles to COULONVILLERS reporting to Staff Officer of 189th Bde at MAIRIE at 10 AM

**Billets** All billets to be inspected by Coy Cmdrs at 9 AM Claims being handed in to OR at 9-15 AM

**Blankets** To be rolled in sectional bundles & to be at QM Stores by 7-30 AM

**Off Baggage** To be at QM Stores at 8 am

**Mess & Medical Cart** To be at HQ Mess & M.I.R. at 8-30 AM

**Dress** Full marching order caps steel helmets to be carried between supporting straps of packs

* 600 yds distance will be kept between Bns

[illegible] Lay

Capt & Adjt

Operation Order 41
by
Lieut-Commdr B. H. Ellis R.N.V.R.
Commanding Anson Bn.

21-11-16.

Move. 1. The Battalion will move to-morrow to the BRAILLY area, route via ST. RIQUIERS & 2nd "E" in ARGENVILLERS. Battalion will be billeted at DOMVAST.

Fatigues 2. 1 N.C.O. and 32 men from A Coy will report to O.C. 188th L.T.M. at 9 am.

1 N.C.O. and 12 men will report to Q.M. at 7.30am sharp.

Order of march. 3. Hdqrs, D. A B. C. Coys, head of column will rest opposite turning near Bgde Hdqrs. Coys to be in position to move at 9-15 am.

Billeting 4 A billeting party consisting of Sub Lt C. H. Hullett and 1 N.C.O per coy with cycles to report to Orderly Room at 7.30am and will report on arrival to Staff Officer of Brigade at the church at DOMVAST.

The same billeting party will report at Bdge Hdqrs DOMVAST at 3-30pm for conveyance by lorry to RUE area, cycles to be taken.

2

Officer to take kit as can be carried on the person, rations for 23rd and 24th will be provided under Bdge arrangements.

March Discipline 5. Same intervals between units as for to-day.
Rear coy to detail 1 Officer, 1 NCO and 4 men to pick up stragglers.

Blankets. 6. To be at QM stores at 7.30am

Transport 7. Transport to be at QM stores at 7.30am sharp
Mess & medical carts to be at Hdqr mess and M.I.R at 8.30am
Officers chargers to be at starting point at 9.30am

Officers Baggage 8. Officers baggage to be at QM stores 8 am.

Billets. 9. To be inspected by Coy Commdrs at 9am. Billeting claims to be handed in to Orderly Room before 9.15am.

[signature]
Captn & Adjt

Operation Order No 42
by
Lieut-Commdr B. H. Ellis R.N.V.R.
Commanding Anson Bn.

22. 11-16

Move 1. The Battalion will move to-morrow to LE TITRE area.

Fall in. 2. At 9 am. Marching order not to be put on until five minutes before the fall in. Coys to be in position to move at 9-15 am. Head of column at church, main road, facing south.

Order of march. 3. Hdqrs, A.B.C.D. Coys.

Officers 4. To be at Hdqrs 9 am.

Blankets. 5. To be at Q.M Stores at 7.30am

Officers Baggage 6. To be at Q.M. stores at 8 am.

Transport. 7. To be at Q.M Stores at 7.30am sharp.

Fatigues 8. 1 Petty Officer and 32 men will report to O.C. L.T.M. Battery at 8.30am. 1 Petty officer and 12 men to report to Q.M. stores at 7.30am sharp. Both parties will be found by duty coy.

Mess & medical Cart. 9. To be at Hdqrs and M.I.R. at 8.30am.

Billeting. 10. Sub. Lt. C.H. Hulbert and 1 man from Hdqrs & Coys will report to Orderly Room at 7am. and will proceed to NOUVION-EN-PONTHIEU and will report to Staff Officer of

2/

Billeting 188th Inf Bdge at the MAIRE at (Contd) 10am.

March Discipline 11. As for to-day.

Billets 12. To be cleaned up and inspected by Coy Commdrs at 8.45am. Billeting claims to be rendered at 8.50am.

[signature]

Capt & Adj

Operation Order No 43
by
Lieut Commander B. H. Ellis RNVR
Commanding Anson Batt.
23-11-16

Move 1 The Battalion will move tomorrow to NOYELLES Fall in on the SAILLY-BRAY road clear of main road ready to move at 10 a.m.
Starting point NOUVION CHURCH
Battalion will move closed up and will follow Brigade Hdqrs.

Order of march 2 Hdqrs B. C. D. & A. Coys.

Billets 3 To be cleaned up and ready for inspection at 9.30 A.M. Billeting reports to be handed in at 9.40 A.M.

Blankets and Officers Baggage 4 To be at Q.M. Stores at 8 A.M.

Transport 5 To be at Q.M. Stores at 8 A.M. keep clear of Main road as far as possible

Fatigues 6 One N.C.O. and 32 men from C. Coy to report to O.C. L.T.M.B. at 9 AM.
One N.C.O. and 12 men from C. Coy to report to Q.M. Stores 7.45 A M

Mess & medical Cart 7 To be at Hdqrs Mess and M.I.R at 8.15 A.M.

Signed D.J. GOWNEY
Capt & Adjt.

Contd.

Mess Cart, 8 To be at Bn HQrs at 8am

*

These Officers will report to Major Miller P.M.

W. J. Gowthey[illegible]

Capt & Adjt.

Operation Order No 44
by
Lieut. Commdr B. H. Ellis R.N.V.R.
Commanding Anson Bn.

25 - 11 - 16

Move. 1. The Battalion, less C Coy. will move to LANNOY & CANTERENE to-morrow.
C Coy. with 1 cooker and 1 water cart will move to BECQUERELLE via MORLAY, FAVIERES, road junction south of T in STEAM.
Billeting representative to meet coy immediately north of W in BRICKWORKS.
Coy will fall in on the road leading to the station NOYELLES ready to move at 10 am
Starting point cross roads at N.E. corner of village.
Fall in on the main street facing North, head of column at the starting point ready to move at 10 am.

Order of March 2. Hdqrs. D. A. B. Coys.

Transport. 3. less 1 cooker and 1 water cart to be in rear, transport to be at Q.M. stores at 7.30am for loading.

Officers Kits and Blankets. 4. That of C. Coy with mens blankets to be loaded first and placed in front of motor lorry. Remaining coys blankets to be loaded in rear of lorry. Lorry will report at Q.M. stores at 8 am and will unload at LANNOY first.

Duty Coy. A Fatigues (Runners) 5. Two runners will be detailed from A Coy as runners for telephone messages at D.H.Q. and will report there on arrival.
1 P.O. and 32 men from A Coy will report to O.C. L.T.M. Battery NOYELLES at 9 am.
1 P.O. and 12 men from A. Coy will report to Q.M. at 7.30 am.

Blankets Baggage. 6. All blankets and Officers baggage to be at Q.M. stores before 8 am.

Mess & Medical Carts 7. To be at Hdqrs Mess and M.I.R. at 8.30 am.

Billets 8. All billets to be inspected at 9.30 am. Billeting claims to be rendered to Orderly Room by 9.40 am.

3

Runners. 9. C. Coy. will detail two runners who will be attached to Hdqrs for messages between Hdqrs and Coy.

Signed – D. J. GOWNEY
Captain & Adj

Anson Battn

Recommendations for Immediate Rewards

| Recommended for | |
|---|---|
| Military Cross | Lieut Commdr J. M. GALLILAND RNVR<br>Commanded Anson Battn 1st wave in the action N. of ANCRE [illegible] Nov 1916 and led his men gallantly forward [illegible] to the attack of German 2nd system lines in times of great doubt & difficulty |
| do | Temp Capt David J. BOWNEY<br>For devotion to duty throughout the action N. of the ANCRE on 13, 14 & 15 Nov. Took command of the remainder of the Anson Battn which had temporarily separated from the C.O. Carried out an advanced reconnaissance with one officer's patrol under fire. Was of the greatest assistance to the C.O. during the whole action. |
| D.C.M. | R.S.M. ALFRE JAMES BANKS RMLI (Ply 4094). For devotion to duty during the attack on the German lines N. of the ANCRE on 13 Nov 1916 and gallantly leading a bombing party until seriously wounded by a bomb. |
| do | (KP.917) George PICKARD (L.S., A.B.) RNVR<br>For gallantry & devotion to duty during the attack on the German position N of the ANCRE on 13–15 Nov 1916. Led his platoon to the attack of a defended part of German 1st Trench with bombs, killed many of the occupants & captured the Trench. Took command of all details near him when his officers had become casualties & kept his men well in hand. |

Rec^d. for (2 L.1479) Ernest Reginald CRUMNER (LSHQ)

D.C.M. For gallantry and devotion to duty during attack on [illegible] [illegible] of the ANCRE 13–15 Nov 1916. When [illegible] officers had become casualties he took command of all [illegible] near him and led them to the assault of [illegible] of the 1^st and 2^nd line with [illegible] [illegible] [illegible] M. G. fire

do. Corp^l JOHN BARRAN [illegible] R A M C [illegible] [illegible]

For devotion to duty during [illegible] [illegible] of the ANCRE [illegible] 13–15 Nov 1916. Attended the wounded gallantly [illegible] [illegible] when the M.G. [illegible] [illegible] [illegible] [illegible] of the [illegible] [illegible] [illegible] [illegible] [illegible] [illegible] [illegible]

(2L.3577) [illegible] [illegible]

For devotion to duty [illegible] [illegible] [illegible] [illegible] ANCRE 13–15 Nov 1916 [illegible] [illegible] [illegible] [illegible] [illegible] very [illegible] [illegible] [illegible] [illegible] [illegible] [illegible]

Military Medal [illegible] [illegible] [illegible] [illegible] For devotion [illegible] [illegible] [illegible] the ANCRE [illegible] [illegible] [illegible] [illegible] [illegible] [illegible] [illegible] very gallantly [illegible] [illegible] [illegible]

Recd. for (KP664) GEORGE COOK AB
D.C.M. For devotion to duty during the action N. of the ANCRE 13–15 Nov 1916. As a runner has untiringly and successfully carried many messages under fire maintaining communication over considerable distances of fire swept ground

B. M. Sllei[illegible]
GOC DNR

Anson Bn.

25.11.16

Notice

Holy Communion will be celebrated at 7.15 am in Padre's Mess tomorrow morning.

Signed R.T. GOWNEY

Capt. & Adjt.

Lt Cdr J.M. Gilliland (Anson)

# 63rd (R.N.) Div. Ancre Attack.

I was in command of the first wave of the Anson Bn. When the barrage lifted at Zero hour on Nov 13th., the Howe Bn. went forward to the enemy's trenches and, after the appointed interval, the Ansons - to whom the first objective, the Green line, had been allotted - advanced to "leap frog" the Howes.

The enemy were stubbornly resisting and part of the first wave and the whole of the second, third and fourth waves of the Anson Bn were engaged in the fighting and held up.

A portion of the first wave, however, succeeded in getting through and we advanced to and occupied the Green line - Station trench, just beyond Station Road. The position here was consolidated.

The composite party I had numbered about 90 and consisted mainly of Ansons with some Howes and Nelsons and later a few Gordon Highlanders.

The Howe Bn should have advanced through us to the second objective, the Yellow line, but by the time the barrage was put down the Howes had not arrived, being held up with the rest of the Ansons in the enemy's front line system.

I, therefore, advanced to the Yellow line. On the way we suffered considerable casualties from Machine gun fire from our right front and the enemy put down a heavy barrage on the Yellow line. We were entirely isolated and enfiladed from the right.

Efforts to get in touch with troops on the flanks were unsuccessful. Messages were sent to head quarters but failed to get through.

The very depleted force I had held on and, under cover of darkness, got in touch with the Hood Bn on the right. No contacts were made on the left. I saw Col Freyberg and explained the position as it existed on the left of his battalion. In the morning I was again wounded and was unable to take further part in the fighting.

----------

No. 1.A.

Anson Bn [illegible] ENDING 2nd December 1918.

| [illegible] | [illegible] | 9am – 12-30pm Stand easy 11–11-15am NATURE of TRAINING | DATE. | NATURE of TRAINING |
|---|---|---|---|---|
| Nov 29th | LAUNOY | Physical training 3/4 hour.<br>Fire orders & fire control 1/2 "<br>Bayonet fighting 3/4 "<br>Close order drill 3/4 "<br>Musketry. use of ground cover and Rapid loading 1/2 " | Dec 1st | 2nd Platoon to use range, and Lewis Gun instruction<br>Physical training 1/2 hour.<br>Indication & recognition of targets 1/2 hour<br>Fire orders. Rapid loading 1/2 "<br>Bayonet fighting 1/2 "<br>Close order drill 1/2 "<br>Extended order drill 3/4 " |
| Nov 30th | " | 1st Platoon to fire on the Range [illegible] to receive instruction in how to load & fire a Lewis Gun L.G. instruction to be detailed to be at range accordingly<br>Physical training 1/2 hour.<br>Extensions from all formations & movement in extended order. (passing orders & [illegible] 1 hour. not to be used)<br>Rifle drill & saluting 1/2 hour<br>Visual training & judging distance 1/2 "<br>Company drill 3/4 " | Dec 2nd | 3rd Platoon to use range & Lewis Gun Inst.<br>Physical training 3/4 hour<br>Company Drill 3/4 "<br>Bayonet fighting 1/2 "<br>Explanation of bombs (Mills "B" & German) & throwing castings 3/4 "<br>Musketry [illegible] loading 1/2 " |

2.

UNIT [illegible] Bn TRAINING PROGRAMME for WEEK ENDING Dec 2nd 1916.

| DATE | COY | PLACE | 9am — 12noon<br>NATURE of TRAINING | PLACE | 2pm — 3pm.<br>NATURE of TRAINING |
|---|---|---|---|---|---|
| 30 Nov | | LANNOY | Physical training 3/4 hour<br>Extensions from all formations movements in extended order 3/4 "<br>Explanation of Lewis Gun & how to use it 3/4 "<br>Visual training & judging distances 3/4 " | LANNOY | Close order drill 1/2 hour<br>Bayonet fighting 1/2 " |
| 1 Dec | | " | Physical training 3/4 "<br>Closing order drill 3/4 "<br>Lecture on Bombs (Mills & German) & throwing casting 3/4 "<br>Semaphore 3/4 " | | Rifle drill & Saluting 1/2 hour.<br>Indication & recognition of targets fire control 1/2 " |
| | A<br>B<br>C<br>D | On ground to be allotted | [illegible] training 3/4 "<br>Company drill 3/4 "<br>Bayonet fighting 3/4 "<br>Extended order 3/4 " | | Lecture on Lewis Guns 1/2 hour.<br>Bayonet Fighting 1/2 " |

Anson Battalion

4.1.17.

Confidential

Vol 7

War Diary

of

Anson Battalion

from

1st Dec 1916

- to -

31st Dec 1916.

H F Kirkpatrick

[illegible]

Anson Battalion

To

The A.G.'s Office

3rd Echelon

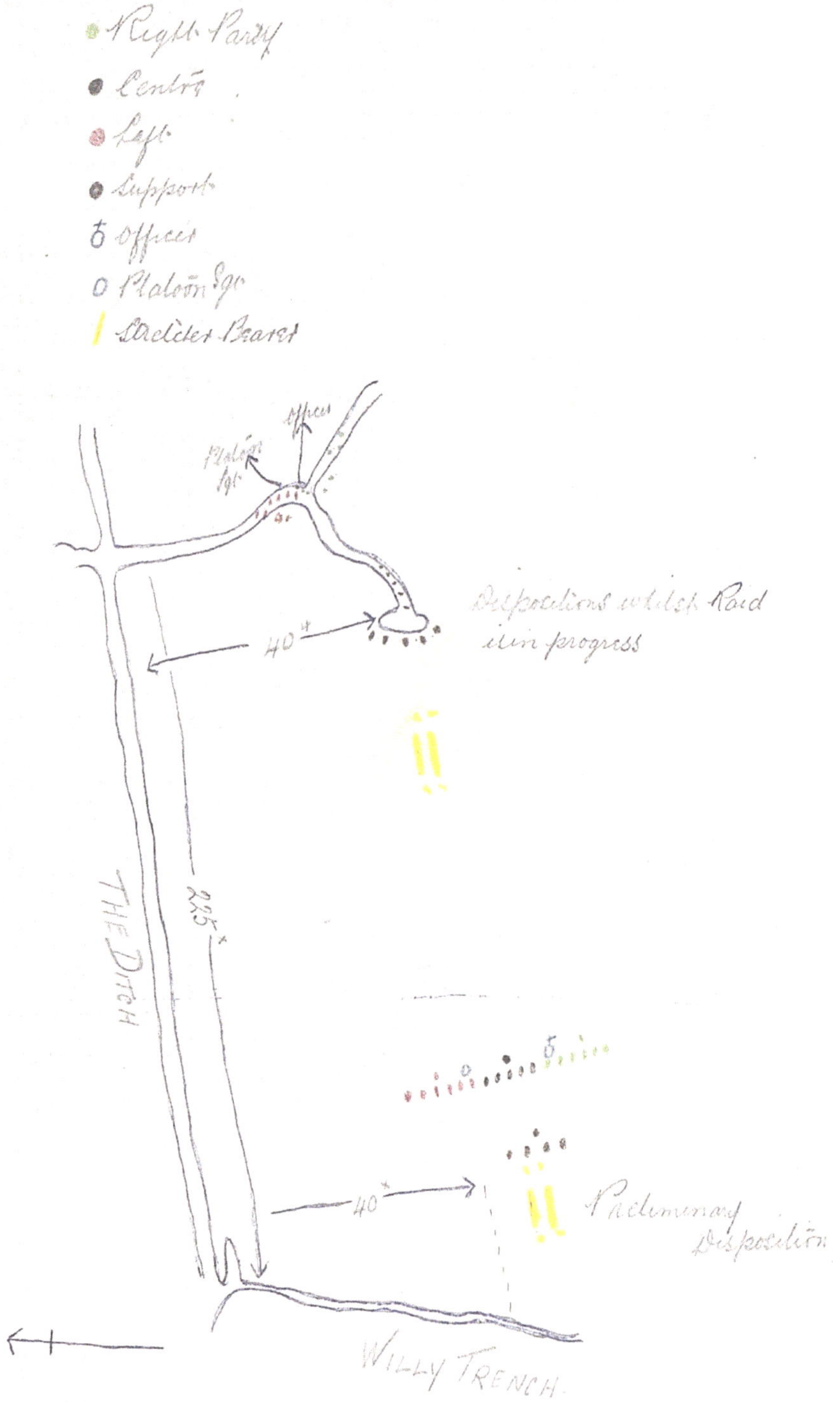
Right Party
Centre
Left
Support
Officer
Platoon Sgt
Stretcher Bearer
Platoon Sgt
Officer
Dispositions whilst Raid is in progress
40x
225x
THE DITCH
40x
Preliminary Disposition
WILLY TRENCH

Instructions regarding War Diaries and Intelligence Summaries are contained in F. S. Regs., Part II. and the Staff Manual respectively. Title pages will be prepared in manuscript.

# WAR DIARY

*or*

# ~~INTELLIGENCE SUMMARY.~~

*(Erase heading not required.)*

Army Form C. 2118.

ANSON. Battalion

| Place | Date | Hour | Summary of Events and Information | Remarks and references to Appendices |
|---|---|---|---|---|
| [illegible] | [illegible] | [illegible] | [illegible] | |

T2134. Wt. W708—776. 500000. 4/15. Sir J. C. & S.

Instructions regarding War Diaries and Intelligence Summaries are contained in F. S. Regs., Part II. and the Staff Manual respectively. Title pages will be prepared in manuscript.

# WAR DIARY
*or*
# ~~INTELLIGENCE SUMMARY.~~
*(Erase heading not required.)*

Army Form C. 2118.

ANSON Batt[n]

| Place | Date | Hour | Summary of Events and Information | Remarks and references to Appendices |
|---|---|---|---|---|
| LANNOY | 1916 Dec 3rd | am ~~11.30~~ | Worcester Battalion [illegible] A Company's billet at LANNOY. | |
| | | 11.30 | Parade Church Service for all denominations except Roman Catholics held on ground just East of RUE CHATEAU with a detachment of the band of the Portsmouth [illegible] R.M.L.I. in attendance. Dress, greatcoats and [illegible]. | |
| | | pm [illegible] | Voluntary [illegible] service [illegible] at [illegible] | |
| | | | [illegible] W.M. [illegible] detached to LE TOUQUET for [illegible] course. | |
| | | | Sub Lieut N. BROWNING returned from course and placed temporarily in charge of [illegible] guns. | |
| | 4th | 9.12.30 / 2.4 pm | Battalion at drill during forenoon. Recreation games in the afternoon. | |
| | | [illegible] | Sub Lieut W G MARSHALL returns from detached duty with 2/RM[t] & assumes the appointment of Assistant Adjutant. | |
| | | 6.30 pm | Comdr B ELLIS lectures to Bn officers on the "Battle of the ANCRE" | |
| | 5th | 1.30 AM | Comdr B ELLIS proceeds on leave from 5th to 15th inclusive. | |
| | | | Capt D. J. COWNEY D.S.C. assumes temporary command of the Battalion | |
| | | | S.L[t] W.G. MARSHALL is appointed acting Adjutant. | |

T2134. Wt. W708—776. 500000. 4/15. Sir J. C. & S.

Instructions regarding War Diaries and Intelligence Summaries are contained in F. S. Regs., Part II. and the Staff Manual respectively. Title pages will be prepared in manuscript.

# WAR DIARY
*or*
# INTELLIGENCE SUMMARY.
*(Erase heading not required.)*

Army Form C. 2118.

ANSON BN

| Place | Date | Hour | Summary of Events and Information | Remarks and references to Appendices |
|---|---|---|---|---|
| | 1916 | | | |
| LANNOY | Dec 5 | 11.30 AM | Surgn Gl. RITCHIE lectures to the Battalion on water. | |
| | | | Sgt Mjr McGEORGE, Army Gymnastic Staff is attached to the Battalion. A Bayonet course is laid out. The whole of the Bn N.C.O.s are instructed in elementary work of the bayonet and physical training. | |
| | | 2. PM | 55 O.R. reinforcements arrive | |
| | 6th | 9. AM | Owing to protests from leaseholder, Bayonet fighting course situated at [illegible] is closed down & a new course made in [illegible]. | |
| | | noon | Instructional class of N.C.O.s commences instruction under the Brigade Gas N.C.O. Battalion Snipers class started under 2nd Lt C.H. JONES. | |
| | | | Lecture to Officers by the Bn Transport officer on care of Horses. | |
| | | | [illegible] commence course of Bombing at Bde H.Q. | |
| | | | C Company commences Musketry. | |
| | 7th | [illegible] | Battalion [illegible] Bombing, Gas, Musketry, Lewis Guns, [illegible] | |
| | | | Average number of Sick for week ending Dec 7th 43 | |

T2134. Wt. W708–776. 500000. 4/15. Sir J. C. & S.

Instructions regarding War Diaries and Intelligence Summaries are contained in F. S. Regs., Part II. and the Staff Manual respectively. Title pages will be prepared in manuscript.

# WAR DIARY
~~or~~
~~INTELLIGENCE SUMMARY.~~
*(Erase heading not required.)*

Army Form C. 2118.

ANSON BN

| Place | Date | Hour | Summary of Events and Information | Remarks and references to Appendices |
|---|---|---|---|---|
| [illegible] ARNCY | 8.12.16 | 9. 12.30 | Very wet day. Battalion at indoor work. Lectures. Etc. Completion of Bayonet fighting course on new area. 20 men on fatigues preparing Bn Bath house, which will probably be ready tomorrow. | |
| " | 8.12.16 | 6.30PM | Captain D. J. COWNEY lecture to Bn officers. PATROLS, REPORTS + RECONNAISANCE. | |
| " | " | 10 PM | S. Lt D. S. ALISON rejoins unit from CAMIERS. | |
| " | 9.12.16 | 9.12.30 | Another wet day. Battalion at drill, Bathing, + Indoor Instruction. | |
| " | " | 9 AM | S. Lt C L JONES + 4 N.C.O proceed to VILLERS-SUR-AUTHIE for billeting Bn. | |
| | | NOON | Recommendation for acting rank for Company Commanders submitted to Bde H.Q | |
| " | 10.12.16 | 7.30 | S. Lt C. L. JONES + 5 N.C.Os proceed to VILLERS-SUR-AUTHIE for billeting Bn. | |
| | | 11 AM | S. Lt [illegible] FUNNELL evacuated to 1st Field Ambulance | |
| | | 11.30AM | Church parade Service at CHATEAU. RUE | |
| | | NOON | 9 O.R inoculated against PARA-TYPHOID + TYPHOID. 4 refusals. | |
| | | 4 PM | Received instructions to hold Bn in readiness to move by road tomorrow to VILLERS-SUR-AUTHIE | |

Instructions regarding War Diaries and Intelligence Summaries are contained in F. S. Regs., Part II. and the Staff Manual respectively. Title pages will be prepared in manuscript.

# WAR DIARY
~~or~~
# ~~INTELLIGENCE SUMMARY.~~
*(Erase heading not required.)*

Army Form C. 2118.

ANSON BN

| Place | Date | Hour | Summary of Events and Information | Remarks and references to Appendices |
|---|---|---|---|---|
| LAUNOY | 10.12.16 | | Received information from 63rd Div Salvage Coy that the body of 2/Lt C.J. HOBBS had been found by them on 5.12.16 | |
| | 11.12.16 | 9-11.30 | In the Valley. Bn [illegible] training [illegible] 50 men of C Coy employed in filling | |
| | | 12.30 | in of Bayonet fighting trenches, rifle ranges, Etc. | |
| | | | Route March in the afternoon to MORLAY. | |
| | | | Orders for move today cancelled. | |
| | | | S. Lt W. [illegible]OFIELD rejoins unit from LE-TOUQUET completing Lewis Gun Course. | |
| | | | Major H.F. KIRKPATRICK assumes command of the Battalion 11.12.16. | |
| | | | [illegible] Commander S.G. JONES, [illegible] & 70 Reinforcements arrive. | |
| | | | Lt Comdr S.G. JONES assumes 2nd in command of Bn 11.12.16 | |
| | | | [illegible] appointed Assistant Adjutant 11.12.16 | |
| | | | [illegible] assumes command of [illegible] Coy vice Sub Lt R. [illegible] | |
| | | | [illegible] FIELD resumes duties of Lewis Gun officer vice S Lt N. BROWNING | |
| | | | S.Lts [illegible] JONES, N. BROWNING, [illegible] to command [illegible] | |
| | | | Platoons respectively. | |

T2134. Wt. W708—776. 500000. 4/15. Sir J. C. & S.

Instructions regarding War Diaries and Intelligence Summaries are contained in F. S. Regs., Part II. and the Staff Manual respectively. Title pages will be prepared in manuscript.

# WAR DIARY
*or*
~~INTELLIGENCE SUMMARY.~~
*(Erase heading not required.)*

Army Form C. 2118.

ANSON. Battalion

| Place | Date | Hour | Summary of Events and Information | Remarks and references to Appendices |
|---|---|---|---|---|
| LANNOY | 12.12.16 | 9.30 AM. | Battalion moved by road to VILLERS | O.O. No 1. |
| VILLERS | | 10.45 AM. | Battalion arrived at VILLERS. Heavy marching, Snow storm all the way. Seven men falling out during march. Companies completed billeting by 11.15 AM. | |
| | 13.12.16 | | Battalion training. Cold damp weather. | |
| | 14.12.16 | | Battalion training with the exception of 40 OR at work at Rifle Range and 60 OR at work on Bayonet Fighting course. Cold damp weather. Avg. Sick week ending 14th 3.2 | |
| | | 4.30 PM | Lt J. F. Odell & Sub Lts. H C Ingle P.A. Shepherd, J Paull, J.V. Williams & H.W. Holmes and 10 OR arrive. Lt J. F. Odell assumes command of A Coy: vice Sub Lt. D. Harrower. Sub Lts D. Harrower, J Paull, H C Ingle, H W. Holmes, P.A Shepherd & J V Williams to command Nos: 1. 2. 8. ~~9~~ 10. 13. & 14 Platoons respectively. | |
| | 15.12.16 | | Wet morning, lectures by Platoon Commanders in Billets. Sub Lt. D Harrower & 3 O.R. proceeded on Gas Course. | |
| | 16.12.16 | | Better weather. Battalion at training with the exception of 40 O.Rs. at work on Rifle Range. | |
| | | 12 Midday | Medical Officer lectured Battalion. | |
| | 17.12.16 | | Church Parade Service on training ground. Cold weather no rain. | |
| | 18.12.16 | | Weather cold & damp. Battalion proceeded at 8.30 AM to a training ground East of | |

T2134. Wt. W708—776. 500000. 4/15. Sir J. C. & S.

Instructions regarding War Diaries and Intelligence Summaries are contained in F. S. Regs., Part II. and the Staff Manual respectively. Title pages will be prepared in manuscript.

# WAR DIARY
or
~~INTELLIGENCE~~ SUMMARY.
(*Erase heading not required.*)

Army Form C. 2118.

ANSON Battalion

| Place | Date | Hour | Summary of Events and Information | Remarks and references to Appendices |
|---|---|---|---|---|
| VILLERS | 18.12.16 | | VERCOURT for trench digging, ~~[illegible]~~ with the exception of Signallers & Lewis Gunners who carried on with instruction, and Sub Lt Ingle + 84 O R employed on Rifle Range & Bombing Ground. Lt Comdr B H Ellis + 13 O R returned from leave. Lt Comdr B H Ellis assumes command of B Coy vice Sub Lt. W H Martin to command 7th Platoon. | |
| | 19.12.16 | 9 AM | Weather, very cold turning to snow at mid-day & clearing up again in afternoon. Battalion at training. Divisional Commander visited training ground. Sub Lt D Hannover + 1 O R returned from Gas Course | |
| | 20.12.16 | 9 AM | Weather Bright & frosty. Battalion proceeded on Brigade Route march, Route VRON-FAVEILLES | |
| | | 1.30 PM | ARRY-VERCOURT, returning to Billets at 1.30 PM. 4. OR falling out. | |
| | 21.12.16 | 9 AM | Weather, cold damp. Battalion training. Sub Lt C L Jones + 2 OR's to [illegible] for course of instruction. [illegible] to [illegible] on leave. Rev W.E.F. Rees to Hospital. Capt D.J. Gourney to England on leave, Lt J COOTE appointed acting Adjutant. Average Sick week ending 21st. 4.9% | |
| | 22.12.16 | 9 AM | Weather very wet in morning. Lectures by Company & Platoon Commanders | |
| | 23.12.16 | 9 AM | Weather, cold & strong gale blowing. Battalion proceeded to Trenches E of VERCOURT for digging & to be inspected by 5th Army Comdr: returning to Billets at 3 PM | |
| | | 5.15 PM | A Fire broke out in buildings partly occupied by ANSON BN, & notwithstanding the high | |

T2134. Wt. W708–776. 500000. 4/15. Sir J. C. & S.

Army Form C. 2118.

Instructions regarding War Diaries and Intelligence Summaries are contained in F. S. Regs., Part II. and the Staff Manual respectively. Title pages will be prepared in manuscript.

# WAR DIARY
or
~~INTELLIGENCE SUMMARY.~~
*(Erase heading not required.)*

ANSON BN.

| Place | Date | Hour | Summary of Events and Information | Remarks and references to Appendices |
|---|---|---|---|---|
| VILLERS | 23.12.16 | 9.30 PM | wind was kept confined to the one building & being finally under control at 9.30 PM | |
| | 24.12.16 | | Weather, milder. Church Parade Service on Training Ground at 12 noon. | |
| | 25.12.16 | | Weather still mild. Church Parade Service on Training Ground at 11.30 PM. | |
| | | | Sub Lts D.S. Allison + L Browning + 27 O.R's on leave to England on 24th inst. | |
| | 26.12.16 | | Weather, frosty. Battalion at Training. Lieut. A.G. HENRY rejoins from 63rd R N Divn Artillery and assumes Command of C Coy: vice Sub Lt J.F. RUSHTON who is appointed to command 11th Platoon to date 27.12.16. Sub Lt J. PAULL + 4 O.R's proceeded on Sniping Course + Sub Lt H.W. HOLMES + 10. O.R's on Bombing Course. | |
| | 27.12.16 | | Weather very Cold. Battalion at Training. | |
| | 28.12.16 | | Weather wet. Lectures by Coy + Platoon Comdrs until 11 o clock, weather cleared up + Battalion training proceeded with. Average sick for Week ending 28th 3.8 | |
| | 29.12.16 | | Weather cold + dry. Battalion at Training | |
| | 30.12.16 | | Weather cold + dry Battalion proceeded to Trenches E of VERCOURT for practice attack, ~~with the [illegible] [illegible] [illegible] [illegible] Sub Lt~~ | |
| | 31.12.16 | | Weather milder. Church Parade Service on Training Ground at 11.30 AM. | |

H.F. Kirkpatrick Lt Col
Commanding Anson Batt.

T2134. Wt. W708—776. 500000. 4/15. Sir J. C. & S.

Instructions regarding War Diaries and Intelligence Summaries are contained in F. S. Regs., Part II. and the Staff Manual respectively. Title pages will be prepared in manuscript.

# WAR DIARY
~~or~~
~~INTELLIGENCE SUMMARY.~~
*(Erase heading not required.)*

Army Form C. 2118.

ANSON BN

| Place | Date | Hour | Summary of Events and Information | Remarks and references to Appendices |
|---|---|---|---|---|
| VILLERS. | 1 1 17 | | Weather fine but cold. Battalion at Training. Capt A.S.K. ANDERSON RAMC joined Bn: took over duties of Surgeon G.L. RITCHIE. RN. on leave to England. Sub Lt. J. F RUSHTON assumes command of C. Coy. vice Lieut: A G HENRY on leave to England. | |
| | 2 1 17 | | Weather milder. Battalion at Training. Capt D J GOWNEY returned from leave. | |
| | 3 1 17 | | Weather damp & windy. Battalion proceeded to Trenches E of VERCOURT for training. | |
| | 4 1 17 | | Weather very wet. Lectures by Battalion Coy Cmdrs. & Platoon Comdrs until 11 AM. weather cleared up, training proceeded with. ~~Capt D.J. Gowney returned from leave~~. Capt D.J. GOWNEY to Hospital. Lieut J. COOTE RNVR performing duties of Adjutant. | |
| | 5 1 17 | | Weather very cold. Battalion at training. | |
| | 6 1 17 | | Weather fine but cold. Battalion proceeded to trenches E of VERCOURT to practice the Brigade attack. returning to Billets at 1.15 P.M. Sub Lts. ALLISON & BROWNING retd from leave. | |
| | 7 1 17 | | Weather dull & cold. Battalion Church parade service on training ground 11.30 A.M. | |
| | 8 1 17 | | Cold windy weather. Battalion at training. Average Sick week ending 6th .58% | |
| | 9 1 17 | 9 AM | Day wet. Lectures by Officers to Companies & Platoons. | |
| | 10 1 17 | | Battalion employed at filling in trenches and clearing the training ground prior to move | |
| | 11 1 17 | 8.20 AM | C & D Coys proceeded to trenches E of VERCOURT to complete work of filling in trenches | |

T2134. Wt. W708–776. 500000. 4/15. Sir J. C. & S.

Instructions regarding War Diaries and Intelligence Summaries are contained in F. S. Regs., Part II. and the Staff Manual respectively. Title pages will be prepared in manuscript.

# WAR DIARY
or
~~INTELLIGENCE~~ SUMMARY.

(*Erase heading not required.*)

Army Form C. 2118.

ANSON BN

| Place | Date | Hour | Summary of Events and Information | Remarks and references to Appendices |
|---|---|---|---|---|
| VILLERS | 11.1.17 | | returning to Billets at 11.15AM. | |
| | 12.1.17 | | Battalion preparing for move back to the Line. | |
| | 13.1.17 | 9.15 | Battalion left VILLERS at 9.15AM for NOUVION arriving at 1PM weather fine | |
| NOUVION | | 1 PM | but cold. 3 men fell out. Average number of sick week ending 13th inst: 1.05% | |
| | 14.1.17 | 9.15AM | Battalion left NOUVION at 9.15AM for MARCHEVILLE arriving at 12.30PM. | |
| MARCHEVILLE | | 12.30PM | weather fine, no men fell out, last 2 miles of road in very bad condition | |
| | 15.1.17 | 8 AM | Battalion left MARCHEVILLE at 8AM for HEUZECOURT arriving at 4PM. | |
| HEUZECOURT | | 4PM | Weather fine, 8 men fell out. | |
| | 16.1.17 | | Battalion rested. Weather bad, snowing nearly all day | |
| | 17.1.17 | 10 AM | Battalion left ~~[illegible]~~ HEUZECOURT at 10AM for TERRAMESNIL arriving at 3.45PM. | |
| TERRAMESNIL | | 3.45PM | Snow & Sleet the whole way. Roads in bad condition. 5 men fell out. | |
| | 18.1.17 | | Battalion resting. Snowing all day. Battalion employed in cleaning gear &c | |
| | 19.1.17 | | Battalion resting. Weather cleared up. Sub Lt E.H. SKEVINGTON joined from 3rd | |
| | | | Entrenching Battn on 16th inst. also Lieut. H M FREWAN & Sub Lt J PATTERSON. | |
| | 20.1.17 | 10.45AM | Battalion left TERRAMESNIL at 10.45AM for ENGLEBELMER in Motor Busses arriving | |
| ENGLEBELMER | | 2 PM | at 2PM. Weather very cold. Average number of sick week ending 20th inst 1.15% | |
| | 21.1.17 | | Sub Lts. H. D. L MATCHAM J.A. BEDFORD F.C. RICHARDSON & C.G. WALKER joined the Battn | |
| | | | Church Service for Church of England at 9.15AM. & Presbyterian Wesleyans at 10.40AM. | |
| | 22.1.17 | | Battalion at training. 150 men provided for R.E. working party at Pioneer Rd. Str. | |

A5834 Wt. W4973 M687 750,000 8/16 D. D. & L. Ltd. Forms/C.2118/13.

Instructions regarding War Diaries and Intelligence Summaries are contained in F. S. Regs., Part II. and the Staff Manual respectively. Title pages will be prepared in manuscript.

# WAR DIARY
*or*
# INTELLIGENCE SUMMARY.
*(Erase heading not required.)*

Army Form C. 2118.

ANSON BN.

| Place | Date | Hour | Summary of Events and Information | Remarks and references to Appendices |
|---|---|---|---|---|
| [illegible] | [illegible] | | Battalion at [illegible]. 150 men provided for R.E. working party at Pioneer Rd Stn. [illegible] LUCE [illegible] the Battalion | |
| | [illegible] | | Battalion provided 150 men for R.E. working party at Pioneer Rd Stn. | |
| Trenches [illegible] [illegible] | [illegible] | [illegible] pm | Battalion relieved HOWE BN in trenches. Relief started at 6 pm and was completed at 10 [illegible] pm. Trenches: Right Sub Sector of Right Sector of Divisional front. Companies disposed as follows: 1 Company in front line, which is a series of detached posts covering a frontage of about 700 yards. 1 Coy in Support, 2 Coys in Reserve in THIEPVAL. [illegible] hard frost. Great difficulty experienced in keeping the front & support lines supplied with water [illegible] all of which has to be carried by the Reserve Companies from THIEPVAL a distance to front line about 3 miles, at night time. [illegible] Four Companies [illegible] addition to their ordinary [illegible] 2 [illegible] Front & Reserve nightly. | |
| | [illegible] | | [illegible] | |
| | [illegible] | | [illegible] in the Sector is very marked. | |
| | [illegible] | | [illegible] Support line by [illegible] | |
| | | | [illegible] Reserve Coy [illegible] | |
| | | | [illegible] in the Reserve. | |
| | | | [illegible] working work for Ration & Carrying | |
| | | | [illegible] enemy [illegible] Observation Post | |

A5834 Wt. W4973 M687 750,000 8/16 D. D. & L. Ltd. Forms/C.2118/13.

Instructions regarding War Diaries and Intelligence Summaries are contained in F. S. Regs., Part II. and the Staff Manual respectively. Title pages will be prepared in manuscript.

# WAR DIARY

~~or~~

~~INTELLIGENCE SUMMARY.~~

*(Erase heading not required.)*

Vol 8 Army Form C. 2118. 63

ANSON BN.

| Place | Date | Hour | Summary of Events and Information | Remarks and references to Appendices |
|---|---|---|---|---|
| Trenches opposite GRANDCOURT | 30.1.17 | | but no large parties. | |
| | 31.1.17 | 5.30 AM | Continued hard frost. Battalion relieved by HOWE BN. Relief commenced at 5.30 pm | |
| | | 8 pm | & completed by 8 pm: On relief 2 Companies proceeded to Billets at ENGLEBELMER | |
| ENGLEBELMER | | 12 Midnight | & 2 to Billets at THIEPVAL. Headquarters to ENGLEBELMER. | |
| | | | Average daily sick for week ending 28th inst ~~[illegible]~~ .85% | |
| | | | Sub. Lt: KEMBLE joined the Battn on 27th inst. and was appointed to C. Coy: | |

H F Kirkpatrick Lt Col
Commdg. Anson Battn.

A5834 Wt. W4973 M687 750,000 8/16 D. D. & L. Ltd. Forms/C.2118/13.

Instructions regarding War Diaries and Intelligence Summaries are contained in F. S. Regs., Part II. and the Staff Manual respectively. Title pages will be prepared in manuscript.

# WAR DIARY
~~or~~
## ~~INTELLIGENCE SUMMARY.~~
*(Erase heading not required.)*

Army Form C. 2118.

Vol 9

ANSON BN.

| Place | Date | Hour | Summary of Events and Information | Remarks and references to Appendices |
|---|---|---|---|---|
| [illegible] | [illegible] 2-17 | | [illegible] 2 Coys [illegible] ENGLEBELMER [illegible] 2 Coys [illegible] THIEPVAL [illegible] (A + B Coys). | |
| | [illegible] | | [illegible] | |
| | [illegible] | | [illegible] | |
| | [illegible] | | [illegible] | |
| | [illegible] | | [illegible] at 11 P.M. | |
| | [illegible] | | [illegible] | |
| | 5 2 17 | | [illegible] | |
| | [illegible] | | [illegible] THIEPVAL [illegible] | |
| [illegible] | | [illegible] | [illegible] H.Q. [illegible] THIEPVAL D Coy [illegible] ENGLEBELMER [illegible] | |
| | [illegible] | | [illegible] | |
| [illegible] | [illegible] | | D Coy [illegible] THIEPVAL [illegible] 5 P.M. | |
| [illegible] | | 5 P.M. | [illegible] | |
| | [illegible] | | [illegible] | |
| | [illegible] | [illegible] | [illegible] | |
| | | | [illegible] H.Q. + 2 Coys [illegible] ENGLEBELMER [illegible] A + C Coy [illegible] RIPLEY + DRAKE | |
| ENGLEBELMER | | | [illegible] H.Q. [illegible] | |
| | [illegible] | | A + C Coy [illegible] B + D [illegible] | |
| | [illegible] | | [illegible] H.Q. [illegible] | |
| | [illegible] | | [illegible] | |
| | 12 2 17 | | [illegible] Sub Lieut J. PAUL [illegible] | |
| | [illegible] | | [illegible] Lieut H.M. FREWEN [illegible] | |

A5834 Wt. W4973 M687 750,000 8/16 D. D. & L. Ltd. Forms/C.2118/13.

Army Form C. 2118.

# WAR DIARY

~~or~~

# ~~INTELLIGENCE SUMMARY.~~

(*Erase heading not required.*)

ANSON BN.

Instructions regarding War Diaries and Intelligence Summaries are contained in F. S. Regs., Part II. and the Staff Manual respectively. Title pages will be prepared in manuscript.

| Place | Date | Hour | Summary of Events and Information | Remarks and references to Appendices |
|---|---|---|---|---|
| ENGLEBELMER | 14.2.17 | 8.30 AM | Battalion relieved 1st HAC in [illegible] BEAUCOURT SECTOR, relief started at 6.30 PM, completed 11.30 PM. disposition of Companies as follows: B. Coy RIVER ANCRE to R3b63. D Coy R3b63 to R3b47 in Sunken Road. C Coy in MIRAUMONT ALLEY, A Coy PUISIEUX TRENCH, Hdqrs PUISIEUX TRENCH R8b66. During relief 4 men slightly wounded by Shrapnel | |
| PUISIEUX TRENCH R8b66 | | 11.30 PM | | |
| | 15.2.17 | | Quiet day. Reserve & Support Companies employed at night in carrying to Front line S.A.A. Bombs, [illegible] Pickets & Trench Stores. | |
| | 16.2.17 | | Enemy artillery [illegible] active, final arrangements made for the forthcoming attack at night [illegible] the HOWE Bn. took up its position preparatory to the assault, which was due to take place at 5.45 AM on 17th inst. Zero time was notified to the C.O. at about midnight. The actual assault is to be carried out by the 1st R.M. & HOWE BNs, whose objective is the SUNKEN ROAD from the left flank of our Advanced Coy (D Coy) to R3.a.0.8. | |
| | 17.2.17 | | From 4 AM onwards the enemy's artillery was very active on our front, at 5.45 AM our Barrage opened & the [illegible] was launched, the objective was gained & the position consolidated during the day. In accordance with the orders on the assault being made C. Coy moved from MIRAUMONT ALLEY to RIVER TRENCH to act as support to the 1st RM & HOWE as might be required. A Coy was held in readiness either to support as above or if so required to cooperate with the left flank of the 18th DIVN: in clearing up the ground in advance of BAILLESCOURT FARM on the N bank of the River ANCRE. During the forenoon ~~the~~ C. Coy came under heavy shell fire, losing 2 Lewis Guns & having a number of casualties by H.E., the Coy was withdrawn first into dugouts in PUISIEUX TRENCH. At 1 PM a Patrol of 1 NCO & 6 men from A Coy was despatched to gain touch with the left flank of the XVIII DIVN: returning at 2 PM having accomplished its object. At 3 PM a Patrol was despatched from B Coy to reconnoitre an old German Trench reported to be on line from R2c94 to R3d1.1. failing to find it the Patrol proceeded further EAST and found a [illegible] completed Trench about 200 Yds EAST of BAILLESCOURT FARM. Percentage of sick week ending 17th 1.03%. | |
| | 18.2.17 | | Heavy enemy shelling on our front all day. At 6 pm we took over the line held by the HOWE BN & our dispositions are now as follows. B Coy from E of BAILLESCOURT FARM to point 100 yards N of Barricade in SUNKEN ROAD from this point to R3A25 being held by D Coy: B Coy was strengthened by 2 Platoons of A Coy & 2 Lewis Guns. C Coy remained in support in PUISIEUX TRENCH, relief completed 4.15 AM 19th | |
| | 19.2.17 | | Heavy shelling on our front especially on D Coys sector, Retaliation asked for & received at 2.30 PM & 8 PM. | |

A5834 Wt. W4973 M687 750,000 8/16 D. D. & L. Ltd. Forms/C.2118/13.

Army Form C. 2118.

Instructions regarding War Diaries and Intelligence Summaries are contained in F. S. Regs., Part II. and the Staff Manual respectively. Title pages will be prepared in manuscript.

# WAR DIARY
*or*
~~INTELLIGENCE SUMMARY.~~
*(Erase heading not required.)*

ANSON BN

| Place | Date | Hour | Summary of Events and Information | Remarks and references to Appendices |
|---|---|---|---|---|
| PUISIEUX TRENCH R.8.b.6.6. | 20.2.17 | | Heavy shelling all day, retaliation asked for at 10.45 A.M. | |
| | 21.2.17 | | Quieter day, Battalion relieved by 4th BEDFORDS, the relief started at 6 AM, and owing to the intense darkness & difficulty of finding ones way was not completed until 9 AM on 22nd. The rationing of the forward companies and the providing of hot meals was one of the greatest difficulty owing to the intense darkness and the difficult nature of the country. Our Total casualties were 1 Officer wounded 21 men killed and 49 wounded. On relief the Battalion proceeded to McKenzie Huts, Martinsart, W.10.c.3.8. | |
| McKENZIE HUTS W.10.c.3.8. | 22.2.17 | | Battalion employed in cleaning up. | |
| | 23.2.17 | | Battalion bathing & generally cleaning, also working parties. 10 Officers & 150 OR's reinforcements joined the Battn. | |
| | 24.2.17 | | The Corps Comdr interviewed all officers & NCO's of the Battalion. Battalion employed on Working Parties. | |
| | 25.2.17 | | Battalion changed [illegible] at 11 PM & working parties. Percentage of daily sick Week ending 24th was 1.5%. | |
| | 26.2.17 | | Training & working parties | |
| | 27.2.17 | | Battalion employed on Working parties & training | |
| | 28.2.17 | | 400 Men of Battalion on working parties. | |

H. J. Kirkpatrick
Lieut Col.
Comdg ANSON BN

A5834 Wt. W4973 M687 750,000 8/16 D. D. & L. Ltd. Forms/C.2118/13.

Instructions regarding War Diaries and Intelligence Summaries are contained in F. S. Regs., Part II. and the Staff Manual respectively. Title pages will be prepared in manuscript.

# WAR DIARY
or
# ~~INTELLIGENCE~~ SUMMARY.

*(Erase heading not required.)*

Army Form C. 2118.

ANSON BN.

Vol 10

| Place | Date | Hour | Summary of Events and Information | Remarks and references to Appendices |
|---|---|---|---|---|
| [illegible] | 1.3.17 | | Battalion engaged on working parties, and Specialists in training. | |
| | 2.3.17 | | Men not engaged on working parties and one company training at Lewis Guns, Signalling & Bombing. | |
| | 3.3.17 | | Working parties for the Battalion on roads at Beaumont Hamel, Beaucourt & remainder of men training. | |
| | | | Average daily sick week ending 3rd inst. 1·4%. | |
| | 4.3.17 | | Church parade service at 11 AM, also working parties. | |
| | 5.3.17 | | Working parties & training. | |
| | 6.3.17 | | Battalion engaged on roads, a few specialists training | |
| | 7.3.17 | | Men not employed on working parties, training as specialists. | |
| | 8.3.17 | | Three Companies working parties, remainder of Battalion training. | |
| | 9.3.17 | | All men not employed on working parties, training. | |
| | 10.3.17 | | Commanding Officer proceeded to DOMART for C.O.'s course under Brig Gen PRENTICE. Battalion on working parties | |
| | | | and training. Average daily sick week ending 10th inst. ·54% | |
| | 11.3.17 | | Church parade service at 11.30 AM, also working parties. | |
| | 12.3.17 | | Working parties and training. | |
| | 13.3.17 | | Specialists training remainder of Battalion on working parties | |
| | 14.3.17 | | Men not employed on working parties, at specialists training. | |

Instructions regarding War Diaries and Intelligence Summaries are contained in F. S. Regs., Part II. and the Staff Manual respectively. Title pages will be prepared in manuscript.

# WAR DIARY
or
# INTELLIGENCE SUMMARY.
(Erase heading not required.)

Army Form C. 2118.

ANSON BN.

| Place | Date | Hour | Summary of Events and Information | Remarks and references to Appendices |
|---|---|---|---|---|
| McKENZIE HUTS at MARTINSART | 15.3.17 | | Working parties for [illegible] Battalion [illegible] | |
| | 16.3.17 | | [illegible] Battalion [illegible] at MARTINSART [illegible] | |
| | | | [illegible] | |
| | 17.3.17 | | Battalion engaged in working parties & [illegible] training. Average daily sick week ending 17th inst ·56 % | |
| | 18.3.17 | | Church Parade service at 11.30 AM. No working parties. Battalion preparing to move on 19th inst. | |
| McKENZIE HUTS | 19.3.17 | 8.30AM | Battalion left McKENZIE HUTS at 8.45AM and arrived at HÉRISSART at 2.15PM. 5 O.R. fell out. | |
| HÉRISSART | | 2.30PM | Weather dull & overcast, cold wind. | |
| HÉRISSART | 20.3.17 | 8 AM | Battalion left HÉRISSART at 8.15AM and arrived at LONGUEVILLETTE at 3 PM. [illegible] O.R. fell out. | |
| LONGUEVILLETTE | | 3 PM | Snow, rain & cold wind. | |
| LONGUEVILLETTE | 21.3.17 | 9.30AM | Battalion left LONGUEVILLETTE at 9.45AM and arrived FORTEL at 3.15PM. 0 Men fell out. A few showers. | |
| FORTEL | 22.3.17 | 9.30AM | Battalion left FORTEL at 9.30AM. and arrived at CROIX at 2.30PM. 0 Men fell out. Changeable weather. Snow & Sun. | |
| CROIX | 23.3.17 | | Battalion rested, inspection of Companies & transport in afternoon. Bright Sunny weather. | |
| CROIX | 24.3.17 | 8.30AM | Battalion left CROIX at 8.55AM and arrived at FIEFS at 1.15PM. 1 Man fell out. Bright Sunny | |
| FIEFS | | 1.15PM | weather very cold winds. Average daily sick week ending 24th inst. ·77 % | |
| FIEFS | 25.3.17 | 10 AM | Battalion left FIEFS at 10AM and arrived at ECQUEDECQUES at 2.30PM 0 Men fell out. Bright Sunny Weather. | |
| ECQUEDECQUES | 26.3.17 | 9.40AM | Battalion left ECQUEDECQUES at 9.40AM and arrived at QUENTIN at 2.45PM. 0 Men fell out. Rained the whole way. | |

A5834 Wt W4973/M687 750,000 8/16 D. D. & L. Ltd. Forms/C.2118/13.

Instructions regarding War Diaries and Intelligence Summaries are contained in F. S. Regs., Part II. and the Staff Manual respectively. Title pages will be prepared in manuscript.

# WAR DIARY

~~or~~

# ~~INTELLIGENCE SUMMARY.~~

*(Erase heading not required.)*

ANSON BN.

Army Form C. 2118.

| Place | Date | Hour | Summary of Events and Information | Remarks and references to Appendices |
|---|---|---|---|---|
| QUENTIN | 27.3.17 | 10 a.m. | Battalion left QUENTIN at 10 o'clock and arrived at NOEUX LES MINES at 2.45 PM. 0 men dropped out. | |
| Noeux les Mines | | 2.45 PM | Raining all the way. Battalion billeted in Huts at L 19.A.0.8. | |
| | 28.3.17 | | Battalion employed at cleaning up. | |
| | 29.3.17 | | Battalion training in morning with the companies, afternoon at specialist training, very wet morning. Training proceeded in Huts. | |
| | 30.3.17 | | Commanding Officer returned from ENGLAND. Battalion carrying out training, Showery weather. | |
| | 31.3.17 | | Battalion training, very dull overcast weather. Cold wind. | |
| | | | Average daily sick week ending 31st inst: ·72 % | |

31/3/17.

H. F. Kirkpatrick Lt Col
Commdg. Anson Battn.

A5834 Wt. W4973 M687 750,000 8/16 D. D. & L. Ltd. Forms/C.2118/13.

63rd

ANSON BATTALION,
(ROYAL NAVAL) DIV.
No. G2/22
Date 6 5 17

A.G.
Base
G.H.Q.

Please receive herewith original copy of war Diary for the month of April 1917.

H G Kirkpatrick
Lieut Colonel
Comd<sup></sup>g Anson Bn

63

Army Form C. 2118.

Instructions regarding War Diaries and Intelligence Summaries are contained in F. S. Regs., Part II. and the Staff Manual respectively. Title pages will be prepared in manuscript.

# WAR DIARY
~~or~~
~~INTELLIGENCE~~ SUMMARY. ANSON BN:

(*Erase heading not required.*)

Vol XI

| Place | Date | Hour | Summary of Events and Information | Remarks and references to Appendices |
|---|---|---|---|---|
| NOEUX LES MINES | 1.4.17 | 9.30AM | Church Parade Service at 9.30AM 11.30AM – 12.30PM Kit inspection. | |
| | 2.4.17 | | Battalion training | |
| | 3.4.17 | | Training for Battalion. Lieut Comdr B.H. ELLIS DSO returned from Course & assumed command of B Coy. | |
| | 4.4.17 | | Battalion training carried out in morning & afternoon. | |
| | 5.4.17 | | ~~Good Friday Church Parade Service at 11.30AM~~ Battalion training | |
| | 6.4.17 | | Good Friday Church Parade Service at 11.30AM. | |
| | 7.4.17 | | Training as usual for Battalion. Daily percentage of sick week ending 7th inst: ·47% | |
| | 8.4.17 | | Church Service for Battalion in Church Army Hut at 11AM | |
| | 9.4.17 | | Battalion training | |
| | 10.4.17 | | Training for Battalion carried out | |
| | 11.4.17 | 9 AM | Battalion training in forenoon. Battalion paraded at 4.45PM to march to MARQUEFFLES FARM under orders of 24th | |
| | | 4.45PM | Division. Order cancelled when Battalion had left parade ground. Battalion to Billets. | |
| | 12.4.17 | | Training carried out as usual | |
| | 12.4.17 | | Inspection of companies under company arrangements. | |
| NOEUX LES MINES. | 14.4.17 | 11.30AM | Battalion left NOEUX LES MINES at 11.30AM arriving at OHLAIN CAMP at 1.45PM. 1 man fell out, fine dry weather | |
| OHLAIN CAMP | " | 1.45PM | Daily sick percentage for week ending 14th inst: ·68% | |

Instructions regarding War Diaries and Intelligence Summaries are contained in F. S. Regs., Part II. and the Staff Manual respectively. Title pages will be prepared in manuscript.

# WAR DIARY ~~or~~ INTELLIGENCE SUMMARY.

(*Erase heading not required.*)

ANSON BN.

Army Form C. 2118.

| Place | Date | Hour | Summary of Events and Information | Remarks and references to Appendices |
|---|---|---|---|---|
| OHLAIN CAMP | 15.4.17 | 10 AM | Left OHLAIN CAMP at 10 AM arriving at MAROEUIL at 3.45 PM. No men fell out, raining the whole march. | |
| MAROEUIL | 16.4.17 | | Inspection of companies by Commanding Officer. | |
| | 17.4.17 | 4 AM | Battalion employed on road repairing on ARRAS-BAILLEUL Road. Very wet weather, returning at 1.30 PM. | |
| | 18.4.17 | 7 AM | Battalion on road repairing work on ARRAS-BAILLEUL ROAD. Rained all the time. Returning 3 PM. | |
| | 19.4.17 | 7 AM | Road repairing work for Battalion on same road as 18th inst. Finer weather. Returning at 3.15 PM. | |
| | 20.4.17 | 11 AM | Battalion left MAROEUIL at 11 AM arriving at St CATHERINES at 12.15 PM. Fine dry weather. No men fell out. | |
| St CATHERINES | 21.4.17 | 6 AM | Companies proceeded independently to MAISON BLANCHE for Road repairing, returning to Billets at 12 NOON. | |
| | | | Percentage of daily sick week ending 21st inst. ·32%. | |
| | 22.4.17 | | Battalion attached to 188th Brigade and standing by under 30 minutes notice to move. | |
| | 23.4.17 | | Battalion left St CATHERINES at 2.15 PM for reserve trenches at LA BOIS de LA MAISON BLANCHE arriving at 4 PM, in reserve | |
| TRENCHES AT LA BOIS DE LA MAISON BLANCHE | | | to 189th Inf Brigade. | |
| POINT DU JOURS | 24.4.17 | | Battalion moved forward to trenches at POINT DU JOURS in reserve to 189th Inf Brigade. Working party of 100 men | |
| | | | to carry ammunition & tools to front line at dusk, returned to 188th Inf Brigade. | |
| | 25.4.17 | | 150 OR's with Officers as carrying party, ammunition &c, from POINT du JOURS to GAVRELLE TRENCHES at dusk | |
| | 26.4.17 | 8.15 PM | Battalion left POINT DU JOURS at 8.15 PM for GAVRELLE to relieve HOWE BN. Relief complete by 2.40 AM. | |
| GAVRELLE | 27.4.17 | 2.40 AM | Disposition of Battalion as follows:— Right flank resting on Sunken Road about 500 yards to the South of Gavrelle | |

T2134. Wt. W708–776. 500000. 4/15. Sir J. C. & S.

Instructions regarding War Diaries and Intelligence Summaries are contained in F. S. Regs., Part II. and the Staff Manual respectively. Title pages will be prepared in manuscript.

# WAR DIARY or ~~INTELLIGENCE~~ SUMMARY.

(Erase heading not required.)

Army Form C. 2118.

ANSON BN:

| Place | Date | Hour | Summary of Events and Information | Remarks and references to Appendices |
|---|---|---|---|---|
| GAVRELLE | 27.4.17 | | when it connected with the left flank of the 37th Division. The Left flank was on the cross roads 250 yards North of GAVRELLE, order of Companies from right to left D. C. A. B. Headquarters in old German Front line 400 yards South of ARRAS-GAVRELLE ROAD. During the day the enemy shelled the village of GAVRELLE and our Front line continuously. | |
| | 28.4.17 | 2 AM | By 2 AM. the following changes had taken place in our dispositions preparatory to the Assault, the 2nd Royal Marines preparatory to attacking had taken over the line held by our A + B Cos. who had moved into Support about 70 yards in rear of C + D Cos. + had dug themselves in. The role assigned to the Battn. was to hold the line at all costs, C Coy being detailed for the special duty of connecting up, by means of small posts, with the right flank of the 2nd ROYAL MARINES on this unit reaching its final objective | |
| | | 4.25AM | some 900 yards to the EAST of GAVRELLE. At 4.25AM our Barrage opened and the assaulting troops went over the top, the enemy artillery replied vigorously, and we suffered some casualties, at 5 AM | |
| | | 5 AM | C. Coy moved out to perform their task of joining up with the 2nd ROYAL MARINES. They came under heavy machine gun fire from their right flank and from a strong point on the main road, moreover a portion of trench running parallel to our front + about 400 yards distant from it, was found to be strongly held by the enemy. The Coy. suffered heavy casualties but in spite of these pressed on and although the position of the flank of the 2nd ROYAL MARINES was not at this time where it had been expected | |

T2134. Wt. W708—776. 500000. 4/15. Sir J. C. & S.

Instructions regarding War Diaries and Intelligence Summaries are contained in F. S. Regs., Part II. and the Staff Manual respectively. Title pages will be prepared in manuscript.

# WAR DIARY
~~or~~
~~INTELLIGENCE~~ SUMMARY.
*(Erase heading not required.)*

Army Form C. 2118.

ANSON BN:

| Place | Date | Hour | Summary of Events and Information | Remarks and references to Appendices |
|---|---|---|---|---|
| GAVRELLE | 28.4.17 | 5 AM | The posts commenced to dig themselves in, & obtained shelter from the heavy fire which was brought to bear on them. Lieut A. G. HENRY the O C C Coy: was wounded and the command devolved on Sub Lt: C G WALKER. At this time the position was somewhat critical and it was deemed necessary to strengthen our front line by moving up B Coy which had previously been in support. By | |
| | | 10 AM | 10 AM it was evident that the posts of C Coy could not be maintained and orders were issued for their withdrawal. Sub Lts ROSS & FRASER with their parties succeeded in carrying out this movement successfully, but Sub Lt WALKER who held the most advanced post of all was forced to remain there all day under the close & accurate fire of the enemy & eventually withdrew at night fall. Our line was now held as follows, our right flank remained in its original position but our left stopped at the Southern edge of the [illegible] House, order of Coys from right to left, D, B C with A Coy in close support in rear of D. Heavy shelling of the village & our line by the enemy | |
| | | 11 4 AM | continued throughout the day. The enemy counter-attacked at 11.45 AM & 5 30 PM but in both cases were dispersed by | |
| | | 5 30 PM | our artillery & machine gun fire, during the night the 14th WORCESTERSHIRE PIONEERS arrived to reinforce the line and were disposed as follows. 1 Coy in support on left flank of our A Coy: 3 Coys in reserve near Battalion Headquarters. Daily percentage of sick week ending 28th inst ·42 %. | |
| | 29.4.17 | [illegible] | At 5 AM the enemy again counter attacked, but was again dispersed & all was quiet by 5 30 AM and barring intermittent shelling of the village, the day was fairly quiet. | |
| | | [illegible] | [illegible] by the 15th W YORKS was commenced at 10 PM and completed by 1 45 AM. | |
| | | | During these two days we were troubled by the enemy snipers who caused a lot of discomfort to our front line & [illegible] the Battalion distinguished itself by its steadiness under very trying circumstances, there being many acts of individual bravery. The outstanding feature being the capture of some 250 Germans by P.O. Scott [illegible] in command of the 5th Platoon, consisting of 15 men. On completion of relief the Battalion moved to | |
| ROCLINCOURT | 30.4.17 | 1 45 AM | [illegible] ROCLINCOURT. At 2 20 PM the Battalion moved on to billets at BRAY arriving at 5.15 PM. | |
| BRAY | | 5 15 PM | [illegible] | |
| | | | Our total casualties were 1 Officer killed 4 wounded 23 O.Rs killed 76 wounded & 6 missing. | |

H. Kirkpatrick
Lieut Col
Commanding ANSON BN:

A5834 Wt. W4973 M687 750,000 8/16 D. D. & L. Ltd. Forms/C.2118/13.

188/63

Vol 12

Instructions regarding War Diaries and Intelligence Summaries are contained in F. S. Regs., Part II. and the Staff Manual respectively. Title pages will be prepared in manuscript.

# WAR DIARY

*or*

~~INTELLIGENCE SUMMARY.~~

*(Erase heading not required.)*

Army Form C. 2118.

ANSON Bn.

| Place | Date | Hour | Summary of Events and Information | Remarks and references to Appendices |
|---|---|---|---|---|
| BRAY | 1/5/17 | 10am | Battalion left for VILLERS BRULIN arriving 1.15pm – no men dropped out.– | |
| VILLERS BRULIN | 2/5/17 | | " rested – Divisional General visited Battalion.– | |
| | 3/5/17 | | " training 9–12 and 2.15 – 3.45 pm – Brigadier congratulated Batt. | |
| | 4/5/17 | 10am | " left for HERMIN arriving 11.20 am – no men fell out.– | |
| HERMIN | 5/5/17 | | " training as above.– | |
| | 6/5/17 | 10am | Church Parade – | |
| | 7/5/17 | | Battalion training 9–12 and 2.15 – 3.45 –<br>Daily percentage of sick for weekending ·63% | |
| | 8/5/17 | 9am | Battalion left HERMIN arrived MONT ST ELOY 12.30 – no men fell out | |
| MONT ST ELOY | 9/5/17 | 1pm | " " for Camp at G10b.5.4 arriving 3.15 pm – | |
| G10b 5.4 | 10/5/17 | | A + B Coys worked on 'Canadian Rly' from 8–12 + 1–4 – Remaining Coys training | |
| | 11/5/17 | | Battalion left at 2.30pm for PONTEFRACT CAMP arriving 3 pm | |
| PONTEFRACT Camp | 12/5/17 | | Battalion worked on GREEN LINE from 9.30 pm – 2.30 am digging.– | |
| | 13/5/17 | | 300 ORs working party as above – Specialists training 9–12 2.15 – 3.45 | |
| | 14/5/17 | | — as above — Daily percentage of sick for weekending ·6 % | |
| | 15/5/17 | | — as above — | |
| | 16/5/17 | | Wet weather – training in the afternoon – no working party – | |
| | 17/5/17 | | Battalion training 9–11 and 2–3 – no working party.– | |
| | 18/5/17 | | — as above — | |
| | 19/5/17 | | training in the forenoon – Batt left for Reserve trenches near BOIS de la MAISON BLANCHE arriving 3 pm.– | |

A5834 Wt. W4973/M687 750,000 8/16 D. D. & L. Ltd. Forms/C.2118/13.

Instructions regarding War Diaries and Intelligence Summaries are contained in F. S. Regs., Part II. and the Staff Manual respectively. Title pages will be prepared in manuscript.

# WAR DIARY

*or*

~~INTELLIGENCE SUMMARY.~~

*(Erase heading not required.)*

ANSON BATT.

Army Form C. 2118.

| Place | Date | Hour | Summary of Events and Information | Remarks and references to Appendices |
|---|---|---|---|---|
| TRENCHES BOIS near MAISON BLANCHE | 20/5/17 | | Battalion in reserve trenches – Inspection by Companies – | |
| | 21/5/17 | | —— as above —— A & B on carrying parties to the line leaving 9 p.m | |
| | | | Daily percentage of sick for week ending ·42% | |
| | 22/5/17 | | Inspection by companies – Coy representatives went up the line to take over – | |
| | 23/5/17 | | Battalion relieved HOWE BATT. in the front line at CAVRELLE. – disposition of Coys was as follows – from right to left C.B.A.D. relief was completed at 2 45 a.m. – On the way up to the trenches four men of A Co were wounded | |
| CAVRELLE | ~~24/5/17~~ | | | |
| | 24/5/17 | | In trenches – Enemy artillery was active and we suffered two casualties from hostile shelling just outside Batt. H.Q. otherwise the day was without incident – At night every available man was engaged on improving and linking up the front line trenches – | |
| | 25/5/17 | | In trenches – hostile shelling less severe than the previous day – At night work was continued on the trenches | |
| | 26/5/17 | | In trenches – a quiet day – work as before | |
| | 27/5/17 | | In trenches. hostile artillery normal – working parties at night as before | |
| | 28/5/17 | | Corps & Divisional Commanders visited the front line and expressed themselves pleased with the work done by the Batt. At night the Batt. was relieved by the HOWE BATT. – Two hours previous to relief a shell fell in D Co front causing us a loss of one killed & three wounded. | |

A5834 Wt. W4973/M687 750,000 8/16 D. D. & L. Ltd. Forms/C.2118/13.

Army Form C. 2118.

Instructions regarding War Diaries and Intelligence Summaries are contained in F. S. Regs., Part II. and the Staff Manual respectively. Title pages will be prepared in manuscript.

# WAR DIARY
*or*
# ~~INTELLIGENCE~~ SUMMARY.

*(Erase heading not required.)*

| Place | Date | Hour | Summary of Events and Information | Remarks and references to Appendices |
|---|---|---|---|---|
| | 28/5/17 contd | | Our total casualties during this tour of duty in the front line amounted to 9 killed and 16 wounded. – | |
| Trenches at BOIS de la MAISON BLANCHE | 29/5/17 | | Batt in reserve trenches 500 yds E of ARRAS-BAIELLEUL ROAD in the vicinity of the BOIS de la MAISON BLANCHE | |
| | 30/5/17 | | In reserve – Carrying parties at night to the front line | |
| | 31/5/17 | | In reserve – Carrying parties at night. – | |

H F Kirkpatrick Lt Col
Commdg. Anson Battn.

A5834 Wt. W4973/M687 750,000 8/16 D. D. & L. Ltd. Forms/C.2118/13.

Instructions regarding War Diaries and Intelligence Summaries are contained in F. S. Regs., Part II. and the Staff Manual respectively. Title pages will be prepared in manuscript.

# WAR DIARY
*or*
# ~~INTELLIGENCE SUMMARY.~~
*(Erase heading not required.)*

Army Form C. 2118.

ANSON

Vol 13

| Place | Date | Hour | Summary of Events and Information | Remarks and references to Appendices |
|---|---|---|---|---|
| | 1/6/17 | | Battn in support. | |
| | 2/6/17 | [illegible] | " relieved "HOWE" Battn in the front line at GAVRELLE relief complete 11.45 pm<br>Percentage of sick per day for week ending ·2% | |
| | 3/6/17 | | Sector appeared to be quiet during Battn. tour in the trenches — | |
| | 4/6/17 | | In reply to our hurricane bombardments the enemy's reply was feeble. | |
| | 5/6/17 | | | |
| | 6/6/17 | | Relieved by the HOWE Battn — relief complete 12.25 am 7/6/17 | |
| | 7/6/17 | | Battn in trenches near BOIS de la MAISON BLANCHE | |
| | 8/6/17 | | Left these trenches 7.15 pm arrived ROCLINCOURT 8 pm — Percentage of sick per day ·5% | |
| | 9/6/17 | | Left 6.15 pm arrived MONT ST ELOI arrived 8.45 pm — no men fell out | |
| | 10/6/17 | | Cleaning up — [illegible] | |
| [illegible] | 11/6/17 | | " " — | |
| " | [illegible] | | Training [illegible] 6 pm — | |
| " | 13/6/17 | | [illegible] — Battn moved to St AUBIN leaving 3.30 pm [illegible] 4.45 pm | |
| [illegible] | 15/6/17 | | " 10.30 [illegible] 6 pm — | |
| | 16/6/17 | | " 10[illegible] Battn left St AUBIN arrived MAROEUIL 4.45 pm | |
| | | | Percentage of sick per day for week ending ·3% | |

A5834 Wt. W4973/M687 750,000 8/16 D. D. & L. Ltd. Forms/C.2118/13.

Instructions regarding War Diaries and Intelligence Summaries are contained in F. S. Regs., Part II. and the Staff Manual respectively. Title pages will be prepared in manuscript.

# WAR DIARY
*or*
~~INTELLIGENCE SUMMARY.~~
*(Erase heading not required.)*

ANSON Batt

Army Form C. 2118.

| Place | Date | Hour | Summary of Events and Information | Remarks and references to Appendices |
|---|---|---|---|---|
| MAROEUIL | 17/6/17 | | Church Parade – | |
| " | 18/6/17 | | Training 7 10-30 & 5-6 p.m. Lecture to Officers 6-7 p.m. – | |
| " | 19/6/17 | | " 7 10-30 a.m. – Lord Charles Beresford inspected Batt. – | |
| " | 20/6/17 | | " 7 10-30 a.m. 5-6 p.m. – Lecture to Officers 6-7 p.m. – | |
| " | 21/6/17 | | " " as above " | |
| " | 22/6/17 | | Batt left for ROCLINCOURT at 8 a.m. arrived 10 a.m. – Working parties at night for 5 off + 231 O.R for 176th + 186th R.E. | |
| ROCLINCOURT | 23/6/17 | | Working parties as above – Percentage of sick per day for week ending ·5 % | |
| " | 24/6/17 | | " " " " | |
| | 25/6/17 | | " " " " | |
| " | 26/6/17 | | " " " " | |
| | 27/6/17 | | No working parties. – | |
| | 28/6/17 | | Training 8-10-30 a.m. – First Army Commander visited & inspected Batt. – | |
| " | 29/6/17 | | " " – Working party 2 off + 70 O.R. for 176th R.E. | |
| | 30/6/17 | | " " – Percentage of sick per day for week ending ·9 % | |

Stuart G. Jones Lieut Comdr RNVR
Comd. ANSON Batt.

A5834 Wt. W4973/M687 750,000 8/16 D. D. & L. Ltd. Forms/C.2118/13

Instructions regarding War Diaries and Intelligence Summaries are contained in F. S. Regs., Part II. and the Staff Manual respectively. Title pages will be prepared in manuscript.

# WAR DIARY
*or*
~~INTELLIGENCE SUMMARY.~~
*(Erase heading not required.)*

"ANSON" Battn.

Army Form C. 2118.

Vol 14

| Place | Date | Hour | Summary of Events and Information | Remarks and references to Appendices |
|---|---|---|---|---|
| ROCLINCOURT | 1/7/17 | | Coys' cleaning up. – Voluntary Church Parade – | |
| | 2/7/17 | | Training 8–8.30 am 9.30–10.30 am – | |
| | 3/7/17 | | Left R'CORT 5.30pm arrived Reserve Trenches in the BLACK LINE 6.15pm | |
| | 4/7/17 | | Inspection of Coys by C.O. – Working party in Trenches 9.30pm – 3.30 am. – | |
| | 5/7/17 | | Training for 'A+D' Co 9.30–11 am – A+D Coys working party as above. – | |
| | 6/7/17 | | " C+B " " " C+B " " " " " " – | |
| | 7/7/17 | | " A+D " " " A+D " " " " " " – | |
| | | | Percentage of sick per day for week ending ·58% – | |
| | 8/7/17 | | Church Service 11.45 am. – B+C working party 9.30pm – 2.30 am. – | |
| | 9/7/17 | | A+D Coys working party 9.30pm – 1.30 am. – | |
| [illegible] | 10/7/17 | | Battn moved into front line to relieve HOWE BATT relief complete 12.45 am. | |
| | 11/7/17 | | Battn in the front line, – a quiet day. – | |
| | 12/7/17 | | " " " " " " " " " | |
| | 13/7/17 | | " " " " " " " " " | |
| | 14/7/17 | | " " " " " Hostile artillery a little more active – | |
| | | | Percentage of sick per day for week ending ·26% | |
| | 15/7/17 | | Battn in the front line. – Fine weather & a quiet day. – | |
| | 16/7/17 | | " " " " " " " " " " " – | |

A5834 Wt. W4973/M687 750,000 8/16 D. D. & L. Ltd. Forms/C.2118/13.

Instructions regarding War Diaries and Intelligence Summaries are contained in F. S. Regs., Part II. and the Staff Manual respectively. Title pages will be prepared in manuscript.

# WAR DIARY
*or*
# ~~INTELLIGENCE SUMMARY.~~ "ANSON" Batt.

*(Erase heading not required.)*

Army Form C. 2118.

| Place | Date | Hour | Summary of Events and Information | Remarks and references to Appendices |
|---|---|---|---|---|
| CAUREUL | 17/7/17 | | Batt. move into support. – HOWE Batt. move into front line. – | |
| | 18/7/17 | | " in support. – Weather fine. – | |
| | 19/7/17 | | " " " . A quiet day & good weather. – | |
| | 20/7/17 | | Batt. moves into front line and HOWE Batt. move into support. – | |
| | 21/7/17 | | " in front line – Percentage of sick per day for weekending ·29% | |
| | 22/7/17 | | " " " " Hostile artillery active on his favourite local targets. – | |
| | 23/7/17 | | " " " " Situation quiet & weather good. – | |
| | 24/7/17 | | " " " " A quiet day – Artillery (hostile) active on back areas – | |
| | 25/7/17 | | Batt. moves into support – HOWE Batt. move into front line. – | |
| | 26/7/17 | | Batt. in support line. – Weather fair – Enemy quiet. – | |
| | 27/7/17 | | " " " " A quiet day. – | |
| | 28/7/17 | | " " " " Percentage of sick per day for weekending ·22%. | |
| | 29/7/17 | | " " " " Enemy quiet. Weather fair. – | |
| | 30/7/17 | | Batt. relieved by HOOD Batt. and move to AUBREY CAMP | |
| | 31/7/17 | | Batt. clean up. Coy Comd. inspection in the afternoon | |

H. Kirkpatrick Lt. Col.
Comd. ANSON Batt.

A5834 Wt. W4973/M687 750,000 8/16 D. D. & L. Ltd. Forms/C.2118/13.

Army Form C. 2118.

Instructions regarding War Diaries and Intelligence Summaries are contained in F. S. Regs., Part II. and the Staff Manual respectively. Title pages will be prepared in manuscript.

# WAR DIARY
*or*
# ~~INTELLIGENCE SUMMARY.~~
*(Erase heading not required.)*

ANSON BATTN

| Place | Date | Hour | Summary of Events and Information | Remarks and references to Appendices |
|---|---|---|---|---|
| [illegible] | 1/6/17 | | Battalion [illegible] up & check Trench Stores after tour in the trenches. | |
| [illegible] | 2/6/17 | | [illegible] day. Inspection & instruction in the huts. | |
| | [illegible] | | Battalion training. Officers reconnoitre Brigade Area. Daily percentage of sick for week ending '32 — Gas mask march by the Battalion at night. | |
| | [illegible] | | " " 8-12-15 — "B" Co. fire on the range. | |
| | [illegible] | | Church Parade. Special parade at [illegible] 2 [illegible] | |
| | 6/6/17 | | Training & [illegible] C. Coy fire on the range. | |
| | 7/6/17 | | Battalion [illegible] for relieving [illegible] Batt. in the front line | |
| [illegible] | [illegible] | | in the front line trenches S. of FRESNES-GAVRELLE ROAD | |
| | | | [illegible] & improving of trenches. | |
| | [illegible] | | Daily percentage of sick for week ending '70 | |
| | | | relieved by [illegible] Batt. relief complete at [illegible] | |
| [illegible] | [illegible] | | in ~~[illegible]~~ BLACK LINE ~~[illegible]~~. [illegible] Coy working parties by night | |
| | | | [illegible] & trenches. C & B Coy working parties by night | |
| | | | [illegible] on trenches during the day & various parties working at night | |
| [illegible] | [illegible] | | relieved [illegible] [illegible] and move into the FRONT LINE | |
| | | | relief complete [illegible] | |

A5834 Wt. W4973/M687 750,000 8/16 D. D. & L. Ltd. Forms/C.2118/13.

Instructions regarding War Diaries and Intelligence Summaries are contained in F. S. Regs., Part II. and the Staff Manual respectively. Title pages will be prepared in manuscript.

# WAR DIARY
*or*
# ~~INTELLIGENCE SUMMARY.~~
*(Erase heading not required.)*

Army Form C. 2118.

ANSON Battn

| Place | Date | Hour | Summary of Events and Information | Remarks and references to Appendices |
|---|---|---|---|---|
| [illegible] | 16/8/17 | | Battn. in FRONT LINE } Work done on trenches & improvements. | |
| | 17/8/17 | | " " " } a very quiet period. — Daily percentage of sick for week ending ·60 | |
| | 18/8/17 | | | |
| | 19/8/17 | | " move into SUPPORT LINE – Relief complete by HOWE Battn at 11 PM | |
| | 20/8/17 | | " in SUPPORT LINE } A very quiet period – little hostile shelling | |
| | 21/8/17 | | | |
| | 22/8/17 | | | |
| | 23/8/17 | | | |
| AUBREY CAMP | 24/8/17 | | Battn relieved by NELSON Battn – Relief complete at 11.30 pm. Battn moved to AUBREY CAMP | |
| | 25/8/17 | | " clean up – 2 officers with camouflage works. Daily percentage of sick for week ending ·32 | |
| | 26/8/17 | | Church Parade. – | |
| | 27/8/17 | | Battalion training in special movement. – | |
| | 28/8/17 | | " " as above. A Co on the range in the afternoon | |
| | 29/8/17 | | " " Wet afternoon. | |
| | | | " perform movement before Brig. General. B Co shoot in the afternoon. Officers on a compass march during afternoon. | |
| | 31/8/17 | | Battalion training 8.30 – 12 noon. C Coy on the range in the afternoon. Daily percentage of sick for week ending ·37 | |

H. Kirkpatrick, Lt Col
Comdg ANSON BATTN.

A5834 Wt. W4973/M687 750,000 8/16 D. D. & L. Ltd. Forms/C.2118/13.

Instructions regarding War Diaries and Intelligence Summaries are contained in F. S. Regs., Part II. and the Staff Manual respectively. Title pages will be prepared in manuscript.

Army Form C. 2118.

# WAR DIARY
*or*
# ~~INTELLIGENCE SUMMARY.~~
*(Erase heading not required.)*

AMSON

Vol 16

| Place | Date | Hour | Summary of Events and Information | Remarks and references to Appendices |
|---|---|---|---|---|
| GAVRELLE | 1/9/17 | | Battalion relieved the NELSON Battn in the front line trenches E. of GAVRELLE. – | |
| " | 2/9/17 | | " in the front line } A very quiet period – Weather good – | |
| " | 3/9/17 | | } No outstanding features of importance. – | |
| " | 4/9/17 | | | |
| " | 5/9/17 | | " " " " " Our front line badly damaged during the night by hostile T.M. fire | |
| " | 6/9/17 | | " " " " " [illegible] day. – Wiring at night for the Defence Scheme. – | |
| | 7/9/17 | | 9.45 pm the Battn carried out a raid against the enemy trench with the object of obtaining an identification – The objective of the raid was a SAP in the enemy's trench to the E. of GAVRELLE – Strength of raiding party 1 Off Sub Lt Russel, [illegible] and 30 O.R. The raid was successful and one prisoner was captured – Our casualties were slight ([illegible] wounded 1 missing). The raiding party was most ably led and all ranks showed great dash and keenness. – Sub Lt Russel was awarded the M.C. P/O [illegible] & [illegible] Brock the M.M. Copies of Battn Orders and report on the results of the raid are attached marked Appendix A. – Daily percentage of sick for week was ·34 %. | |
| | [illegible] | | Battn in the front line. A quiet day. | |
| | [illegible] | | " moved into Support line – relieved by HOWE Battn – | |
| | [illegible] | | " in Support. A & C Coys occupy MARINE & NAVAL TRENCH. – | |
| | [illegible] | | " } B & D [illegible] RED LINE – | |
| | [illegible] | | " } An uneventful period. Improvement & upkeep of trenches during the day. Carrying parties at night for the front line Battn. | |
| | [illegible] | | " moved to the BLACK LINE into [illegible] CAMP – | |
| | [illegible] | | " [illegible] Battn. Inspection by Coys. Daily percentage of sick | |
| | [illegible] | | " [illegible] Battn inspection and [illegible] for week [illegible] | |

(A7092). Wt W12839/M1293 75,000. 1/17. D. D. & L., Ltd. Forms/C.2118/14.

Army Form C. 2118.

Instructions regarding War Diaries and Intelligence Summaries are contained in F. S. Regs., Part II. and the Staff Manual respectively. Title pages will be prepared in manuscript.

# WAR DIARY
*or*
# ~~INTELLIGENCE SUMMARY.~~
*(Erase heading not required.)*

ANSON

| Place | Date | Hour | Summary of Events and Information | Remarks and references to Appendices |
|---|---|---|---|---|
| ROUNDHAY CAMP | 16/9/17 | | Church Parade – Inspection of Coys by C.O. | |
| ROCLINCOURT | 17/9/17 | | Batt. moved into billets in the Railway cutting S.W. of BAILLIEUL and came under command of 190th Inf Bde | |
| | 18/9/17 | | Battn in the Railway cutting } Clean up and inspection by Coys & work on improvement of billets in the Cutting by day. – | |
| | 19/9/17 | | " " " " } 3 Coys on working parties at night. – | |
| | 20/9/17 | | " " " " } Removal of material from railhead to front line | |
| | 21/9/17 | | " } and construction of Defensive Posts. – | |
| | | | Daily percentage of sick for week end. 3%. – | |
| | 22/9/17 | | Battn in the Railway Cutting } Work as above – | |
| | 23/9/17 | | " " " | |
| | 24/9/17 | | Battn. relieved by 23rd London Regt. and moved by train and bus to CHELERS – | |
| | 25/9/17 | | " cleaned up and prepared for training. – | |
| | 26/9/17 | | " Training 8.30 am – 12 noon – and 2.30 pm – 3.30 pm. | |
| | 27/9/17 | | " " " " " " | |
| | 28/9/17 | | " " | |
| | | | Daily percentage of sick for week end. 57%. | |
| | 29/9/17 | | Battn training [illegible] and 2.30 pm – 3.30 pm – | |
| | 30/9/17 | | Church Parade. Battn Sport in the afternoon – | |

H Kirkpatrick
Lieut Col
Comd. 'ANSON' Battn.

(A7092). Wt W12839/M1293 75,0.0. 1/17. D. D. & L., Ltd. Forms/C.2118/14.

S E C R E T                                                    APPENDIX A

BATTALION ORDER
BY
Lieut Colonel H.F. Kirkpatrick
Commanding Anson Battalion.

1. D Company will carry out a raid on the enemy's trenches - date to be notified later.

OBJECT 2. To obtain an identification.

OBJECTIVES 3. The enemy's sap at O.25.b.10.15.

STRENGTH 4. 1 Officer 30 O.Rs.

FORMATION 5. In two lines at 15 yards distance.
<u>First Line</u>. A line of three parties extended at 1 yard interval.

Right Party - 6 men and a group leader.
Centre " - 5 men " " " "
Left " - 6 " " " " "

The Officer Commanding party will move with the Right Party.

Platoon Sergeant will move with the left party.

<u>Second Line</u> consisting of 4 men and a group leader will move 15 yards in rear of first line. This party will move in extended order at 1 yard interval.

4 stretcher bearers × will move 25 yards behind the second line.

Parties will consist of an equal number of bombers and riflemen. × with 2 stretchers.

DRESS & EQUIPMENT 6. Steel helmets will be worn.
SBR's in "ALERT" position.
All ranks will carry a rifle and bayonet with the exception of 1 bomber per party who will carry a Knobkerry. In addition all ranks will carry wire cutters and two Mills grenades, one in each side pocket.
All men will carry a sandbag - bombers - 8 bombs in Waistcoat pattern carriers. Riflemen - 1 bandolier SAA in first line, magazines will be charged, 1 round in chamber. In second line - magazines charged, no rounds in chamber. Faces will be blackened.

METHOD OF CARRYING OUT ATTACK 7 A forming up tape will be laid out 40 yds in advance of our trench, the left of the taped line being 30 yds south of the Ditch. The raiding party will be formed up on this line by ZERO - 10.

O.C. - "C" Company will provide a covering party of 1 section. This party will take up its position at ZERO - 60 minutes and withdraw through the raiding party at ZERO - 10.

At ZERO the raiders will advance and follow the barrage as closely as safety permits. Immediately the barrage lifts off the sap and enemy's front line, the first line will dash up to the sap and endeavour to obtain an identification.

The action of the various parties will be as follows :-

<u>Centre party</u> will jump into the sap at the sap head and make their way down the sap.

<u>Right and left parties</u> will continue along the top on either side of the sap and jump into the main trench 3 yds to the right and left respectively of the point at which the sap joins the main trench.

2 men from each of these parties will not enter the trench but will lie down on the top of the enemy parapet and cover the operations of the remainder. Of the remainder, 3 men of each party will form a block to the right and left flank respectively.

Remaining 3 of each party will block the exit to the main trench from the sap.

SECRET

Reference Map: Special 1/10,000 GAVRELLE "B" Ed 6.

REPORT on raid carried out by ANSON Battalion against Sap-head in German Trench at C.25.b.10.15, on night of 7th September.

---

1. Strength of Raiding party. 1 Officer -Sub Lieut J.G. Russell- and 30 O.R's.

2. Preliminary arrangements. Were all carried out as laid down in ANSON Battalion Order of the 2nd of September'17 in accordance with 188th Inf Brigade Order No 138 of the 2nd Sept '17.

3. Forming up. The raiding party was formed up and in position on the tape at 9.35 pm.

4. Time Table. -Observed from Battalion Headquarters.-

| | |
|---|---|
| ZERO 9.45 pm | Our barrage opened. |
| plus 2.30 | A Few Bosche whit lights were going up but not on front of raid. |
| plus 4. | Our red lights were put up, guiding signal for raiders. |
| plus 4.20 | Boche retaliation, slight, apparently directed on TOWY ALLEY. |
| plus 5 | Boche putting up double green lights |
| plus 5.30 | Retaliation, still slight. |
| plus 6.10 | More double green lights from enemy's line. |
| plus 7 | Boche retaliating with 5.9. |
| plus 8.50 | Double green lights from enemy's line. |
| plus 12 | Our red lights cease. |
| plus 12.50 | Our lights recommence. |
| plus 15 | Our red lights cease. |
| plus 15.30 | Slight retaliation by enemy. |
| plus 16.30 | Our barrage slackens. |
| plus 18 | Our barrage ceases. |
| plus 18.50 | Slight machine gun fire, hostile. |
| plus 19 | Hostile machine gun fire rather heavier. |
| plus 23 | Quiet, situation normal. |

5. Our Barrage. The opening of the barrage was ragged, some guns being inadavnce of the scheduled time. It was however, taken up by everyone, and having started, proved most effective. Our raiding party advanced under it with the utmost confidence, and much appreciated its accuracy, as also that of the machine guns, and Trench Mortars.

6. German wire. Had been very effectively dealt with by our artillery and proved no obstacle.

7. Action of raiding Party. Arrived at their objective as pre-arranged. The right party, led by Sub Lieut Russell and PO Simpson, jumped into the trench on the right of the sap, almost on to a Boche who was emerging from the mouth of the shaft of a dug out about 3 yards from the junction of the sap and the main trench. This man was taken prisoner, by the above mentioned.

Another Boche bolted out down the trench and was shot by A.B. Widdows.

The object of the raid having been accomplished, the order was given to get back to our trenches, and the party withdrew and returned.

/8 Enemy Trench.

The second will lie down round the head of the sap and take over prisoners or assist casualties.

If the sap and portion of trench entered is found unoccupied the whole party will immediately withdraw and return to our trenches.

If an identification is obtained the raiding party will at once withdraw, by order of the Officer Commanding the party.

In either case the withdrawal will only take place by order of the senior person present.

The second line will cover the withdrawal.

BARRAGE 8. Artillery, T.M's and Machine Guns will co-operate. Details and time table will be issued later.

CUTTING OF OUR OWN WIRE. 9. O.C. "C" Company will arrange for this to be carried out on the 2 nights previous to the raid.

VERY LIGHTS 10. To assist in guiding the party on their return - RED Very Lights will be fired continuously from our trench at the point of exit. These lights will be fired from ZERO plus 4 until all the raiders are in. These lights will be fired by 3 men, each armed with a Very pistol, men will fire in rapid succession. A reserve party of 3 men, each armed with a Very Pistol, will be kept ready about 30 yds away in the trench in case of a breakdown, when they would move up and continue the signals.

The necessary arrangements to be made by OC "C" Company.

ACTION OF BATTALION 11. From ZERO, until completion of raid, the Battalion will "Stand To", but with the exception of sentries will not get on the fire steps.

ESCORT TO PRISONERS 12. OC "C" Company will detail and hold in readiness escorts to take over charge of prisoners on arrival in our trenches. They will be immediately despatched to Headquarters of the Battalion.

GENERAL 13. No identifications of any sort will be worn. No papers of any description will be carried, identity discs will be withdrawn and a number issued to everyone taking part in the raid.

Nominal roll of those taking part will be prepared by OC "D" Company and against each name will be entered the number with which the person has been issued. This roll will be handed in to Battalion Headquarters by 6. 0 pm. the day before the raid.

All ranks taking part are to be warned that in the event of capture they should disclose nothing but their rank and name.

CODE WORD 14. Code word for raid - "M A R T I N".

2 /9/ 17

Sgd. H.F. Kirkpatrick
Lieut Colonel,
Commanding Anson Battalio[n]

8. Enemy Trench. Had been very badly knocked about by our artillery deep, no parapet, no duckboards.

9. Enemy action. Practically nil, slight machine gun fire pursued the party on their return journey, which increased after the party had re-entered our trenches. A few shells fell in their vicinity.

10. Our withdrawal signal. Proved satisfactory, could be plainly seen but the quality of our ammunition is indifferent. The cessation of our red lights between plus 12 and plus 12.50 was due to a succession of "Duds" and numerous gaps were noticed in the succession of lights.

11. Prisoners. One was captured.

12. Casualties - Ours - 4 slightly wounded, 1 O.R. missing, was last seen halfway across "No Man's land" whilst our party was returning. He was then unwounded.

13. General. All ranks carried out their work with dash and keenness and were most capably led.

Sgd. H.T. Kirkpatrick
Lieut Colonel,
Commanding Anson Battalion

8th Sept. '17.

Instructions regarding War Diaries and Intelligence Summaries are contained in F. S. Regs., Part II. and the Staff Manual respectively. Title pages will be prepared in manuscript.

# WAR DIARY
~~or~~
# ~~INTELLIGENCE~~ SUMMARY.
(*Erase heading not required.*)

ANSON BN.

Army Form C. 2118.

| Place | Date | Hour | Summary of Events and Information | Remarks and references to Appendices |
|---|---|---|---|---|
| NOUVEAU MONDE | 23.10.17 | | Battalion moved from NOUVEAU MONDE to YPRES by Bus at 12 Noon arriving at 3.30 PM | |
| YPRES | 24.10.17 | | into front line taking over from the 12th Royal Scots, relief complete by 10 PM. SOUTH OF POELCAPELLE. | |
| S. of POELCAPELLE | 25.10.17 | | Holding the line | |
| | 26.10.17 | | in action. Zero at 5.40 AM we attacked on a frontage of 520 yds. with D Coy on the right, half of B Coy in support, A Coy on left, C Coy in ~~[illegible]~~ reserve, remainder of B Coy was detailed for carrying duties. The [illegible] hour to Zero, steady rain fell which [illegible] over which we had to advance was indescribably [illegible] filled with mud [illegible] difficulty & stiff resistance [illegible] the men [illegible] their knees, in spite of [illegible] part of its objective. A Coy on the left were held [illegible] D Coy on the right, in spite of the fact that [illegible] its objectives, but ~~[illegible]~~ were compelled to fall back owing to the [illegible] on their right [illegible] having got into touch with the troops on their right, they dug in and remained there until relieved. SUB LIEUT STEVENSON with 7 men, all that remained of his Platoon [illegible] VARLET FARM where they hung on although nearly surrounded by the enemy until [illegible] when they were relieved by the HOOD BN. Such portions of the Battalion [illegible] IRISH FARM / the remainder were relieved on the following night [illegible] the 189th Brigade. Our Casualties were [illegible] 2 [illegible] killed 7 wounded 1 missing the total losses [illegible] killed wounded & missing [illegible] 260. The Officers killed were LIEUT F.C. MUNDY M.C. + SUB LIEUT J.G. RUSSELL, M.C. | |
| DAMBRE CAMP | 27.10.17 | | Battalion [illegible] to DAMBRE CAMP | |
| | 28.10.17 | | " resting & cleaning up. [illegible] Daily [illegible] week ending .67% | |
| | 29.10.17 | | " " " reorganisation | |
| | 30.10.17 | | " " | |
| | 31.10.17 | | " " [illegible] congratulated the Battalion on its magnificent work | |

H F Kirkpatrick Lt Col.
Comdg. ANSON BATT^n

Instructions regarding War Diaries and Intelligence Summaries are contained in F. S. Regs., Part II. and the Staff Manual respectively. Title pages will be prepared in manuscript.

# WAR DIARY
*or*
~~INTELLIGENCE SUMMARY.~~
(*Erase heading not required.*)

"ANSON" BAT.

Army Form C. 2118.

183/63

Vol 18

| Place | Date | Hour | Summary of Events and Information | Remarks and references to Appendices |
|---|---|---|---|---|
| DAMBRE CAMP NEAR BRIELEN | 1/11/17 2/11/17 3/11/17 | | Reorganising and refitting of Battalion after returning from action. | |
| | 4/11/17 | | | |
| | 5/11/17 | | Battalion proceeded to the line relieving the HOOD Battn. Relief started at 5.30 pm but was not completed until 2.30 a.m. Delay was due in the initial stages to the HOOD guides not being in readiness and later to the great difficulty experienced in relieving the garrison of VAPOUR FARM owing to the intense darkness and the almost impossible condition of the ground. – | |
| | 6/11/17 | | I. Canadian Div. immediately on our right attacked, as a result the Battn. suffered a heavy shelling by the enemy our casualties approximately 50 – of these some 8-10 were caused by shells from our own guns | |
| | 7/11/17 | | The Battn. was relieved at night by I WELSH REGT and M.R.A. – The relief was complete at 3 am and Battn. marched to IRISH CAMP Daily percentage of sick for week ending 3.1% | |
| | 8/11/17 | | Battn. entrained at 9.30 a.m. and detrained close to POPERINGHE from thence to SCHOOL CAMP by road | |
| SCHOOL CAMP | 9/11/17 10/11/17 | | In camp. | |
| | 11/11/17 | | Left SCHOOL CAMP at 8.45 am reaching WINNEZEELE at 11.15 am – | |
| | 12/11/17 | | " WINNEZEELE at 9 am arrived ARNEKE 12.20 pm – | |
| ARNEKE | 13/11/17 | | Battn. in billets over a very scattered area | |

A5834 Wt. W4973/M687 750,000 8/16 D. D. & L. Ltd. Forms/C.2118/13.

Instructions regarding War Diaries and Intelligence Summaries are contained in F. S. Regs., Part II. and the Staff Manual respectively. Title pages will be prepared in manuscript.

# WAR DIARY
*or*
# INTELLIGENCE SUMMARY.
*(Erase heading not required.)*

Army Form C. 2118.

| Place | Date | Hour | Summary of Events and Information | Remarks and references to Appendices |
|---|---|---|---|---|
| [illegible] | 14/10/17 | | Battn clean up — Daily percentage of sick for week ending ·20% | |
| | 15/10/17 | | Training — | |
| | 16/10/17 | | | |
| | 17/10/17 | | | |
| | 18/10/17 | | | |
| | 19/10/17 | | | |
| | 20/10/17 | | | |
| | 21/10/17 | | Battn was visited by Capt Backhouse C.B. R.N. formerly Comd 2nd R.N. Bde. Daily percentage of sick for week ending ·30% | |
| | 22/10/17 | | " proceeded by bus to MURAT CAMP near YPRES for [illegible] parties and came under orders of 35th Div. | |
| MURAT CAMP | 23/10/17 | | In camp — | |
| | 24/10/17 | | Battn was engaged on work for the H.A. II Corps work consisting chiefly in shifting ammunition | |
| | 25/10/17 | | As above — | |
| | 26/10/17 | | | |
| | 27/10/17 | | Daily percentage of sick for week ending ·20% The area in which the camp is situated was considerably shelled by the enemy throughout the day — one shell falling in the middle of the camp killing 2 wounding [illegible] | |
| | 28/10/17 | | | |
| | 29/10/17 | | | |
| | 30/10/17 | | Battn on working parties — | |

H. F. Kirkpatrick
Lt Col.
Comd ANSON Battn

A5834 Wt. W4973/M687 750,000 8/16 D. D. & L. Ltd. Forms/C.2118/13.

Instructions regarding War Diaries and Intelligence Summaries are contained in F. S. Regs., Part II. and the Staff Manual respectively. Title pages will be prepared in manuscript.

# WAR DIARY
*or*
~~INTELLIGENCE SUMMARY.~~
*(Erase heading not required.)*

Army Form C. 2118.

"ANSON" Battn

| Place | Date | Hour | Summary of Events and Information | Remarks and references to Appendices |
|---|---|---|---|---|
| MURAT CAMP YPRES | 1/12/17 | | Working parties for CRA. Building dugouts – moving guns and ammunition – Specialist training | |
| | 2/12/17 | | " " " " " do " " " " | |
| | 3/12/17 | | " " " " " do " " " | |
| | 4/12/17 | | No work – Battn under short notice to move by train. – | |
| | 5/12/17 | | " " " do " " " | |
| SCHOOL CAMP | 6/12/17 | | Battn marched to SCHOOL CAMP arriving at 2.30 pm – | |
| | 7/12/17 | | Clean up and inspection by Coy Comd. – | |
| | 8/12/17 | | Training 9 – 12.30. – Recruits taken in [illegible] Drill – Specialist Training " | |
| | 9/12/17 | | Battn receives orders to entrain. – | |
| | 10/12/17 | | Left SCHOOL CAMP 5.30 am marched to PESELHOEK then entrained for ACHIET LE GRAND detraining at ACHIET-LE-GRAND Battn marched to BEAULENCOURT at 3.50 am. 11/12/17 | |
| BEAULENCOURT | 11/12/17 | | Clean up and inspection by O.C. Coys during the afternoon. – | |
| | 12/12/17 | | Training 9–12 – Specialists and ordinary. – Battn bathed during the day. – | |
| | 13/12/17 | | " " " " – | |
| ROCQUIGNY | 14/12/17 | | Battn marched to ROCQUIGNY leaving at 2 pm arriving 3 p.m. – | |
| ETRICOURT | 15/12/17 | | " " " ETRICOURT 13 reinforcement officers joined the Battn | |
| | 16/12/17 | | Church parade. – | |

Army Form C. 2118.

Instructions regarding War Diaries and Intelligence Summaries are contained in F. S. Regs., Part II. and the Staff Manual respectively. Title pages will be prepared in manuscript.

# WAR DIARY
*or*
# ~~INTELLIGENCE SUMMARY.~~

*(Erase heading not required.)*

ANSON Battn

| Place | Date | Hour | Summary of Events and Information | Remarks and references to Appendices |
| --- | --- | --- | --- | --- |
| METZ | 17/10/17 | | Left ROCQUIGNY 12.30 pm arrived METZ 2.45 pm Battn in billets [illegible] | |
| | [illegible] | | Training 9 – 12.30 – Specialists under specialist officers – | |
| | [illegible] | | [illegible] Lieut Comr Buckle joined the Battn. | |
| | [illegible] | | Lieut-Comdr Buckle assumes command [illegible] | |
| | | | [illegible] temporary command [illegible] | |
| | [illegible] | | Training [illegible] – Specialists under their Specialist Officers. | |
| | [illegible] | | [illegible] taken over from 1 [illegible] | |
| | | | [illegible] Battn – | |
| | [illegible] | | [illegible] area [illegible] | |
| | | | Battn [illegible] the day in improving the occupied portion of the trenches [illegible] improving [illegible] and cleaning [illegible] – | |
| | [illegible] | | [illegible] by HOWE BATTN | |
| | | | [illegible] SUPPORT Battn were employed in digging new SUPPORT TRENCH [illegible] and generally improving and strengthening the area. – | |
| | | | Salvage [illegible] to Brigade Dump – | |
| | [illegible] | | [illegible] it was reported the Germans had attacked and [illegible] by HOWE Battn – At [illegible] the Support Coys moved up into [illegible] put down a "hurricane" on the [illegible] in the morning and at [illegible] pm A Coy supported by C Coy counter attacked [illegible]. The attack was successful and [illegible] | |

A5834 Wt. W4973/M687 750,000 8/16 D. D. & L. Ltd. Forms/C.2118/13.

Instructions regarding War Diaries and Intelligence Summaries are contained in F. S. Regs., Part II. and the Staff Manual respectively. Title pages will be prepared in manuscript.

# WAR DIARY
*or*
# INTELLIGENCE SUMMARY.
*(Erase heading not required.)*

Army Form C. 2118.

| Place | Date | Hour | Summary of Events and Information | Remarks and references to Appendices |
|---|---|---|---|---|
| In the line | 30/12/17 | | opposition was encountered 2 M.G. and 3 prisoners. — Casualties during the whole day amounted to 4 Killed 28 wounded 4 missing — after touch had been gained with the NELSON Battn on our left the situation quietened down — | |
| | 31/12/17 | | Battn relieved the HOWE Battn in the front line. — Except for artillery activity at times by the enemy the situation was normal — | |

A.W. Buckle
Lieut Comd
Comd ANSON Batt

31/12/17

A5834 Wt. W4973/M687 750,000 8/16 D. D. & L. Ltd. Forms/C.2118/13.

Army Form C. 2118.

Anson Bn

# WAR DIARY
*or*
# INTELLIGENCE SUMMARY.
*(Erase heading not required.)*

Instructions regarding War Diaries and Intelligence Summaries are contained in F. S. Regs., Part II. and the Staff Manual respectively. Title pages will be prepared in manuscript.

| Place | Date | Hour | Summary of Events and Information | Remarks and references to Appendices |
|---|---|---|---|---|
| [illegible] TRENCH | 1.1.18 | | Holding the line – Quiet day. Lt COOTE Rejoined from HOWE Bn | |
| | 2.1.18 | | Quiet day: work concentrated on improvement of wire. Inter-Coy relief. | |
| | 3.1.18 | | Quiet day – Sub Lt HUNTER killed. | |
| | 4.1.18 | | Quiet day. Relieved by RMLI. Occupied billets vacated by HOWE Bn in METZ. Bn in Brigade Reserve. | |
| METZ. | 5.1.18 | | Resting & cleaning up. Sub Lt MATCHAM left Bn. sick. | |
| | 6.1.18 | | Range, [illegible] and Co. inspections. Baths. Lt COOTE rejoined HOWE Bn as 2nd in Command. Lt COL. KIRKPATRICK WENT ON LEAVE FROM Brigade. | |
| | 7.1.18 | | Co. Commanders [illegible] front line. | |
| LINE. | 8.1.18 | | [illegible] HOWE Bn in Right Sub Sector of Brigade front. [illegible] commenced wiring HOLLY TR. between FIFTEEN [illegible] SAP and [illegible] SAP | |
| | 9.1.18 | | [illegible] quiet. Continued wiring as above. Active Patrolling commenced [illegible] Trenches [illegible] | |
| | 10.1.18 | | [illegible] patrol [illegible] in VILLAGE ROAD (in no man's land) west of LA VACQUERIE [illegible] | |

A5834 Wt. W4973/M687 750,000 8/16 D. D. & L. Ltd. Forms/C.2118/13.

Instructions regarding War Diaries and Intelligence Summaries are contained in F. S. Regs., Part II. and the Staff Manual respectively. Title pages will be prepared in manuscript.

# WAR DIARY
*or*
# INTELLIGENCE SUMMARY.
*(Erase heading not required.)*

Army Form C. 2118.

| Place | Date | Hour | Summary of Events and Information | Remarks and references to Appendices |
|---|---|---|---|---|
| | 10.1.18. | | all idea of salvage was therefore abandoned. | |
| | 11.1.18 | | Our Barrage on whole Corps front 5.17 – 5.32 am. Bn holding R. Sector HQ at FARM RAVINE. Unit on Right reports alteration of defence scheme; ie. outposts in front line and main line of defence in rear. (21st Brigade on right – 189th Brigade on left). Still thawing and showery – much mud. | |
| VILLERS-PLOUICH | 12.1.18 | | Relieved by 1 RMLI – took over billets in support from 1 RMLI. Sub Lt LLOYD left Bn sick. | |
| | 13.1.18 | | Whole Bn out from 6.0 pm for 4 hours wiring NEWPORT TR. Quiet day. Weather [illegible] – commenced freezing during evening and a little snow fell. | |
| [illegible] | 14.1.18 | | Relieved HOWE Bn in Left Sub Sector. [illegible] thawing hard. | |
| | [illegible] | | Position normal. [illegible] – trenches very muddy, up to waist in places. Sub Lts LANGDON, WHITTAKER and PATTERSON left Bn sick. Sub Lt McLAREN joins Bn | |
| | 16.1.18 | | Position unaltered – quiet. Lt COOKE left Bn sick. Sub Lt MALLETT returned from leave. Sub Lt OFIELD takes command of B Co vice Lt COOKE. Sub Lt RIDLER assumes command of A Co | |

A5834 Wt. W4973/M687 750,000 8/16 D. D. & L. Ltd. Forms/C.2118/13.

Army Form C. 2118.

Instructions regarding War Diaries and Intelligence Summaries are contained in F. S. Regs., Part II. and the Staff Manual respectively. Title pages will be prepared in manuscript.

# WAR DIARY
*or*
# INTELLIGENCE SUMMARY.

(*Erase heading not required.*)

| Place | Date | Hour | Summary of Events and Information | Remarks and references to Appendices |
|---|---|---|---|---|
| [illegible] | [illegible] | | Position normal. Night patrols and wiring continued. Trenches almost untenable and communication possible only by "overland" route. Scheme of holding the line by system of posts commenced - owing to existing conditions. | |
| | [illegible] | | Position and conditions unaltered. Bn relieved by [illegible] and occupied [illegible] in Support. Posts were completed and [illegible] | MAP attached. |
| [illegible] | [illegible] | | Bn [illegible] track across open from QUARRY (Support) to [illegible] TR. (Front Line). | |
| METZ | [illegible].1.18 | | Relieved by [illegible]. Bn occupied billets vacated by HOWE Bn in METZ. [illegible] returned from leave. | |
| | [illegible] | | Cleaning up and inspection by [illegible]. [illegible] returned from course. | |
| | [illegible] | | [illegible] and Baths. [illegible] inspection. Lt Col BUCKLE awarded D.S.O. | |
| [illegible] | [illegible] | | Relieved by [illegible]. Bn moved to [illegible] [illegible] NELSON Bn. | |
| | [illegible] | | Moved by train and march to [illegible]. Took over billets vacated by 17 [illegible]. | |
| | [illegible] | | [illegible] | |

A5834 Wt W4973/M687 750,000 8/16 D. D. & L. Ltd. Forms/C.2118/13.

Instructions regarding War Diaries and Intelligence Summaries are contained in F. S. Regs., Part II. and the Staff Manual respectively. Title pages will be prepared in manuscript.

# WAR DIARY
*or*
# INTELLIGENCE SUMMARY.
*(Erase heading not required.)*

Army Form C. 2118.

| Place | Date | Hour | Summary of Events and Information | Remarks and references to Appendices |
|---|---|---|---|---|
| [illegible] Camp | 26.1.18 | | Reorganisation – training in Saluting and Arm Drill. Bn visit Theatre at BAPAUME. ~~[illegible]~~ (22.1.18) | |
| | 27.1.18 | | Church Parade 10.0 am. Commenced building Range in afternoon. Lieut Capt GORDON USA, MORC, posted to this Bn for duty. | |
| | 28.1.18 | | Training, and Huts protected against hostile aircraft. | |
| | 29.1.18 | | Training 9 am to 1.0 pm. as per Programme | |
| | 30.1.18 | | Training 9 am to 1.0 pm. as per Programme. | |
| | 31.1.18 | | Training – as yesterday – Sub Lt INGLE left Bn for course of duty in England. Sub Lt BARKER assumes duties of Adjutant. | |
| | | | H F Kirkpatrick Lt Col<br>Commanding Anson Battn. | |

A5834 Wt. W4973/M687 750,000 8/16 D. D. & L. Ltd. Forms/C.2118/13.

Instructions regarding War Diaries and Intelligence Summaries are contained in F. S. Regs., Part II. and the Staff Manual respectively. Title pages will be prepared in manuscript.

# WAR DIARY
*or*
# ~~INTELLIGENCE SUMMARY.~~
*(Erase heading not required.)*

Army Form C. 2118.

Anson Bn

Vol 21

| Place | Date | Hour | Summary of Events and Information | Remarks and references to Appendices |
|---|---|---|---|---|
| BEAULEN COURT | 1.2.18. | | Training – 9.0am to 1.0pm Sub Lt MORTON rejoined from 188th Brigade. | |
| | 2.2.18. | | — ditto — | |
| | 3.2.18. | | Church Parade, 10am. | |
| | 4.2.18 | | Training – 9.0am to 1.0pm. | |
| | 5.2.18 | | — ditto — Sports in afternoon. Lecture by Divn Gas Offr 6.0pm. | |
| | 6.2.18. | | Working Parties on New Camp ROCQUIGNY – whole Bn less 3 Platoons C Co. – 9.30 – 2.0pm. | |
| | 7.2.18. | | Training 9.0am to 1.0pm. Voluntary Range Practice and games during afternoon. Lt Comr J. COOTE posted to Bn. Sub Lts GOWAN and HOBSON join Bn from HOWE Bn. | |
| | 8.2.18 | | Training – as above. Afternoon as above. C.P.O. A. STODDART awarded Croix de Guerre (Belgium) | |
| | 9.2.18 | | Training – as above. Lecture by Rev J.H. Roberts – noon. Afternoon Brigade Sports. | |
| | 10.2.18 | | Church Parade 10.30am. Lt Col. KIRKPATRICK to 189th Brigade. Hon Lt & QM. KANE sick. | |
| | 11.2.18 | | Training – 9.0am to 1.0pm – less A & B. Coys on Working Party at New Camp ROCQUIGNY. Lt Comr J. COOTE assumes Command of Bn vice Lt Col KIRKPATRICK to 188th Brigade. | |
| | 12.2.18. | | Training – as above – whole Bn. Sub Lt WHITTAKER to Course. | |
| | 13.2.18 | | Training – as above. Afternoon presentation of prizes for Div. Sports. Baths | |
| LECHELLE. | 14.2.18. | | Move to GRAZING CAMP. LECHELLE and occupy camp vacated by ARTISTS RIFLES. | |
| | 15.2.18. | | Preparation for Line. Sub Lt McLAREN to Hospital. | |
| | 16.2.18 | | Training – 9.30am to noon. Special feet & scabies inspection | |

A5834 Wt W4973/M687 750,000 8/16 D. D. & L. Ltd. Forms/C.2118/13.

Instructions regarding War Diaries and Intelligence Summaries are contained in F. S. Regs., Part II. and the Staff Manual respectively. Title pages will be prepared in manuscript.

# WAR DIARY
*or*
# INTELLIGENCE SUMMARY.
*(Erase heading not required.)*

Army Form C. 2118.

| Place | Date | Hour | Summary of Events and Information | Remarks and references to Appendices |
|---|---|---|---|---|
| LECHELLE | 17.2.18 | | Church service 11.45 am. WAR STORES issued. | |
| LINE. | 18.2.18 | | Relieved DRAKE Bn in ~~Support~~ LINE. COUILLET LEFT sub sector. 1/RMLI on our RIGHT. 4/BEDS on left. After relief – wiring and improving Posts carried on. 1 casualty during relief. | |
| | 19.2.18 | | Quiet day. Slight minenwerfer activity causing 4 casualties. Wiring continued. Lt Com. BUCKLE rejoined from leave. Sub Lt JENKINS rejoined from Course. Lt HENRY and Sub Lt PATERSON joined Bn. | |
| | 20.2.18 | | Quiet except for occasional salvos of Gas shells and more than usual M.G. fire. Improvement of Posts & trenches and wiring carried on. | |
| | 21.2.18 | | Position unchanged – slightly more E. artillery activity. Lt ROSS to England (duty). Relieved by 2/HLI and take over billets at LECHELLE (GRAZING CAMP) vacated by HAWKE Bn. | |
| LECHELLE | 22.2.18 | | Clean up and Baths. Lt Com BUCKLE resumes command of Bn vice Lt Com COOTE. Sub Lt NESBITT rejoined from course. | |
| LINE (SUPPORT) | 23.2.18 | | Relieve 19/Lond. Regt. in ~~Support~~ RIBECOURT LEFT sector. Sub Lt OGLE?? to Course. Sub Lt HOBSON to course. | |
| | 24.2.18. | | Quiet day – much work (wiring, improving etc.) done on defences & salvage. Sub Lt AULD to LEAVE. | |
| | 25.2.18 | | Situation unchanged – work as above continues. Sub Lt TREMHOLM joined Bn from leave. | |
| | 26.2.18 | | No change – work as above. Lt ODELL to D.F.S. Coy. RE DHQ. Sub Lt LANGDON to course. | |
| FRONT LINE | 27.2.18 | | Relieved by 10th RMLI and relieve 2/RMLI in Line. 4/E YORKS on left. HOOD on right. Lt Col KIRKPATRICK rejoined from Brigade (188) assumes command. 2 casualties (OR) | |
| | 28.2.18 | | Position unchanged except for slightly increased E. arty activity. 1 Casualty (O.R.) T/Surgeon ~~E~~ SHAW RN. joins as M.O. vice Lt GORDON MORC USA. | |

O. W. L. Beak
~~Commander~~ RNVR.
Commanding ANSON Bn.

A5834 Wt. W4973/M687 750,000 8/16. D. D. & L. Ltd. Forms/C.2118/13.

188th Brigade.

63rd Division

------

"A N S O N" BATTALION

M A R C H 1 9 1 8

Army Form C. 2118.

# WAR DIARY
*or*
# INTELLIGENCE ~~SUMMARY~~.
*(Erase heading not required.)*

ANSON Bn 63rd (RN) Divn

10/63

Vol 22

* Instructions regarding War Diaries and Intelligence Summaries are contained in F. S. Regs., Part II. and the Staff Manual respectively. Title pages will be prepared in manuscript.

| Place | Date March | Hour | Summary of Events and Information | Remarks and references to Appendices |
|---|---|---|---|---|
| Front Line | 1st | | Bn in Front Line - FLESQUIERES. Situation quiet. | |
| | 2nd | | Situation unchanged | |
| HAVRINCOURT WOOD. | 3rd | | Bn relieved by 1 RMLI and proceeded to take over billets in EASTWOOD CAMP. | |
| | 4th | | Clean up - Coy inspection. | |
| | 5th | | Work in camp and Specialist training. | |
| | 6th | | Working parties and Specialist training | |
| Support Line | 7th | | Bn relieved 1/RMLI in Support Line. | |
| | 8th | | Working parties for BROWN LINE and MTM positions and carrying parties | |
| | 9th | | — ditto — | |
| | 10th | | — ditto — | |
| Front Line | 11th | | Bn relieved by 1 RMLI and proceeded to relieve 1/RMLI in Front Line. | |
| | 12th | | Quiet day | |
| | 13th | | Slight enemy artillery activity and gas shelling of rear lines. | |

A7092 Wt W123 o/M1293 750,000 1/17 D. D. & L. Ltd. Forms/C2118/14.

Instructions regarding War Diaries and Intelligence Summaries are contained in F. S. Regs., Part II. and the Staff Manual respectively. Title pages will be prepared in manuscript.

# WAR DIARY
*or*
# ~~INTELLIGENCE SUMMARY.~~
*(Erase heading not required.)*

Army Form C. 2118.

| Place | Date MARCH | Hour | Summary of Events and Information | Remarks and references to Appendices |
|---|---|---|---|---|
| Front line | 14th | | Heavy gas shelling in TRESCAULT area. Front line quiet. | |
| EASTWOOD CAMP | 15th | | Relieved by [illegible] and proceeded to EASTWOOD CAMP taking over billets vacated by [illegible]. | |
| | 16th | | Clean up – Baths – Coy inspections. | |
| | 17th | | Working Parties – Specialist instruction. | |
| | 18th | | – ditto – | |
| | 19th | | – ditto – | |
| | 20th | | – ditto – | |
| | 21st | 5 am | Stand to. Heavy bombardment. At 10.30am Bn proceeded to new support line S. of HAVRINCOURT VILLAGE. | |
| | 22nd | | Bombardment continues. At dusk R.M. Battalions withdrew through us. Lt Comdr [illegible] posted to command 1 R.M.L.I. | |
| | 23rd | 1.0 am | Bn [illegible] to positions immediately N. of HAVRINCOURT WOOD – [illegible] 33 b and K 34 a (Sheet 57c) | During the withdrawal all operation orders [illegible] etc. were destroyed. |
| | | 12 noon | Withdrew to positions behind HAVRINCOURT VILLAGE; in support of 1 and 2 RMLI. [illegible] (Sheet 57c) | |
| | 24th | 9 am | Withdrew through BARASTRE and VILLERS AU FLOS to MARTINPUICH, occupying positions in M.27d and M.33 b (Sheet 57c). Sub Lt KETTENHOLM missing. Lt Cdr KIRKPATRICK rejoined from 63rd Div HQrs & assumed command. | |

A7092 Wt. W12839/M1293 750,000 1/17 D. D. & L. Ltd. Forms/C.2118/14

Army Form C. 2118.

Instructions regarding War Diaries and Intelligence Summaries are contained in F. S. Regs., Part II. and the Staff Manual respectively. Title pages will be prepared in manuscript.

# WAR DIARY
*or*
~~INTELLIGENCE SUMMARY.~~

*(Erase heading not required.)*

| Place | Date | Hour | Summary of Events and Information | Remarks and references to Appendices |
|---|---|---|---|---|
| | MARCH | | | |
| MARTINSART | 25th | | Rear Guard actions to THIEPVAL – Outpost positions taken up at back in R 20 and R 26 (Sheet 57D). Lt Col H KIRKPATRICK wounded. Lt G S RIDLER and | |
| THIEPVAL | 26th | 3.30am | Withdrew across R. ANCRE, and held RAILWAY Line in Q 29 + 35 (Sheet 57D). Sub Lt H. KENNY killed, Sub Lt J WHITLEY wounded. Sub Lts SARLOTTE, H.A. CASSIDY, and E.A. FENNER wounded. Sub Lt W JOHNSTONE missing. | |
| MARTINSART | | 8.30pm | Relieved by 6/R.W.K. Regt at about 8.30pm and proceed to Billets in MARTINSART. Lt Comdr A.W. BUCKLE assumes command. | |
| | 27th | | Enemy broke through on left flank and Bn counter attacked and restored line; afterwards returning to MARTINSART. Lt E G WALKER and Sub Lt J. CATON killed. | |
| FORCEVILLE | 28th | | Bn relieved by 2/HLI and proceeded to MAILLY-MAILLET about 2.30am marching thence at 1.0pm to FORCEVILLE. Sub Lt H.F. LANGDON to Hospital. | |
| | 29th | | Clean up and re-organise. | |
| | 30th | | Clean up and inspections by Brigadier and C.O. | |
| | 31st | | Church Services. | |

A. W. Buckle
Comd. RNVR
Comd ANSON Batt

A7092 Wt. W128 9/M1293 750,000 1/17 D. D. & L. Ltd. Forms/C2118/14

188th Inf.Bde.
63rd Div.

# A N S O N   B A T T A L I O N .

## A P R I L

## 1 9 1 8

Instructions regarding War Diaries and Intelligence Summaries are contained in F. S. Regs., Part II. and the Staff Manual respectively. Title pages will be prepared in manuscript.

Army Form C. 2118.

# WAR DIARY
*or*
# ~~INTELLIGENCE SUMMARY.~~
*(Erase heading not required.)*

ANSON Bn 63rd (RN) Divn. WM 23

| Place | Date 1917 | Hour | Summary of Events and Information | Remarks and references to Appendices |
|---|---|---|---|---|
| FORCEVILLE | 1/4 | | Bn in billets at FORCEVILLE – Training for 2 hours in morning: Digging at night | |
| TOUTENCOURT | 2/4 | | Route march to TOUTENCOURT – via LEALVILLERS. | |
| ENGLEBELMER | 3/4 | | Route march to ENGLEBELMER – via VARENNES. Sub Lt PATERSON rejoined from Course. | |
| | 4/4 | | Artillery active in village. [illegible] Lt J.S. FLEMING/RWK Regt and 2/Lt C.K. MARTIN/5S Staffs Regt joined Bn for duty | |
| | 5/4 | | Bn moved forward to banks EAST of Village (about 3 pm). E Artillery still active; mixture of yellow & gas shells & H.E. Sub Lt GOWAN to Hosp. (gas) | |
| AVELUY WOOD | 6/4 | | Bn moved to close support in Railway embankment W. of AVELUY WOOD. B Company took over part of front line held by 1/4th BEDFORDS. Following officers joined Bn for duty Lt C.E. MALPASS RWK Regt; 2/Lt HOME GALL RF; 2/Lts A.C. GOODSON, L. PHILLIPS, S. GRAHAM, A.V. HURDIDGE, D.J. EDWARDS, L.A. TUGBY – all Welsh Rgt, and Lt C.A. SCOTT Staffs Regt – also following ORs 66 RWK Regt, 46 RF, 35 Staff. Rgt + 31 3rd RWK Regt. 2/Lt SOUTHGATE joined Bn for duty; also Sub Lts DUNNING and COOKE. | |
| | 7/4 | | Bn relieved 1/RMLI in [illegible] in AVELUY WOOD. D Coy HOOD Bn attached to Bn [illegible] S[illegible]. Following officers wounded: Lt SHEPHERD and Sub Lts NESBIT and COOKE. | |
| | 8/4 | | Enemy MGs and snipers [illegible] active. 2/Lt SOUTHGATE killed in action. Sub Lts STACEY and MALLETT wounded. | |
| ENGLEBELMER | 9/4 | | Bn relieved by 1/RMLI and proceeded to billets in ENGLEBELMER. Sub Lt DUNNING missing – Sub Lt HAWORTH wounded. | |
| | 10/4 | | Reinforcements finding Outposts [illegible] [illegible] of Village. Bn [illegible] [illegible] | |
| | 11/4 | | Bn relieved by 7/R[illegible] and proceeded to billets at FORCEVILLE. | |

A7092 Wt. W128,9/M1293. 750,000. 1/17. D. D & L., Ltd. Forms/C2118/14.

Instructions regarding War Diaries and Intelligence Summaries are contained in F. S. Regs., Part II. and the Staff Manual respectively. Title pages will be prepared in manuscript.

# WAR DIARY
*or*
# INTELLIGENCE SUMMARY.
(*Erase heading not required.*)

Army Form C. 2118.

| Place | Date | Hour | Summary of Events and Information | Remarks and references to Appendices |
|---|---|---|---|---|
| [illegible] | 11/11 | | Cleaning up and kit inspections. Lt BLACKHALL, MC and 2nd Lt WILLIAMS joined Bn. | BH. |
| | 12/11 | | Training – winter [illegible] arrangements – kit inspections etc. | |
| ARGUEVES | 14/11 | | [illegible] to ARGUEVES. | |
| | 15/11 | | Working parties – Specialists training. Lt PARKES joined Bn | |
| | 16/11 | | Working parties – Specialists training. | |
| | 17/11 | | Training – 9.30 to 12 pm – General & Specialists. | |
| | 18/11 | | Training as above. | |
| | 19/11 | | Working parties. Specialists training. | |
| | 20/11 | | Training – as above. 2/Lt L TUBBY, Welsh Regt joined LTM Battery. | |
| | 21/11 | | Church Services – [illegible] Staffs Regt joined Bn from leave. | |
| | 22/11 | | Training – as above. | |
| | 23/11 | | Working parties – Specialists training. Following officers joined Bn for duty. 2nd Lts H RADNEY, J E LLOYD, C KEMBLE, J MATTHEW, E J EVANS. | BH. |
| | 24/11 | | Training as above. Capt J. FLEMING left Bn for [illegible]. | |

A7092 Wt W128,9/M1293 750,000. 1/17. D. D & L., Ltd. Forms/C2118/14.

Instructions regarding War Diaries and Intelligence Summaries are contained in F. S. Regs., Part II. and the Staff Manual respectively. Title pages will be prepared in manuscript.

# WAR DIARY

~~or~~

~~INTELLIGENCE SUMMARY.~~

*(Erase heading not required.)*

Army Form C. 2118.

| Place | Date | Hour | Summary of Events and Information | Remarks and references to Appendices |
| --- | --- | --- | --- | --- |
| APROVES | 25/4 | | Working Parties – Specialists training. | |
| | 26/4 | | Training – as before. | |
| | 27/4 | | Training – ditto – and Special tactical scheme. | |
| | 28/4 | | Church Services. Sub Lt J. BEDFORD posted to LTM Battery. | |
| | 29/4 | | Working Parties – Specialists training. Sub Lts J NEIL and E OSBURN joined Bn from 1/RMLI. | |
| | 30/4 | | Special Tactical Scheme – ie Practice occupation of RED and BROWN Line. Following officers left Bn for 190th Inf Bde:- Lt C.E. MALPASS, 2/Lts HOMEGALL, J GRAHAM, L. PHILLIPS, L.A. TUGBY, R.W. HURDIDGE, D.J. EDWARDS & A.C. GOODSON. | |

A.W. Buckle
Lt Comdr RNVR, DSO,
Commanding
ANSON

A5092 Wt W128,9/M1293 750,000. 1/17. D. D & L., Ltd. Forms/C2118/14.

Instructions regarding War Diaries and Intelligence Summaries are contained in F. S. Regs., Part II. and the Staff Manual respectively. Title pages will be prepared in manuscript.

# WAR DIARY
*or*
~~INTELLIGENCE SUMMARY.~~
*(Erase heading not required.)*

Army Form C. 2118.

Vol 24

ANSON Bn 63rd (RN) Divn

| Place | Date May 1918 | Hour | Summary of Events and Information | Remarks and references to Appendices |
|---|---|---|---|---|
| ARQUÉYES | 1st | | Bn in Rest at ARQUÉYES. Working parties for digging at FORCEVILLE. D Coy carry out attack Practice before Divisional Commander. | |
| | 2nd | | Training 9.0am to 1.0pm. SBRs tested at Gas Chamber. | |
| | 3rd | | Working parties - Specialist training. | |
| | 4th | | Training - 9.0am to 1.0pm. | |
| | 5th | | Working parties, - Church Services. Sub Lts R. WHITTAKER and J. BEETHAM rejoined Bn from Signal Course. | |
| | 6th | | Training 9.0am to 1.0pm. Preparation for move into Line. | |
| Line | 7th | | Route march starting 9.0am to ACHEUX WOOD - remain there until dusk when Bn proceeds to relieve 12th MANCHESTER REGT. in Front Line HAMEL LEFT sector. Trench Strength of Bn 21 Officers and 654 ORs. - Surplus Battle Personnel of 40 ORs sent to Divl wing. | |
| | 8th | | Quiet day - Weather fine and sunny. A/WO1 A.I. BANKS promoted Hon Lt & QM. to date 4.5.18. | |
| | 9th | | Quiet day. Short bursts of hostile artillery fire. E. snipers active. Sub Lt W.F. LANGDON rejoined Bn from Divl wing. | |
| | 10th | | Situation unchanged. " - " J. MATTHEW D.C.M. wounded. | |
| | 11th | | — ditto — | |

A7092 Wt W128.9/M1293 750,000 1/17. D. D. & L., Ltd. Forms/C2118/14.

Instructions regarding War Diaries and Intelligence Summaries are contained in F. S. Regs., Part II. and the Staff Manual respectively. Title pages will be prepared in manuscript.

# WAR DIARY

*or*

~~INTELLIGENCE SUMMARY.~~

*(Erase heading not required.)*

Army Form C. 2118.

| Place | Date | Hour | Summary of Events and Information | Remarks and references to Appendices |
|---|---|---|---|---|
| FRONT LINE "HAMEL LEFT" Sector | MAY 1918 12th | | Situation quiet. Slight hostile shelling and sniping. Weather fine - changing to rain. Sub/Lt S. ROSSITER proceeded to Army Rest Camp | |
| Reserve Line | 13th | | Situation unchanged. Bn relieved by R.M. Bn and proceeded to take over Billets in Reserve Line vacated by 2/R. IRISH. 'B' Coy in intermediate (PURPLE) Line. | |
| | 14th | | Cleaning up - company and Kit Inspections. Sub/Lt J CROWTHER joined Bn | |
| | 15th | | Working Parties on cableburying. | |
| | 16th | | Cleaning up - Baths and medical inspection. Training - 2 hours. 'A' Coy relieve 'B' in PURPLE LINE. | |
| | 17th | | Training - 2½ hours. 'B' Coy cleaning up. Baths and medical inspection. Specialist instruction. | |
| | 18th | | Training and Specialist instruction. Sub/Lts T. YOUNGER and L FARMBOROUGH proceed on Courses. Rev. B.M. KENNETT to Hospital | |
| Support Line. | 19th | | Church Services. Bn relieve 2/R. IRISH in Support line. | |
| | 20th | | Hostile artillery and aircraft active. | |
| | 21st | | Increased enemy artillery and aircraft activity. Sub/Lt W. BARNETT joined Bn from Divl Wing. | |
| | 22nd | | Situation unchanged. | |
| Front Line. | 23rd | | Bn relieved 2/R. IRISH in Front Line. Revd J. McCARDEL left Bn to report ABANCOURT for duty. | |

A5092 Wt. W1283/M1293 750,000. 1/17. D. D & L., Ltd. Forms/C2118/14.

Instructions regarding War Diaries and Intelligence Summaries are contained in F. S. Regs., Part II. and the Staff Manual respectively. Title pages will be prepared in manuscript.

# WAR DIARY

*or*

# ~~INTELLIGENCE~~ SUMMARY.

*(Erase heading not required.)*

Army Form C. 2118.

| Place | Date MAY 1918 | Hour | Summary of Events and Information | Remarks and references to Appendices |
|---|---|---|---|---|
| Front Line | 24th | | Quiet day. Bn carried out a Raid on enemy positions – copy of Operation Order No 81 attached. Number taking part – 15 Officers, 500 ORs. Captures: 1 Officer 22 ORs Prisoners and 6 machine guns. Lt KE PARKES, Lt AG HENRY and Lt GL HAWKINS wounded. Sub Lt J. CROWTHER killed. ORs 9 K. 42 W. 8 M. | |
| Reserve | 25th | | Enemy artillery very active. Bn relieved by RM Bn and proceeded to take over billets in Reserve vacated by RM Bn. – D Coy in 'PURPLE LINE.' Sub Lt H.C. INGLE and Lt C.E. MALPASS (RWK) rejoined Bn. Sub Lt S ROSSITER rejoined Bn | |
| | 26th | | Cleaning up + Baths. Sub Lt DEWDNEY left Bn for course. | |
| | 27th | | Inspection by Corps Comdr. Lecture by Divl Gas Officer. 2/Lts D.J. EDWARDS and S. GRAHAM rejoined Bn | |
| | 28th | | Coy inspections and Anti-Gas Training. C Coy relieve 'D' Coy in PURPLE LINE. Sub Lt H C GOWAN rejoined Bn from Divl Wing. | |
| | 29th | | Working parties on Cable Bury. 'D' Coy cleaning up + Baths. | |
| | 30th | | Bn relieve RM Bn in Front Line. | |
| | 31st | | [illegible] | |

A W Buckle

Instructions regarding War Diaries and Intelligence Summaries are contained in F. S. Regs., Part II. and the Staff Manual respectively. Title pages will be prepared in manuscript.

# WAR DIARY
~~or~~
~~INTELLIGENCE SUMMARY.~~
(Erase heading not required.)

Army Form C. 2118.

ANSON BATTN. 63rd (RN) DIV

Vol 23

| Place | Date JUNE 1918 | Hour | Summary of Events and Information | Remarks and references to Appendices |
|---|---|---|---|---|
| LINE. | 1st. | | Battalion in the line - MESNIL - LEFT - SECTOR. On the right - HAWKE BATTN. On the left - 10th LANCS. FUS. In support - R.Ms. In reserve 2nd R.I.R. Operations on the right commence at 3.25 AM. slight enemy barrage on our front line - one man wounded. Capt. Scott proceeds to England on leave. Lieuts Edwards & Graham leave Battalion to join 4th K.S.L.I. Battalion strength in the line. 20 Officers & 585 ORs. | |
| | 2nd. | | Situation unchanged. | |
| | 3rd. | | Situation unchanged. | |
| | 4th. | | Enemy raid Battn on left - 10th LANCS. FUS (17th Div) barrage from 2/30 AM. slight bombardment on our left front. two casualties (one killed, one wounded). HAWKE Battn on right relieved by 10TH WELCH REGT. | |
| | 5th. | | Battalion relieved in the line by 13th. R.W.F. 11/30 pm. then proceeded to ACHIEUX WOOD | |
| | 6th. | | Battalion leave Achieux Wood 10.30 AM and arrive at Hervissart 2/15 pm. under canvas. New Pres. Padre joins Battalion. - Rev. J. Gowdie. | |
| HERISSART | 7th. | | Re-organization by Companies - checking of War stores &c. Lt. K. E. Parkes transferred to England & struck off strength of Battalion as from 24/5/18. T. Sub-Lt. (A. Lt.) R. Donaldson M.C. promoted to Temp rank of Lt. as from 24/1/18. Battn. bathing. | |
| | 8th. | | Training 8/30 AM to 12/30 pm. T. Sub Lt G. Paterson promoted to A Lt (additional) 26/5/18. T. Lt. J. F. Odell - struck off the establishment 26/2/18. Following awards for services in the field. T. Sub Lt (A.Lt.) C. G. Walker RNVR (since killed) M.C. C.Z. 4894 P.O. Gallagher J. M.M. KX 206 A.B. Charlton R. M.M. 20596 L/Cpl Edwards G. W. (S. Staffs) M.M. Special order of the day issued No 1000. copy of which is attached. | |

A7092 Wt W12839/M1293 750,000 1/17 D. D & L. Ltd. Forms/C2118/14.

Army Form C. 2118.

# WAR DIARY
~~or~~
~~INTELLIGENCE SUMMARY.~~ ANSON BATTN. 63rd (R.N.) DIV.

(Erase heading not required.)

Instructions regarding War Diaries and Intelligence Summaries are contained in F. S. Regs., Part II. and the Staff Manual respectively. Title pages will be prepared in manuscript.

| Place | Date JUNE 1918 | Hour | Summary of Events and Information | Remarks and references to Appendices |
|---|---|---|---|---|
| HERRISSART | 9th | | Church services. Commanding Officer's inspection of Companies. | |
| | 10th | | Training 8/30 to 12/30 pm. Specialist training in afternoon. Sub Lt Farnborough rejoins Battn from Course. | |
| | 11th | | Training 8/30 to 12/30 pm. do do {T Sub Lts H C Ingle & C H Barker to wear rank of [illegible] H C Ingle 25/5/18 C H Barker 1/2/18 to 24/5/18. | |
| | 12th | | Training 8/30 to 12/30 pm. do do Sub Lt Farnborough to Hospital | |
| | 13th | | Training 8/30 to 12/30 pm. Officers on L. G range in afternoon. Letter of congratulation received from G.O.C on the salvage work of the Battalion for week ending 8/6/18. Following Officers to wear badges of rank pending approval T Lt. J A Green (S. Staffs) to be A/Capt 9/6/18. T Sub Lt T V Williams to be A/Lt (Addl) 10/6/18. | |
| | 14th | | Training 8/30 to 12/30 pm. Specialist training in afternoon. | |
| | 15th | | Training 8/30 to 12/30 pm. | |
| | 16th | | Church Services. Commanding Officer's inspection by Companies. T Sub Lt (A/Lt) [illegible] Hawkins RNVR awarded M.C. | |
| | 17th | | Battalion Sports. | |
| | 18th | | Training 8/30 to 12/30. Special party on wiring. | |
| | 19th | | Training 8/30 to 12/30. Battn bathing by companies. T Sub Lt D B Harrower RNVR to be Temp Lt. 26/2/18. A/Capt T A Green and T Sub Lt Rossiter and 2nd Lt Martin (S. Staffs) proceeded to Rest Camp. | |
| | 20th | | Training 9/30 to 12/30 pm. Reorganization of Companies 8/30 to 9/30 AM. Sub Lt K M Evans M.C. transferred to England & struck off strength of Unit 12/6/18. | |
| | 21st | | Training 8 AM to 11/30 AM. Brigade Sports in afternoon. | |

D. D. & L., London, E.C.
(A10260) Wt W5300/P713 750,000 2/18 Sch. 52 Forms/C2118/16

Instructions regarding War Diaries and Intelligence Summaries are contained in F. S. Regs., Part II. and the Staff Manual respectively. Title pages will be prepared in manuscript.

# WAR DIARY

~~or~~

~~INTELLIGENCE SUMMARY.~~ ANSON BATTN. 63rd (R.N.) DIV.

(*Erase heading not required.*)

Army Form C. 2118.

| Place | Date JUNE 1918 | Hour | Summary of Events and Information | Remarks and references to Appendices |
|---|---|---|---|---|
| HERRISSART | 22nd | | Training 8/30 AM. to 12/30 pm. Preparation for move into the line. Lt H.C. Dyke to Hospital | |
| ACHIEUX WOOD | 23rd. | | Battalion leave at 11/30 AM. to relieve of the Border Regt. in Acheux Wood arriving 3 pm. (Bgde in reserve). American M.O joins Batt in place of Surgeon Shaw (to Hospital) 22/6/18. | |
| | 24th. | | Improving bivouacs & cleaning up generally. | |
| | 25th. | | Two Companies supply working party for C.R.E. - remainder of Batt. bathing | |
| | 26th. | | Batt. supply working party for 247 Field Co. R.E. | |
| | 27th. | | N.C.O.s & Officers (Platoon Commanders) Map reading. - L.G. instruction for Lewis Gunners. T/Sub Lt G. Maycock RNVR struck off strength of Establishment 12/5/18. Meritorious Service Medal awarded to following for valuable services during present War CZ. 1544 AB L/S McKinlay J. Attd M.G.C.C. T.Z. 2326 P.O. Meyers H.T. (now C.P.O.) {Lt H. C. Dyke rejoins Battalion. | |
| | 28th. | | Two Companies supply working parties for C.R.E. remainder bathing. Surg. Shaw M.O. rejoins Batt. American M.O. leaves to join 1487 Ambce. | |
| | 29th. | | Sub Lt Langdon leaves for course. Batt. on Working parties | |
| | 30th. | | Church Services. S.B.R's tested in Gas chamber under Gas Officer | |

A. W. Buckle
Commander RNVR
Commanding. ANSON Battn.

A7092 Wt. W128.9/M1293. 750,000. 1/17. D. D & L., Ltd. Forms/C2118/14.

ANZAC BATTALION. [illegible]

[illegible]

[illegible] of the ANZAC Battalion, the following notes on the history of the Battalion are published for the information of all ranks. The Commanding Officer desires to thank all those who [illegible] to this record, and to express his confidence that those now serving with the Battalion will at least maintain the [illegible] of the unit.

---

21st August [illegible] Battalion formed [illegible]

October, [illegible] Battalion [illegible] in defence of [illegible], this being the first [illegible] active service in the [illegible] War.

[illegible] February [illegible]

[illegible]

25th April [illegible]

[illegible] April [illegible]

[illegible] May [illegible]

[illegible] May [illegible] Attack on Turkish [illegible]

[illegible] June [illegible] [illegible] Objectives [illegible]

[illegible] August [illegible]

[illegible] August [illegible]

October, [illegible]

[illegible]

[illegible] February [illegible]

3rd April [illegible]

[illegible]

July, [illegible]

[illegible] Sept. [illegible]

[illegible] Sept. [illegible]

[illegible] November [illegible]

February [illegible]

[illegible] April [illegible] in front of [illegible]

[illegible]

December [illegible]

[illegible]

Special Order of the Day (Continued)

| | |
|---|---|
| Feb.- March,1918. | In line at FLESQUIERES. |
| 21st March to 25th March,1918. | Took part in withdrawal to RIVER ANCRE. Rearguard actions fought at [illegible], [illegible], COURCELETTE and THIEPVAL. |
| 26th March, 1918 | Counter-attack in AVELUY WOOD. Enemy ~~positions~~ driven back through [illegible] to the River. [illegible] M.G's and [illegible] prisoners captured. |
| May, 1918. | In line at HAMEL. |
| 24th May, 1918. | Successful raid on enemy positions in HAMEL by whole Battalion. [illegible] M.G's, with one officer and [illegible] other ranks, captured. |

NAMES OF COMMANDING OFFICERS.

| | |
|---|---|
| August, 1914. | Commander Strickland, R.N. |
| September, 1914. | Lt-Col. G.Cornwallis West. |
| November, 1914. | Lt-Commdr. [illegible], R.N.V.R. |
| February, 1915. | Col. Moorhouse, C.M.G., D.S.O. |
| May, 1915. | Major Roberts, R.[illegible] |
| June, 1915. | Major Bridges, R.M.L.I. |
| October, 1915. | Lt-Commdr. G.G.Jones, R.N.V.R. |
| February, 1916. | Lt-Commdr. B.H.Ellis, R.N.V.R. |
| June, 1916. | Lt-Col. Saunders, D.S.O. |
| November, 1916. | Lt-Commdr. B.H.Ellis, R.N.V.R. |
| December, 1917. | Lt-Col. H.F.[illegible] |
| March, 1918. | Commander A.S.Buckle, D.S.O., R.N.V.R. |

HONOURS AND AWARDS.

The following Honours have been gained by Officers and Men whilst serving with the Battalion.

Officers.

| | |
|---|---|
| V.C. | 1 (Sub-Lt. Tisdall RNVR) |
| D.S.O. | [illegible] |
| Bars to D.S.O. | [illegible] |
| D.S.C. | 1 |
| M.C. | [illegible] |
| Mentioned | [illegible] |

Other Ranks.

| | |
|---|---|
| C.G.M. | [illegible] |
| D.C.M. | [illegible] |
| D.S.M. | [illegible] |
| M.M. | [illegible] |
| Bars to M.M. | [illegible] |
| Croix de Guerre (Belgian) | 1 |

Signed/

[illegible]

Sub-Lieut. & Adjutant.

Army Form C. 2118.

Instructions regarding War Diaries and Intelligence Summaries are contained in F. S. Regs., Part II. and the Staff Manual respectively. Title pages will be prepared in manuscript.

# WAR DIARY
or
~~INTELLIGENCE SUMMARY.~~

(Erase heading not required.)

ANSON Bn July 1918.

| Place | Date | Hour | Summary of Events and Information | Remarks and references to Appendices |
|---|---|---|---|---|
| ACHEUX | July 1st | | Bn in Reserve at ACHEUX WOOD - supplying working parties for R.E. Cmdr. A.W. BUCKLE leaves for C.O.s conference at PORT MAHON. Lt Cmdr. J. CHOTE assumes command. | |
| | 2nd | | Working parties. 2nd Lt. H. KENNY joins Bn after recovering by sea. | |
| | 3rd | | Working parties - L.G. specialist training. 2nd Lt. J. McKie joins Bn | |
| | 4th | | Working parties. L.G. and [illegible] specialist training. C Coy proceed to [illegible] area. 2nd Lt. L. NESBITT and 1 OR proceed to UK on leave. | |
| | 5th | | Working parties. Observing specialist instruction. 2nd Lt. T. JENKINS and 10 ORs to UK on leave. | |
| MAILLY-MAILLET | 6th | | [illegible] [illegible] move to [illegible]: relieve 4/Bedfordshire Regt in Reserve. 29 Reinforcements arrive. Trench strength Offrs 14, ORs 491. } First party leave ACHEUX WOOD at 10.30 pm. Relief completed 12.45 am. 5th MANCHESTERS (42nd Div) on left; DRAKE Bn on right. 2nd RF in support, HAWKE in front line. 2nd Lt. H. HAMMAKER joins Bn. HQ as Signal officer. | |
| | 7th | | Working parties - Lt. PATERSON proceeds on French leave; 2nd Lt. BARNET takes command of C Coy. Hostile shelling of HQ every 2 hours from 9 am to 10 pm. | |

D. D. & L., London, E.C.
(A10266) Wt W5300/P713 750,000 2/16 Sch. 52 Forms/C2118/16

Instructions regarding War Diaries and Intelligence Summaries are contained in F. S. Regs., Part II. and the Staff Manual respectively. Title pages will be prepared in manuscript.

# WAR DIARY
or
INTELLIGENCE SUMMARY.
(Erase heading not required.)

ANSON Bn — July 1918 — (contd) — Army Form C. 2118.

VR 26

| Place | Date | Hour | Summary of Events and Information | Remarks and references to Appendices |
|---|---|---|---|---|
| MAILLY-MAILLET | July 8th | | Working parties – Situation quiet. | |
| | 9th | | – ditto – & Bathing. Situation quiet. 47 Reinforcements join Bn | |
| | 10th | | – ditto – " " " 29 Casuals etc. join Bn (including Archd Guard) | |
| | 11th | | – ditto – 5th MANCHESTERS in left relieved by 7th Lanc. Fusiliers, early morning. HAWKE Bn in Front Line relieve DRAKE Bn in Reserve. Sub Lt E ROSSITER Lt HENRY and Capt. J. GREEN join Bn. | |
| | 12th | | Working Parties. Casualties 2 ORs (slight) | |
| | 13th | | " " 1st R.I. from Support relieve R.M.L.I. Bn in Front Line. Sub Lt H. Gowan rejoins Bn from Course | |
| | 14th | | Working Parties. Lt. J FLEMING rejoined Bn | |
| | 15th | | " " Major F SANDILANDS RM rejoins Bn. Casualties – Killed 2, Wounded 19 (Gas), " 2 (Shell) | |
| | 16th | | " " Lt Comdr J. COOTE proceeds to U.K. for 6 months tour of duty. MAJOR F. SANDILANDS assumes command. Sub Lt Barnett proceeds to Course. "A" Coy relieve C & D Coys. R.Irish in Front Line. Casualties Killed 1, Missing 1, Wounded 2, Wounded (accidentally) 1 | |
| | 17th | | Working Parties. • Sub Lt R. YOUNGER and 1 O.R. wounded. HAWKE Bn relieve DRAKE Bn in Support. Died of Wounds (Gas) 1 | |

D. D. & L., London, E.C.
(A10260) Wt W5300/P713 750,000 2/18 Sch. 52 Forms/C2118/16

Instructions regarding War Diaries and Intelligence Summaries are contained in F. S. Regs., Part II. and the Staff Manual respectively. Title pages will be prepared in manuscript.

# WAR DIARY
or
~~INTELLIGENCE~~ SUMMARY.

(Erase heading not required.)

Army Form C. 2118.

ANSON Bn July 1918.

| Place | Date | Hour | Summary of Events and Information | Remarks and references to Appendices |
|---|---|---|---|---|
| MAILLY-MAILLET | July 18th | | Working parties. "A" Coy rejoin Bn and relieve C & D Coys R Irish | |
| | 19th | | " " "A" Coy baths. Sub Lt J NEIL transferred to R.M. Bn. Sub Lt McKee to F.A. sick | |
| | 20th | | Relieved 2/R Irish in Front Line. MAILLET-Left sector: 1st party leave Reserve at 10.30pm; relief completed by 12.30pm. Casualties – wounded 1. Trench Strength Offrs 14, ORs 530. Lt J. FLEMING to UK on leave | |
| Front Line | 21st | | Bn in Front Line. Lt PATERSON rejoins Bn. Sub Lt E KENNY to [illegible] for [illegible] | |
| | 22nd | | " " " working parties. Casualties – wounded 3 (2 [illegible]) Sub Lt N NESBITT rejoins Bn. Operation on our left by 42nd Divn (7th L.F.); slight retaliation on our left Coy front. | |
| | 23rd | | Sub Lt E OSBORN and 2/Lt C MARTIN rejoin Bn. 1 OR to Paris on leave. 25 reinforcements arrive from Base Wing. – Casualties – wounded 3. Advance party of relief arrive. Sub Lt E KENNY to HOOD Bn | |
| [illegible] | 24th | | Relieved by 12/13 N.F. and proceed to LEALVILLERS; arrive 3.30am. Casualties – wounded [illegible] | |
| ARQUEVES | 25th | | March to ARQUEVES and occupy billets vacated by 12/13 N.F. | |
| | 26th | | Cleaning up – bathing and kit inspections; [illegible] U.K. | |
| | 27th | | Training as per programme – and Bathing. | |
| | 28th | | Church Service – Coys inspected by C.O. Sub Lt H WHITAKER proceeds on Course of Signalling at Corps S.C. | |

D. D. & L., London, E.C.
(A10266) Wt W5300/P713 750,000 2/18 Sch. 52 Forms/C2118/16

Army Form C. 2118.

Instructions regarding War Diaries and Intelligence Summaries are contained in F. S. Regs., Part II. and the Staff Manual respectively. Title pages will be prepared in manuscript.

# WAR DIARY or ~~INTELLIGENCE SUMMARY.~~

(*Erase heading not required.*)

ANSON Bn. July 1918.

| Place | Date | Hour | Summary of Events and Information | Remarks and references to Appendices |
|---|---|---|---|---|
| AUTHIE | 29th | | Battn march to AUTHIE and occupy camp: Leave ARQUÈVES at 12.30pm; Route – via RAINCHEVAL; arrive 3.45pm. | |
| " | 30th | | Training – as per programme. | |
| | 31st | | Training – as per programme. Comdr. A.W. BUCKLE rejoins Bn. from Leave | |

A.W.Buckle
Comdr. R.N.V.R.
Commanding
ANSON Bn.
63rd (RN) Div.

A5834 Wt. W4973 M687 750,000 8/16 D. D. & L. Ltd. Forms/C.2118/13.

Instructions regarding War Diaries and Intelligence Summaries are contained in F. S. Regs., Part II. and the Staff Manual respectively. Title pages will be prepared in manuscript.

# WAR DIARY
*or*
# INTELLIGENCE SUMMARY.

*(Erase heading not required.)*

Army Form C. 2118.

Anson Bn

Vol 27

| Place | Date | Hour | Summary of Events and Information | Remarks and references to Appendices |
|---|---|---|---|---|
| | Aug 1 | | Bn carry out practice in taking up assembly position in Cenin Valley from Camp at AUTHIE. Commander A.W. Buckle, D.S.O. assumes command of Bn on return from leave. 1 Lt Commdr and 5 Sub Lieuts join Bn. 11 O.R. to Hosp. | |
| | Aug 2 | | Training as per programme. Lt Commdr Sprang appointed to command "B" Coy to date 5/8/16 | |
| | Aug 3 | | Training as per programme & bathing. Sub Lt Younger struck off strength from 25/7/18 (wounded - to England). Sub Lt Beetham proceeded on course. | |
| | Aug 4 | | Church services and bathing. Lt Blackhall to Div Hqrs & 47 O.R. 2 O.R. on French leave. Battalion leave AUTHIE 10.15 pm to camp at VAUCHELLES. | |
| | Aug 5 | | Battalion left VAUCHELLES at 6 pm and moved into Brown System. ABC Coys in ACHEUX WOOD. D Coy & Hqrs in billets in ACHEUX. Take over from Hood Bn. | |
| | Aug 6 | | Training as per programme in morning. Improving bivouacs in afternoon. Lt Williams left for 14 days rest at ST. VALERIE. | |
| | Aug 7 | | Two Coys (A & B) working in Brown System. C & D Coys training as per programme. All officers under Commanding Officer for tactical schemes in afternoon. Sub Lt Heslop admitted into Hospital. | |
| | Aug 8 | | A & B Coys training as per programme in morning. C & D Coys working under R.E.s in Brown System. At night Battalion marched to CONTAY and settled down in field on CONTAY - BEAUCOURT ROAD (3rd Corps 4th Army) | |
| | Aug 9 | | Inspection and re-adjustment of fighting order equipment during morning. Battalion rested during afternoon. | |
| | Aug 10 | | As per August 9th | |
| | Aug 11 | | Naval Sunday Church Parades during morning. Bn fired on range from 4 pm to 8 pm (platoon competitions). A Lieut deported from England. Lt Young returned to Bn. | |
| | Aug 12 | | Bn tactical training during morning (attack through wood). Observers & scouts fired on range in afternoon. Sub Lt Young joined Bn and posted to "A" Coy. | |
| | Aug 13 | | Training as per programme. Bn bathed in afternoon. | |

D. D. & L., London, E.C.
(A10266) Wt W5300/P713 750,000 2/15 Sch. 52 Forms/C2118/16

Army Form C. 2118.

# WAR DIARY
*or*
# INTELLIGENCE SUMMARY.
*(Erase heading not required.)*

Instructions regarding War Diaries and Intelligence Summaries are contained in F. S. Regs., Part II. and the Staff Manual respectively. Title pages will be prepared in manuscript.

| Place | Date | Hour | Summary of Events and Information | Remarks and references to Appendices |
|---|---|---|---|---|
| | Aug 14 | | Tactical scheme during morning. Bn in attack. Sub Lt Gowan went on leave. Bn did night march to HENU. Camped in orchard with only 42 tents for Bn. Lt Luce took over Adjutant. Sub Lt Auld went on French leave | |
| | Aug 15 | | Inspection in morning & Bn rested during remainder of day. | |
| | Aug 16 | | Training as per programme. Officers riding instruction in early morning. Sub Lt Ingle went to Bde as Bde Intelligence Officer. Sub Lt McLaren went on leave | |
| | Aug 17 | | Training as per programme. Two platoons per Company digging revetments in horse lines in afternoon. Five new officers arrived (Sub Lieuts). Lt Fleming returned from English leave & took over intelligence. | |
| | Aug 18 | | Usual Sunday Routine (Church Parades) Work in Transport Lines completed by B & C Coys. | |
| | Aug 19 | | Companies on the range in the morning. Stand by to move. Move to CHATEAU DE LA HAIE SWITCH. Hqrs in SOUASTRE. Preliminary orders for attack on 21st inst received | |
| | Aug 20 | | Coys & I.O. reconnoitre assembly positions in TOP and HALIFAX trenches. | Ref 57.D.N.E. and 57.C.N.W. |
| | Aug 21 | | Bn moves from CHATEAU DE LA HAIE SWITCH to assembly positions. B.H.Q. in Top TRENCH. following capture of ABLAINZEVILLE by 37th Div. 63rd Division attack from line L 4 b. 3.2 – A 20 a 5.1. ANSON Bn left Bn of left Bde. 3rd Division operates on our left. Royal Marines and Royal Irish on our right. Bn front A 19 d. 0.1 – A 20 a. 5.1<br>1st Objective brown line. sunken road G. 2. b. 3.0 – A 27 a. 3.2.<br>2nd Objective red line – railway (ACHIET-LE-GRAND). G. 4. c. 5. 0 – G. 4. a. 0. 7. at zero (4.45am)<br>Coys went through to jumping off line A. 19. d 0.1 – A 20. A. 5.1. Thick mist prevailed.<br>Right front Coy. B Coy. Lt C.R. SPRANSE, M.C. } to take first objective<br>Left front Coy. C Coy. Lt G. PATERSON }<br>Right support D Coy. Sub Lt DEWDNEY<br>Left A Coy Capt. G.A. SCOTT, M.C. (South Staffs Regt) } to take second objective<br>First objective gained by a.m. A & C Coys held up 200 yards beyond first objective by heavy infantry fire. Attack resumed at 5.30 pm without tank or artillery support. After suffering heavy losses line advanced within 50 yards of objective | |

D. D. & L., London, E.C.
(A10266) Wt W5300/P713 750,000 2/18 Sch. 52 Forms/C2118/16

Army Form C. 2118.

Instructions regarding War Diaries and Intelligence Summaries are contained in F. S. Regs., Part II. and the Staff Manual respectively. Title pages will be prepared in manuscript.

# WAR DIARY
*or*
# INTELLIGENCE SUMMARY.
*(Erase heading not required.)*

| Place | Date | Hour | Summary of Events and Information | Remarks and references to Appendices |
|---|---|---|---|---|
| | Aug 21 [illegible] | | when a field gun opened fire at point blank range. line withdrawn about 250 yards and took up outpost line in shell holes. Coy H.Q. at Bank in G.3.[illegible] Earlier in the day Lt. C.R. SPRANGE, MC had actually reached railway but was forced to withdraw on finding himself unsupported. Casualties heavy including the following:– | |
| | | | Killed: Sub. Lt DEWDNEY D Coy | |
| | | | Sub Lt NESBITT B Coy | |
| | | | Wounded: Sub. Lt FOX C Coy | |
| | | | Sub Lt LAWSON A Coy | |
| | Aug 22 | | Enemy counter-attacked three times – repulsed with heavy losses. Relieved by 13th Rifle Bde. 37th Div. | |
| | Aug 23 | | Bn took up reserve position in BADEN AV. and VERY TRENCH W of ABLAINZEVILLE. Rested for the day and reorganised. | |
| | Aug 24 | | Breakfast 4 a.m. about [illegible] to move from open position in F.39.d. till noon. At noon moved to G.3.c. moving from this point at 4 p.m. via ACHIET-LE-PETIT to [illegible] of positions SW of GREVILLERS and NE of Loupart Wood. Bn ordered to attack [illegible] 7.30 p.m. objectives ① Main BAPAUME–ALBERT ROAD M6.c.[illegible] H31.c 9.0 [illegible] THILLOY | |
| | | | Right front Coy B Lt. C.R. SPRANGE MC | |
| | | | Left front C Lt G. PATERSON | |
| | | | Right support D Sub Lt S. ROSSITER | |
| | | | Left A Capt C.A. SCOTT MC | |
| | | | Operation postponed till following morning. night spent in the open. | |
| | Aug 25 | | [illegible] 6 a.m. attack opened as above [illegible] between GREVILLERS and LOUPART [illegible] by ANSON Bn. Left Royal Marines. Right New Zealand Troops [illegible] to conform to our movements. Heavy mist prevailed. First objective gained by [illegible] and line advanced to outskirts of THILLOY but was forced to withdraw to Sunken Road in N1A 4 C | |

D. D. & L., London, E.C.
(A10266) Wt W5300/P713 750,000 2/18 Sch. 52 Forms/C2118/16

# WAR DIARY
*or*
# INTELLIGENCE SUMMARY.
*(Erase heading not required.)*

Army Form C. 2118.

Instructions regarding War Diaries and Intelligence Summaries are contained in F. S. Regs., Part II. and the Staff Manual respectively. Title pages will be prepared in manuscript.

| Place | Date | Hour | Summary of Events and Information | Remarks and references to Appendices |
|---|---|---|---|---|
| | Aug 25 cont | | Enemy counter-attacked during afternoon and again at 9 pm. beaten off with heavy loss, our Artillery doing particularly heavy damage. A number of prisoners taken mostly of 3rd Naval Division including a Staff surgeon & a medical officer ~~[illegible]~~ with other officers and men | |
| | Aug 26 | | Attacked THILLOY from SUNKEN ROAD at 7.30 am. after advancing 200/300 yds were forced to withdraw to original line being subjected to heavy M.G. fire from front & flanks. Officers & men very tired. Casualties during the operation 25/26th very heavy including the following officers:- | |
| | | | Killed. T/Lt & Adjt RICE, R S | |
| | | | Missing believed killed Capt SCOTT, C.A, M.C. (South Staffs Regt) | |
| | | | " PATERSON, G | |
| | | | Wounded Lt. Comdr SPRANSE, E.A., M.C | |
| | | | Sub. Lt WESTBROOK, T.H | |
| | | | INGLIS, D.A | |
| | | | HIRSCHFELD, C.R | |
| | | | BUTTERS, J.R | |
| | | | McKAIN, G | |
| | | | OSBURN, E | |
| | | | YOUNG, A | |
| | | | ROBERTSON, | |
| | | | HARDY, W.E, M.M. | |
| | Aug 27 | | Attack renewed by 190th Bde who passed through our line | |

D. D. & L., London, E.C.
(A10266) Wt W5300/P713 750,000 2/18 Sch. 52 Forms/C2118/16

Instructions regarding War Diaries and Intelligence Summaries are contained in F. S. Regs., Part II. and the Staff Manual respectively. Title pages will be prepared in manuscript.

# WAR DIARY
*or*
# INTELLIGENCE SUMMARY.
*(Erase heading not required.)*

Army Form C. 2118.

5

| Place | Date | Hour | Summary of Events and Information | Remarks and references to Appendices |
|---|---|---|---|---|
| | Aug 28 | | Relief orders received. Relieved by 5th Manchester 42nd Division. Rest billets MIRAUMONT. Sgn. in Quarry – Coys in open fields opposite. Estimated casualties 21/28 Aug. 416. | |
| | Aug 29 | | Rest, clean up, reorganise | |
| | Aug 30 | | C O inspects Coys. Reconnaissance of THILLOY (now captured) by I.O with B.I.O. Stand by to move to BOIRY-ST-RICTRUDE. | |
| | Aug 31 | | March off from MIRAUMONT [illegible] reach BOIRY ST RICTRUDE 5.15am [illegible] CO + IO reconnoitre forward in area T.5. | |

A J Banks

[illegible] RM
for Commander RNVR
Commanding Howe Bn

D. D. & L., London, E.C.
(A10260) Wt W5300/P713 750,000 2/18 Sch. 52 Forms/C2118/16

Instructions regarding War Diaries and Intelligence Summaries are contained in F. S. Regs., Part II. and the Staff Manual respectively. Title pages will be prepared in manuscript.

# WAR DIARY
~~or~~
~~INTELLIGENCE SUMMARY.~~
(*Erase heading not required.*)

Army Form C. 2118.

ANSON BATTN
63rd (R.N.) DIV

V8 28

| Place | Date 1918 | Hour | Summary of Events and Information | Remarks and references to Appendices |
|---|---|---|---|---|
| BOIRY-STE RICTRUDE | Sept 1st | | Moved to assembly position in D6d at 1800 hrs where Battn remained for the rest of the day | |
| | " 2nd | | At 0430 Battn moved to 2nd assembly position in U9d. At 0745 boys move off in artillery formation from HENDECOURT where Battn came under artillery fire moved off by platoons in artillery formation & advance continued South of CALLING CARD WOOD. Bombs were dropped by enemy planes & 4 men were wounded. On reaching the DROUCOURT-QUEANT line it was necessary to extend owing to MG fire from about V26. About V20a the Battn in extended order changed direction with left on Rd junction at T31d & advanced towards the final objective. Heavy M.G fire was encountered here & MG guns were immediately brought up & posted in the trench in V20a & opened a fire on V26 & on the ridge which formed our objective. At 1110 one Coy was established along the road V21d72. V27a73 with a forward position on side of ridge about V28a25. The right Coy occupied a line along the [illegible] in V20 c & a. At 1255 the RM Battn advanced & on reaching our line the whole attack proceeded. The trench in V27b was reached & 2 heavy & 4 light M.Gs captured & the crews killed. By this time numbers of the RM & RI had appeared in our trench & reorganization was at once commenced preliminary to the assault on the final objective. At 1655 reorganization was reported complete & orders prepared by the C.O. of the Anson for the taking of the ridge line. It was found that the DRAKE Battn had been ordered for this work, so the line as held was consolidated & patrols sent forward to gain touch with the enemy. 290 PGs were captured including 6 heavy M.G & 3 LTMs. | |
| | Sept 3rd / 4 | | Spent in support ready to move forward if required. Coy Officers made reconnaissance of the forward position. | |
| | 5 / 6 | | Salvage and burial parties were sent out daily & salvage returned to Div. dump. Casualties - 4 Officers wounded (including M.O.) 7 ORs killed 49 wounded 10 missing. | |
| | 7 | | Moved back to CROISELLES area remained in that area | |
| | 8 | | Marched to BOYELLES & at 1900 hrs entrained arriving at BAVINGCOURT 0400 | |
| | 9 | | Kit inspecting - cleaning up & bathing | |

A7092 Wt. W12839/M1293 750,000. 1/17. D. D & L., Ltd. Forms/C2118/14.

Instructions regarding War Diaries and Intelligence Summaries are contained in F. S. Regs., Part II. and the Staff Manual respectively. Title pages will be prepared in manuscript.

# WAR DIARY or ~~INTELLIGENCE SUMMARY~~. ANSON BATTN. 63rd (R.N.) DIV.

(Erase heading not required.)

Army Form C. 2118.

| Place | Date 1918 | Hour | Summary of Events and Information | Remarks and references to Appendices |
|---|---|---|---|---|
| | Sept 10 | | Battn at BAVINCOURT reorganising & cleaning up. Lieut T V WILLIAMS rejoins Battn from leave to U.K. Sub Lieut Whittaker proceeds to ENGLAND on leave | |
| | " 11 | | Training as per programme & Bathing | |
| | " 12 | | Training as per programme. Sub Lieut Scott to course with Tank Battn. | |
| | " 13 | | Training as per programme | |
| | " 14 | | Training as per programme | |
| | " 15 | | Usual Church parades. Sub Lieut Scott rejoins from course. | |
| | " 16 | | Training as per programme | |
| | " 17 | | Battn move to BLAIRVILLE and carry out practice attack en route on position at BLAIRVILLE | |
| | " 18 | | Battn move to BOISELLES & practice attack on that position. Sub Lt Barker rejoins Battn from leave to U.K. | |
| | " 19 | | Training as per programme. Lieut Henry proceeds to ENGLAND on leave | |
| | " 20 | | Training as per programme | |
| | " 21 | | Training as per programme. Working party 8 NCO & 76 men on salvage work | |
| | " 22 | | Usual church parades. Battn inspected by M.O. | |
| | " 23 | | Training as per programme | |
| | " 24 | | Training as per programme. Sub Lieut Auld to ENGLAND on leave. | |
| | 25 | | Training as per programme. Rev. J Goodie returns from leave to ENGLAND. Sub Lieuts Southam, Jackson & Holland & [illegible] men join Battn. 19 awards for good work in the field (list attached herewith) | |
| | " 26 | | Battn move to concentration area at QUEANT. Strength 636 OR and 17 Officers. | |
| | " 27 | | 00.10 Battn moved off from QUEANT to concentration area No 2 WEST OF MOEUVRES (Map Ref 57C NE 1/20000 E13c). At Zero + 15 the Battn moved off in file & crossed the CANAL DU NORD in E15c & companies formed up EAST of the CANAL. Opposition was met along the HINDENBERG SYSTEM & the Battn moved up this area in going forward. The ROYAL MARINES were on the left & the ROYAL IRISH in support with the 190th Bde on the right – | |

A5834 Wt. W4973 M687 750,000 8/16 D. D. & L. Ltd. Forms/C.2118/13.

Instructions regarding War Diaries and Intelligence Summaries are contained in F. S. Regs., Part II. and the Staff Manual respectively. Title pages will be prepared in manuscript.

# WAR DIARY
*or*
# INTELLIGENCE SUMMARY.
*(Erase heading not required.)*

ANSON BATTN
63rd (RN) DIV

Army Form C. 2118.

| Place | Date 1918 | Hour | Summary of Events and Information | Remarks and references to Appendices |
|---|---|---|---|---|
| | Sept 27 (Contd) | | The advance was continued and in crossing the ridge in E23a and E22b heavy machine gun fire was encountered. Artillery support was arranged & the advance continued capturing the FACTORY in E23c & E29a and GRAINCOURT. The Battn taking up position in the BROWN LINE in F25c and K6b. Enemy Counter attack was driven off here. Casualties - Killed Sub Lt Southern "B" Coy. Wounded Sub Lt Langdon A Coy, Sub Lt McLaren A Coy, Sub Lt Smith C Coy | |
| | " 28th | | Reorganization of Coys carried out in Sunken Rd in E29d. The 57th Div having gone through our own line. The Battn marched to concentration area in F27c where the Battn remained overnight in support to the R.I. & R.M. ready to move off at a moments notice. | |
| | " 29 | | at 11.15 hrs the Battn moved off to position EAST of CANAL DESCAUT in F30 & b. The night was spent there. The R.I. & R.M. having previously crossed the CANAL and taken the ridge west of PROVILLE. | |
| | 30 | | In conjunction with the attack made by the 190th Bde the Battn moved up to assembly position at 16.00 hrs in A26a & b & attacked the enemy line in A20c & d A21c & A27a. A number of men of different companies reaching the line immediately SW of PROVILLE A20d65 to A20b57. At night time reorganization was carried out & the line established from A20d35 to A21c30 and one Coy in support in trench in A26a74 to A26a93.<br>Casualties - Wounded: Sub Lt HAWKINS D Coy; " GOWAN B; (since died of wds) - STONE D; SCOTT D.C.M. C; ALLMAN A. Missing: Sub Lt BARNETT C Coy; " WILD C<br>A. W. Buckle<br>Commander RNVR<br>Commanding Anson Battn | |

A5834 Wt. W4973 M687 750,000 8/16 D. D. & L. Ltd. Forms/C.2118/13.

OCTOBER 1918.

Instructions regarding War Diaries and Intelligence Summaries are contained in F. S. Regs., Part II. and the Staff Manual respectively. Title pages will be prepared in manuscript.

# WAR DIARY
*or*
# ~~INTELLIGENCE SUMMARY.~~
*(Erase heading not required.)*

ANSON BATTN
63rd (R.N.) DIV.

Army Form C. 2118.

| Place | Date | Hour | Summary of Events and Information | Remarks and references to Appendices |
|---|---|---|---|---|
| CAMBRAI [illegible] | Oct 1st | | Battalion in the line BOURLON [illegible]. At 1800 hrs the 57th Division attacked through our line. The Battalion then came out to rest in ANNEUX AREA. | |
| | 2nd | | Reorganization by companies and cleaning up. Sub Lieut. Barker - Assistant Adjt [illegible] "A" Company & assumes command. 10 new officers join Battalion from [illegible]. | |
| | 3rd | | Training according to programme issued. Sub Lt Phillips report sick to 1st F.A. | |
| | 4th | | Training according to programme and bathing. Sub Lieut Brooks takes over duties of Assistant Adjutant. | |
| | 5th | | Training as per programme. Sub Lieut Rowe to FORT MAHON on [illegible] course. | |
| | 6th | | [illegible] church parade services. Sub Lieut CUNNINGTON appointed Assistant Adjutant vice Sub Lieut BROOKS to D Coy. | |
| | 7th | | Battalion moved off from ANNEUX AREA at 1600 hours to concentration area No. 1 in Sunken Road G5a arriving there at 1900 hours. (Map Ref. 57B N.W. 1/20000). | |
| | 8th | | At 0100 the Battn [illegible] moved to concentration area No 2 in C16a E of RUMILLY [illegible] 0220 hours. The 189th Brigade on the left - 2nd Division on the right & 190th Brigade in reserve. At 04.50 hours the Battalion moved off by companies. One officer, R.S.M. & 6 O.Rs were killed before moving off. The 2 R.I.R. were leading followed by the 1st R.M. The ANSON being in reserve ready to go forward whenever required. The R.I. reached their objective without much opposition. The R.M.s then went through the R.I. followed by the ANSON. The R.M.s and 2 Coys of the ANSON reached their objective by 0840 hours. One platoon mopped up the village of NIERGNIES and took about 50 prisoners. By this time the HOOD BATTN formed a line on the NE side of the village. | |

A7092 Wt. W128,9/M1293. 750,000. 1/17. D. D & L., Ltd. Forms/C2118/14.

OCT 1918

Instructions regarding War Diaries and Intelligence Summaries are contained in F. S. Regs., Part II. and the Staff Manual respectively. Title pages will be prepared in manuscript.

# WAR DIARY
*or*
# ~~INTELLIGENCE SUMMARY.~~
*(Erase heading not required.)*

ANSON BATTN
63rd (R.N.) DIV

Army Form C. 2118.

| Place | Date | Hour | Summary of Events and Information | Remarks and references to Appendices |
|---|---|---|---|---|
| NIERGNIES | Oct 8th | | At 0930 four enemy tanks were observed making their way towards their line [illegible] our troops on the right were seen to be withdrawing. A line running through G6d occupied by the 2nd (R.I.R.) was taken up & from here the enemy tanks were successfully driven off. Commander Buckle of the ANSON BATTN himself put one of these tanks out of action with anti-tank rifle he found in the trench. The men of the ANSON and R.Ms then went forward to their objective but were unable to occupy the roadway owing to heavy artillery & M.G. fire so a position was taken up 200 yards west of the road & some troops occupying the road in G6d & H1b. At 1500 hours artillery support was arranged & a barrage put down when we again advanced our line & occupied shell holes slightly west of the road. | |
| | | | At 1700 hours the enemy again made a counter attack but was successfully driven off our line established as above when it was handed over at 1800 hours to the relieving Unit - 7th BATT EAST SURR REGT. | |
| | | | Casualties. Killed: [illegible] Sub-Lieut A.E. ROSS RNVR, " P.R. SHINKFIELD RNVR; O.R. 8. Wounded: Commdr A.W. BUCKLE DSO RNVR, Sub-Lieut J.E. WHITLEY RNVR, " F.R. LESSELLS RNVR; O.R. 57. Captures: Officers 3, O.R. 132, M. Guns 2 | |
| | | | The Battalion then moved back by companies to camp in ANNEUX arriving there by 2400 hours. | |

A7092 Wt. W12839/M1293. 750,000. 1/17. D. D & L., Ltd. Forms/C2118/14.

OCT 1918

Instructions regarding War Diaries and Intelligence Summaries are contained in F. S. Regs., Part II. and the Staff Manual respectively. Title pages will be prepared in manuscript.

# WAR DIARY
*or*
# ~~INTELLIGENCE SUMMARY.~~
*(Erase heading not required.)*

ANSON BATT<sup></sup>N
63rd (RN) DIV

Army Form C. 2118.

| Place | Date | Hour | Summary of Events and Information | Remarks and references to Appendices |
|---|---|---|---|---|
| | Oct 7 | | Battalion marched to MORCHIES leaving ANNEUX at 1200 hours arriving at MORCHIES at 1550 hours. Lieut Cdr G H HENRY rejoined Battalion from leave to UK & assumed Command of the Batt<sup></sup>n | |
| MORCHIES | 10 | | Battalion cleaning up & resting. | |
| do | 11 | | Battalion marched to VAULX VRAICOURT & entrained there at 1750 hours & proceeded to [illegible] St. POL arriving there at 0600 hours (12th) [illegible] with the Battalion. Remainder of transport by road. [illegible] | |
| | [illegible] | | at 0630 hours Batt<sup></sup>n marched to HERNICOURT arriving there at 0800 hours. Transport arrived at 1800 hours. | |
| | | | [illegible] RNVR to ENGLAND on duty. | |
| | 13th | | [illegible] CO's inspection of companies. | |
| | 14th | | Training according to programme. Bathing. Sub Lieut [illegible] RNVR rejoined Batt<sup></sup>n. | |
| | 15th | | CO & Company Commanders attend Conference at Brigade HQ. Batt<sup></sup>n training as per programme. | |
| | [illegible] | | Training as per programme. Lieut [illegible] Phillips RNVR rejoined Batt<sup></sup>n from hospital. [illegible] RNVR is appointed Adjutant ANSON BATT<sup></sup>N with effect from 26/9/18 vice T/Lieut P S LUCE RNVR killed in action 27/9/18. [illegible] Lieut Comdr R H SHELTON DSO RNVR assumes Command of the ANSON BATT<sup></sup>N. | |

A7092 Wt W12839/M1293 750,000. 1/17. D. D & L., Ltd. Forms/C2118/14.

OCT. 1918.

Instructions regarding War Diaries and Intelligence Summaries are contained in F. S. Regs., Part II. and the Staff Manual respectively. Title pages will be prepared in manuscript.

# WAR DIARY
*or*
# INTELLIGENCE SUMMARY.
*(Erase heading not required.)*

ANSON BATT<sup></sup>N
63rd (RN) DIV

Army Form C. 2118.

| Place | Date | Hour | Summary of Events and Information | Remarks and references to Appendices |
|---|---|---|---|---|
| HERNICOURT | Oct 1st/18 | | The undermentioned Officers - transferred to ENGLAND - are struck off the strength of the Battalion. T/Sub Lieut G SCOTT DCM RNVR 3/10/18<br>" H GOWAN DCM RNVR 3/10/18<br>" J. HAWKINS RNVR 4/10/18<br>" W. ALLMAN RNVR 4/10/18.<br>Honours & awards for Gallantry in the Field:-<br>Second Bar to the D.S.O. T/Comdr A W BUCKLE DSO RNVR<br>Military Cross T/Sub Lieut C M ROBERTSON RNVR<br>" W BARNETT RNVR.<br>Distinguished Conduct Medal KW 149 AB. B. POLLARD. RNVR.<br>Bar to the C G M. R/3146 A/CPO A BLORE CGM RNVR | |
| " | Oct 18th | | Training according to programme. | |
| " | " 19th | | Training according to programme. The u/m. Officers transferred to ENGLAND are struck off the strength of this Battalion.<br>T/Sub Lieut W F LANGDON RNVR 30/9/18<br>" M McLAREN RNVR " | |
| " | 20th | | Church Parade Services. Companies inspected by C.O. | |
| | 21st | | Training according to programme. Sub Lieut S L ARLOTTE appointed L.G. Officer on H.Q. | |
| " | 22nd | | Battalion moved to MAIZIERES leaving HERNICOURT at 1000 hours arriving at MAIZIERES at 15.15 hours | |

A/092. Wt. W12839/M1293. 750,000. 1/17. D. D & L., Ltd. Forms/C2118/14.

Oct^r 1918

Instructions regarding War Diaries and Intelligence Summaries are contained in F. S. Regs., Part II. and the Staff Manual respectively. Title pages will be prepared in manuscript.

# WAR DIARY
*or*
# INTELLIGENCE SUMMARY.
*(Erase heading not required.)*

ANSON BATT^N
63^rd (RN) DIV

Army Form C. 2118.

| Place | Date | Hour | Summary of Events and Information | Remarks and references to Appendices |
|---|---|---|---|---|
| [illegible] | Oct 23^rd | | Training according to programme. | |
| " | 24^th | | do do | |
| " | 25^th | | do do | |
| " | 26^th | | do do | |
| " | 27^th | | Church Parade Services & bathing. 4 new Officers join Battalion | |
| " | | | Inspection of Companies by C.O | |
| " | 28^th | | Training as per programme | |
| | | | Honours awarded: | |
| | | | Bar to M.M. L.Z/1951 C.P.O. KNIGHTLEY E | |
| | | | Military Medal: L 3/3146 C.P.O. BLORE A. C.G.M. [illegible] | |
| | | | PLY/15176 A/B [illegible] H RMLI S/162 P.O. EVANS J – ZB 145 L.S. REES G – SS 168 [illegible] McCOURT C [illegible] | |
| | | | [illegible] AB WINTRIP E – LZ 6304 AB MOLLETT J – R5601 AB FOX A – CZ 7029 AB SPENCE F.B. | |
| | | | PO 15717 [illegible] E RMLI – CH 1376 Pte BEER W.C. RMLI – 20439 Pte YOUNG J.G. R.M.K. – | |
| | | | [illegible] EN APBANT RNVR joins Battalion [illegible] "B" Coy. | |
| | 29^th | | Training according to programme. [illegible] BURGESS RNVR joins Battn to "D" Coy. | |
| | 30^th | | Training according to programme | |
| | 31^st | | Training according to programme. | |

R. H. [illegible]
Lieut Com^dr RNVR
Commanding ANSON Battalion

A5092 Wt. W128.9/M1293. 750,000. 2/17. D. D. & L., Ltd. Forms/C2118/14.

Honours & Awards gained by men of ANSON Battalion during operations 21st Aug. to 2nd. Sept.

MILITARY MEDAL.

| No. | Rank | Name | Unit |
|---|---|---|---|
| TZ 9860 | P.O. (A/CPO) | Bone T. | D Co. |
| LZ 1931 | " " | Knightley E. | A Co. |
| WZ 542 | " " | Evans C. | A Co. → Bar to M.M. |
| TZ 1556 | " | Martin T. | A Co |
| KP 565 | " | Chapman J. | Trans. |
| TZ 199 | " | O'Brien N. | A Co. |
| CZ 3054 | L/S. A/PO. | Bruce G. | A Co. |
| S 3086 | Cpl | Salisbury T. (Medical) | H.Q. |
| TZ 1844 | A.B. A/LS | Downe W.A. | C Co. att. Bde HQ. |
| TZ 2063 | " | Purkiss F. | A Co |
| R 1839 | " | Roberts W. | A Co. att.Trans. |
| KP 661 | " | Buchan A. | HQ |
| KW 15 | " | Davis S. | HQ. |
| BZ 4115 | " | Brewin G. | C Co. |
| TZ 2819 | " | Allan W.L.G. | ~~att.188th L.T.M.Bty.~~ TRANSPORT |
| CZ 2605 | " | Macfarlane J. | B Co. |
| R 4561 | " | Miles W.J. | A Co. |
| KP 477 | " | Buckingham J. | HQ. |

Bar to M.M.

| No. | Rank | Name | Unit |
|---|---|---|---|
| TZ 1066 | LSHG | Murphy J.W., (M.M.) | B Co. |

NOV. 1918.

Instructions regarding War Diaries and Intelligence Summaries are contained in F. S. Regs., Part II. and the Staff Manual respectively. Title pages will be prepared in manuscript.

# WAR DIARY
~~or~~
~~INTELLIGENCE SUMMARY.~~
*(Erase heading not required.)*

ANSON BATT. 63rd (R.N.) DIV.

Army Form C. 2118.

| Place | Date NOV | Hour | Summary of Events and Information | Remarks and references to Appendices |
|---|---|---|---|---|
| MAIZIERS | 1st. | | Battalion left MAIZIERS at 07.30 hrs embussing for EVIN-MALMAISON arriving at 10.00 hrs. Transport moving under Brigade T.O. Ration strength 567. | |
| EVIN-MALMAISON | 2nd | | Cleaning up of billets. Transport arrive 17.00 hrs. | |
| do | 3rd | | [illegible] Church parade services. C.O.s inspection of Companies. | W.A. |
| do | 4th | | Training as arranged. Sub Lieut [illegible] return from course. Ration Strength 563 | |
| do | 5th | | Battalion embuss at 08.00 hrs for HULCHIN. arriving at 13.00 hrs. | |
| HULCHIN | 6th | | Battalion leave HULCHIN 07.30 hrs marching to AULNOY arriving 12.00 hrs. | |
| AULNOY | [illegible] | | Battalion leave AULNOY 09.00 hrs march to SAULTAIN arriving 11.30 hrs. At 15.00 hrs Battalion march to SEBOURQUAIN arriving 18.00 hrs. Sub Lieut Hunt [illegible] Batt. [illegible] U.K. Ration Strength - 584. | |
| [illegible] | 8th | | Batt. leave SEBOURQUAIN 09.00 hrs march to ANGRE arriving 12.00 hrs. At 13.00 hrs Batt. move to ANDREGNIES arriving at 15.30 hrs. [illegible] C. MARTIN (S. STAFFS) join Batt. from DIV REST CAMP. Sub Lieut EDWARDS to 1st ARMY SCHOOL for course. | W.A. |
| ANDREGNIES | 9th | | Batt. leave 07.30 hrs for BLAUGIES arriving at 11.30 hrs. At 14.30 hrs leave for SARS-LA-BRUYERE arriving at 16.00 hrs. | |
| SARS-LA-BRUYERE | 10th | | Batt. leave SARS-LA-BRUYERE 07.00 hrs for concentration area near SUNKEN ROAD - ASQUILLIES where dinner was served. Ration Strength 564. | |

D. D. & L., London, E.C. (A10266) Wt W5300/P713 750,000 2/18 Sch. 52 Forms/C2118/16

NOV. 1918.

Instructions regarding War Diaries and Intelligence Summaries are contained in F. S. Regs., Part II. and the Staff Manual respectively. Title pages will be prepared in manuscript.

# WAR DIARY
*or*
~~INTELLIGENCE SUMMARY.~~
*(Erase heading not required.)*

ANSON BATT
63rd (R.N.) DIV

Army Form C. 2118.

| Place | Date | Hour | Summary of Events and Information | Remarks and references to Appendices |
|---|---|---|---|---|
| VILLERS-ST-GHISLAIN. | 11th | | Battalion attacked enemy position. Summary of operations attached. | WA. |
| | | | HOSTILITIES CEASE. 11.00 HRS. | |
| VILLERS-ST-GHISLAIN. | 11th | | Batt. occupy billets in VILLERS-ST-GHISLAIN. Sub Lieut HUCKLEBRIDGE RNVR joins Batt. | WA |
| | 12th | | Cleaning & tidying up billets &c. Lieut Comdr. WARBLASTER takes command of Batt. vice Lieut Comdr SHELTON to HAWKE. RSM HAWKER to UK leave. P.O KNIGHTLEY acting RSM. Ration Strength 481. | |
| | 13th | | Training as arranged. Sub Lieut BARKER RNVR proceeds on L.G. course. Sub Lieut NOWELL on course (S.O.S.) | |
| | 14th | | Training as arranged. | |

D. D. & L., London, E.C.
(A10266) Wt W5300/P713 750,000 2/18 Sch. 52 Forms/C2118/16

NOV. 1918.

Instructions regarding War Diaries and Intelligence Summaries are contained in F. S. Regs., Part II. and the Staff Manual respectively. Title pages will be prepared in manuscript.

# WAR DIARY
*or*
~~INTELLIGENCE SUMMARY.~~
*(Erase heading not required.)*

ANSON BATT
63rd (RN) DIV.

Army Form C. 2118.

| Place | Date | Hour | Summary of Events and Information | Remarks and references to Appendices |
|---|---|---|---|---|
| VILLERS-ST GHISLAIN | 15th | | 300 men & 5 Officers proceed to MONS - ARMY COMMANDERS inspection. Remainder carry on training as arranged. Ration Strength 467. | |
| do | 16th | | A+B Coys relieve C+D Coys [illegible] in outpost line. complete by 1200 hrs. C+D Coys training as arranged. Sub Lieut ROSSITER RNVR joins Batt. from U.K. | |
| | 17th | | Brigade Church parade service. Ration Strength 467 | WA. |
| do | 18th | | A+B Coys withdrawn from outpost line return to billets by 1500 hrs. C+D Coys training as arranged. The ff/m. Officers to be Acting Lieuts (Actg.) T/Sub Lieut C H BARKER RNVR 10/9/18. T/Sub Lieut A ROSSITER RNVR 22/[illegible]/18. A/Lieut BARKER return from course. Sub Lieut LOWE RNVR joins Batt. from D.R.C. | |
| do | 19th | | Training as arranged. Sub Lieut HASLOP RNVR return from leave to UK | |
| | 20th | | Training as arranged. Ration Strength 565. (90 Reinforcements arrive) | |
| | 21st | | do do Sub Lieut JACKSON return from Hospital | |
| do | 22nd | | do do | |
| | 23rd | | do do Ration Strength 580. | |
| | 24th | | Church Parade Services | |
| do | 25th | | Batt. Bathing. | |
| | 26th | | Training as arranged. Ration Strength 588 | |
| VILLERS-ST-GHISLAIN | | | Batt. leave VILLERS-ST-GHISLAIN 0830 hrs march to SARS-LA-BRUYERE arriving [illegible] hrs. LIEUT. ADJT. F.A. JENKINS to U.K. leave. Sub Lieut CONNINGTON takes over duties of ADJUTANT. Surgeon G.K. SHAW RN. joins Batt. & takes over duties of M.O. vice LT R.O. SUMNER M.O.R.C. U.S.A. | |

D. D. & L., London, E.C.
(A10266) Wt W5300/P713 750,000 2/18 Sch. 52 Forms/C2118/16

NOV. 1918.

ANSON BATT.
63rd (R.N.) DIV.

Army Form C. 2118.

# WAR DIARY
or
~~INTELLIGENCE SUMMARY.~~
(Erase heading not required.)

Instructions regarding War Diaries and Intelligence Summaries are contained in F. S. Regs., Part II. and the Staff Manual respectively. Title pages will be prepared in manuscript.

| Place | Date | Hour | Summary of Events and Information | Remarks and references to Appendices |
|---|---|---|---|---|
| SARS-LA-BRUYERE | 28th | | Training as arranged. | |
| | 29th | | Recreational training (Battn paper chase). | W.A. |
| | 30th | | Training as arranged. Ration Strength - 582. | |
| | | | The U/M. Officers struck off strength of this Unit | |
| | | | A/LIEUT COMDR. H K DOUGLAS RNVR | |
| | | | T/Sub Lieut T. DIXON RNVR | |
| | | | The following decorations are awarded. | |
| | | | M.C. T/Sub Lieut C B WHEELER DCM. MM. RNVR att 1/LTMB. | |
| | | | T/Sub Lieut C A RICHARDS RNVR (since killed in action) | |
| | | | D.C.M. CZ/6977 AB (LG) RUSSELL RNVR | |

W. Ashcroft
LIEUT COMMANDER RNVR
COMMANDING ANSON BATTN.

D. D. & L., London, E.C.
(A10266) Wt W5300/P713 750,000 2/18 Sch. 52 Forms/C2118/16

Copy No.....
3rd. [illegible]ov. [illegible]

S E C R E T.

[illegible]th. INF. [illegible] (A[illegible]) ORDER No. [illegible]

1. The [illegible]rd. (R[illegible]) Division (less Artillery) is being transferred from the [illegible] Corps to the XXIInd. Corps on 4th. and 5th. instant.

2. Move of [illegible]th. Inf. Bde. [illegible] will probably be by bus on the 5th. inst.

3. Detailed orders will be issued later.

4. ACKNOWLEDGE.

[illegible]
Issued through Signals at 16.15.

Captain,
Brigade Major,
[illegible] Inf. [illegible]

Copies to :-
[illegible]

## ANSON BATTALION.

## SUMMARY OF OPERATIONS 10, 11 NOVR., 1918.

Orders were received at 08.30 on 10 November, 1918, that the Anson Battalion would attack the enemy positions that morning. The Battalion was to form up on a line W 10 a. 5.8 to W 3, d, 0.3 ready to advance as soon as possible. It was arranged with O.C. Royal Irish Regiment and 188th M.G's. that the attack ~~would~~ should commence at 12.30.

First Objective - main MONS - GIVRY ROAD between W 4 a. 7.2 - Q 35 b. 5.6.

Second Objective - the Village of VILLERS ST GHISLAIN and to establish posts on farther side.

The First London Regiment were on ~~xxx~~ right and the Royal Irish Regiment were on left. The Royal Marines in support. The Battalion had 4 mobile sections of Artillery attached - A Coy. 63 (R.N.) M.G.Battalion and two L.T.M's. of the 188th L.T.M. BatTERY.

The Battalion assembled in sunken road in W . 3. d and it was decided to attack with B. and D. Coys. in front, C. Coy in support and A Coy. in reserve. B. Coy on right and D Coy. on left. B Coy. from W 10 b.8 to W 10 a. 0.5. D Coy. from 10 a 0.5 - W 3 d. 0.3. The Battalion left the sunken road at 11.45 and were in position by 12.15. A fair amount of shelling was encountered during the approach march and heavy M.G. fire was opened on troops' assembly position. The advance commenced at 12.30 under heavy M.G. fire from post at W 10 b. 7.7 and cliffs W 5 b. 5.8 - Q 34 d.5.8. In spite of considerable casualties the advance continued. M.G. post at W 10. b. 7.7 retired from their position leaving one man killed. The advance was temporarily held up going down forward slope towards railway from enemy M.G's in HARMIGNIES. D. Coy were held up by swamp in W 5 a.3. Q 34 d and C Coy. were pushed in to assist B Coy. at 13.00. They also encountered heavy T.M. and M.G. fire. A Coy. were ordered to endeavour to outflank these points via the village. The First London Regiment had not advanced. A Coy. were unsuccessful but D Coy. by 13.45 had forced a crossing over the lake capturing

4 prisoners. The crossing was held by a party of C Coy. while D and B Coys. crossed and stormed the cliffs, C Coy. following. A Coy. had advanced to the outskirts of HAR[illegible]IGNIES at [illegible] [illegible] fire from [illegible] continued throughout the [illegible] position [illegible] At [illegible].45 the enemy [illegible] top of the cliffs but was driven off. One officer being killed and other [illegible] troops on right not [illegible] could not continue. [illegible] were captured and two [illegible]'s on cliffs. Shortly after the enemy in [illegible] in village continued [illegible] first objective was taken and posts established [illegible] At [illegible].30 [illegible] [illegible] [illegible] driven off. Posts were put out [illegible] of village. No troops [illegible] relieved by the [illegible] billets [illegible].

C[illegible] [illegible] Killed, 1 Wounded.

O[illegible] [illegible] Killed, [illegible] Wounded.

Instructions regarding War Diaries and Intelligence Summaries are contained in F. S. Regs., Part II. and the Staff Manual respectively. Title pages will be prepared in manuscript.

DEC. 1918.

# WAR DIARY
*or*
~~INTELLIGENCE~~ SUMMARY.
*(Erase heading not required.)*

ANSON BATTN
63rd R.N. DIV

Army Form C. 2118.

| Place | Date Dec | Hour | Summary of Events and Information | Remarks and references to Appendices |
|---|---|---|---|---|
| SARS-LA BRUYERE | 1st | | Church parade services. Ration strenght. Officers 29. O.Ranks 546. | |
| do. | 2nd | | Training as arranged. | |
| do | 3rd | | do. do. Awards :- 3rd Bar to D.S.O. - T.Comdr. A.W. Buckle DSO. RNVR.<br>Bar to the Military Medal - CZ1163 P.O. Caldow. J. M.M.<br>Military Medal - TZ2707 L.S. Newport. J. R.1743 AB. Bewley. G.<br>R.775 AB. Bigley. J.W. TZ3635 L.S. Robinson S.<br>TZ 3493 AB. Thompson. J. K.P 1003 AB. Adams. E. CZ1811 AB. Patterson J. | |
| do. | 4th | | Educational classes and training as arranged. Sub-Lieut Beagant RNVR proceed to ENGLAND to No 1 School of Aeronautics.<br>Ration Strength :- Officers 29. ORs 535. | |
| do | 5th | | Battalion march to BOIS DE TILLEUL to view H.M. THE KING touring the 1st ARMY area. | |
| do | 6th | | Ceremonial drill and bathing | |
| do. | 7th | | Ceremonial drill. Ration Strength Officers 28. ORs 530. | |
| do | 8th | | Church Parade Services. Sub-Lieut Holland to PARIS PLAGE Rest House | |

DEC 1918.

# WAR DIARY
*or*
# INTELLIGENCE SUMMARY.
*(Erase heading not required.)*

ANSON BATT^N
63^rd (R.N.) DIV

Army Form C. 2118.

Instructions regarding War Diaries and Intelligence Summaries are contained in F. S. Regs., Part II. and the Staff Manual respectively. Title pages will be prepared in manuscript.

| Place | Date Dec | Hour | Summary of Events and Information | Remarks and references to Appendices |
|---|---|---|---|---|
| SARS-LA-BRUYERE | 9th | | Training as arranged. | |
| do | 10th | | [illegible] to WASMES leaving SARS-LA-BRUYERE at 1030 hrs arriving WASMES at 1230 hrs. [illegible] R. LOWE [illegible] on leave. | |
| WASMES | 11th | | [illegible] as arranged. [illegible] Officers 28. O.R.s 594. | |
| do | [illegible] | | [illegible] training as arranged. [illegible] to VIII Corps [illegible] (Miners proceeding to U.K.). | |
| do | [illegible] | | [illegible] and one Coy on [illegible] work. [illegible] Officers 37 O.R.s 564. | |
| | | | Training [illegible] | |
| | | | Church [illegible] | |
| | | | [illegible] | |
| | | | [illegible] RNVR [illegible] | |
| | | | [illegible] Officers 30 O.R.s 558 | |
| | | | [illegible] BRUYERE. | |
| | | | [illegible] Officers 31 O.R.s 5[illegible] | |
| | | | [illegible] RNVR. | |
| | | | [illegible] RNVR. | |
| | | | [illegible] RNVR. | |

A7092 Wt. W.1845/M1301 750,000 1/17 D. D. & L., Ltd. Forms/C.2118/14

DEC 1918

Instructions regarding War Diaries and Intelligence Summaries are contained in F. S. Regs., Part II. and the Staff Manual respectively. Title pages will be prepared in manuscript.

# WAR DIARY
*or*
~~INTELLIGENCE SUMMARY.~~
*(Erase heading not required.)*

ANSON BATTn
63rd (R.N.) DIV.

Army Form C. 2118.

| Place | Date Dec | Hour | Summary of Events and Information | Remarks and references to Appendices |
|---|---|---|---|---|
| WASMES | 20th | | Educational classes and bathing | |
| do | 21st | | Training as arranged | |
| do | 22nd | | Church parade services. Sub Lieut R Burgess from R.A.F. course<br>Ration strength – Officers 33 OR 543. Lieut F A Jenkins (Adj) [illegible] [illegible] OR [illegible] | |
| do | 23rd | | Battalion march to SARS-LA-BRUYERE for salvage work.<br>Comdr A W Buckle DSO RNVR [illegible] Battn [illegible] command<br>Lieut Comdr W Ambler MC RNVR relinquishes command and [illegible]<br>duties of 2nd i/c. 2nd Lieut C Martin (S. STAFFS) [illegible] [illegible] | |
| do | 24th | | Educational classes and training as arranged.<br>Sub Lieut [illegible] RNVR joins Battn from [illegible] R [illegible] | |
| do | 25th | | X Mas Day. Church parade service in morning<br>Battn dinner in afternoon. Ration strength Officers 3[illegible] OR [illegible]73 | |
| do | 26th | | No training. | |
| do | 27th | | Training as arranged. Sub Lieut Jackson to [illegible] School, on course. | |

A7092 Wt. W128 9/M1293 750,000. 1/17. D. D. & L., Ltd. Forms/C2118/14.

DEC 1918

# WAR DIARY

*or*

# INTELLIGENCE SUMMARY.

*(Erase heading not required.)*

ANSON BATTN
63rd (R.N.) DIV.

Army Form C. 2118.

Instructions regarding War Diaries and Intelligence Summaries are contained in F. S. Regs., Part II. and the Staff Manual respectively. Title pages will be prepared in manuscript.

| Place | Date | Hour | Summary of Events and Information | Remarks and references to Appendices |
|---|---|---|---|---|
| [illegible] | [illegible] | | [illegible] | |
| do | [illegible] | | [illegible] | |
| do | [illegible] | | [illegible] | |
| do | [illegible] | | [illegible] | |

A. W. Buckle

[illegible]

A7092 Wt. [illegible] D. D. & L., Ltd. Forms/C2118/14.

JAN 1919

Instructions regarding War Diaries and Intelligence Summaries are contained in F. S. Regs., Part II. and the Staff Manual respectively. Title pages will be prepared in manuscript.

# WAR DIARY
*or*
# INTELLIGENCE SUMMARY.
*(Erase heading not required.)*

Army Form C. 2118.

Vol 32

| Place | Date | Hour | Summary of Events and Information | Remarks and references to Appendices |
| --- | --- | --- | --- | --- |
| [illegible] | [illegible] | | [illegible] | |

D. D. & L., London, E.C.
(A10260) Wt W5300/P713 750,000 2/18 Sch. 52 Forms/C2118/16

Instructions regarding War Diaries and Intelligence Summaries are contained in F. S. Regs., Part II. and the Staff Manual respectively. Title pages will be prepared in manuscript.

JAN 1919

# WAR DIARY
*or*
# ~~INTELLIGENCE~~ SUMMARY.
*(Erase heading not required.)*

ANSON. BATTN.
63rd (R.N.) DIV.

Army Form C. 2118.

| Place | Date JAN. | Hour | Summary of Events and Information | Remarks and references to Appendices |
|---|---|---|---|---|
| WASMES | 12. | | Church Parade services. Lieut Comdr. J Coote MC RNVR. assumes Command of Battalion during the absence of Comdr. A.W. Buckle DSO. RNVR | |
| " | 13. | | Educational Classes Lecture. Ration strength officers 26. O.Rs. 464. | |
| | 14. | | Training Lecture. Sub Lieut [illegible] to U.K. (draft conducting) | |
| | 15. | | Training Bathing as arranged under Company arrangements. | |
| | 16. | | Educational classes & training Lecture. Ration Strength officers 27. O.Rs [illegible] | |
| | 17. | | Battalion Route March Lecture. Lieut. T.V. Williams. RNVR to U.K. leave. Sub Lt. J. Cook RNVR Town Major during Lieut. T.V. Williams RNVR. absence. | |
| | 18. | | Training under Company arrangements. Lecture by M.O. Sub Lieut. P. Gaymard RNVR. from Corps Educational Centre. | |
| | 19. | | Church Parade services. Sub Lieut. W.E. Pentreath. RNVR. to 1st Army "Rifle training school". | |
| | 20. | | Training under Company arrangements. C.O. inspection Debate "Prohibition of Drink" Sub Lieut. [illegible] RNVR from 1st Army Rifle training school. Comdr A.W. Buckle D.S.O. RNVR. from U.K. Ration strength officers. 25. O.Rs 350 | |

D. D. & L., London, E.C.
(A10260) Wt W5300/P713 750,000 2/18 Sch. 52 Forms/C2118/16

Army Form C. 2118.

Instructions regarding War Diaries and Intelligence Summaries are contained in F. S. Regs., Part II. and the Staff Manual respectively. Title pages will be prepared in manuscript.

JAN 1919.

# WAR DIARY
or
# INTELLIGENCE SUMMARY.
(Erase heading not required.)

ANSON. BATTN.
63RD (RN) DIV.

| Place | Date JAN | Hour | Summary of Events and Information | Remarks and references to Appendices |
|---|---|---|---|---|
| WARMES | 21. | | Training under Coy arrangements. D Coy. Salvage work. M.O. Inspection for H.Q. + C. Coy. Sub Lieut. J.H. Low. M.C RNVR TO U.K (draft conducting.) | |
| " | 22 | | Inspection by M.O. of A.B&D Coys. Debate. Should professionalism in Sport be abolished. Lieut (addl) S. Rossiter R.N.V.R. to VIII Corps. concentration Camp for duty as entraining officer. | |
| " | 23. | | A&B Coy + H Q move to new allotted areas. Sub Lieut. C J Price RNVR to U.K. (draft conducting) Ration strength officers 24 O.Rs. 334. | |
| " | 24. | | Battn. Route March. Battn reorganised. 4 Coys amalgamated. Debate. "Should English marry foreigners." Sub Lieut C Holland RNVR. rejoined from U.K. | |
| " | 25. | | Training + lecture by Sub Lieut. Rowe RNVR. Sub Lieut. T.S. O'Brien to U.K. on leave | |
| " | 26. | | Church Parade Services. Ration strength Officers 24. O.Rs. 326. | |
| " | 27 | | Training + Debate. 'Whippet versus Horse racing'. | |

D. D. & L., London, E.C.
(A10266) Wt. W5300/P713 750,000 2/18 Sch. 52 Forms/C2118/16

Instructions regarding War Diaries and Intelligence Summaries are contained in F. S. Regs., Part II. and the Staff Manual respectively. Title pages will be prepared in manuscript.

JAN. 1919

# WAR DIARY
*or*
# INTELLIGENCE SUMMARY.
*(Erase heading not required.)*

ANSON. BATTN.
63RD (R.N.) DIV.

Army Form C. 2118.

| Place | Date JAN | Hour | Summary of Events and Information | Remarks and references to Appendices |
|---|---|---|---|---|
| WASMES | 27 | | Sub Lieut G. Jackson RNVR to concentration Camp. Conducting officer | |
| | 28. | | Bathing Lecture Sub. Lt. L.P. Hunt to U.K for Demobilisation. | |
| | 29. | | Educational Classes & Training Debate "Should Bachelors be taxed" Sub Lieut V.H. Powell RNVR. to U.K. Conducting officer. Ration strength Officers 21. ORs. 305. | |
| | 30. | | Battalion Route march Lecture. | |
| | 31. | | Educational Classes & Training. Debate "Should ladies be allowed in smoking Compartments." | |

A. W. Buckle
[illegible] RNVR
[illegible]

D. D. & L., London, E.C.
(A10266) Wt W5300/P713 750,000 2/18 Sch. 52 Forms/C2118/16

Feb 1919

Instructions regarding War Diaries and Intelligence Summaries are contained in F. S. Regs., Part II. and the Staff Manual respectively. Title pages will be prepared in manuscript.

# WAR DIARY
*or*
# INTELLIGENCE SUMMARY.
*(Erase heading not required.)*

Army Form C. 2118.

ANSON BATTN
63rd (RN) Div

WO 33

| Place | Date | Hour | Summary of Events and Information | Remarks and references to Appendices |
|---|---|---|---|---|
| | FEB | | | |
| WATOMES | 1 | | Training. Ration strength Officers 21 ORs 200 | |
| | 2 | | Church Services Parade | |
| | 3 | | Training. Lecture "British Navy in Action" by Sub Lt H W Turner RNVR Sub Lt G E C Edwards RNVR to UK conducting officer. Ration strength Officers 20. ORs 285 | |
| | 4 | | Educational Classes Training Lecture. Sub Lt H H D Phillips RNVR from leave. Sub Lt E B Tiny RNVR to Brigade H.Q | |
| | 5 | | Educational Classes Training – Organised Games | |
| | 6 | | Bathing under company arrangements. Lieut [illegible] A J Davy RNVR to UK for demobilisation. Ration strength Officers 19 ORs 277 | |
| | 7 | | Ceremonial Drill. Educational Classes. Organised Games | |
| | 8 | | Educational Classes Organised Games. Pte C H Smith RNVR from UK leave. Sub Lt T E Rose RNVR attached to 22 Brigade RFA | |

D. D. & L., London, E.C.
(A10266) Wt W5300/P713 750,000 2/18 Sch. 52 Forms/C2118/16

Instructions regarding War Diaries and Intelligence Summaries are contained in F. S. Regs., Part II. and the Staff Manual respectively. Title pages will be prepared in manuscript.

FEB 1919

# WAR DIARY
*or*
# INTELLIGENCE SUMMARY.

*(Erase heading not required.)*

ANSON BATTN
63rd (R.N.) DIV.

Army Form C. 2118.

| Place | Date | Hour | Summary of Events and Information | Remarks and references to Appendices |
|---|---|---|---|---|
| [illegible] | 9 | | [illegible] | |
| | 10. | | [illegible] | |
| | 11. | | [illegible] | |
| | 12. | | [illegible] no. 13. Offrs 249. | |
| | | | [illegible] | |
| | 13 | | [illegible] | |
| | | | [illegible] to UK Conducting officer. | |
| | | | [illegible] to UK Conducting officer. | |
| | | | F. [illegible] RNVR to UK Conducting officer. | |

D. D. & L., London, E.C.
(A10266) Wt W5300/P713 750,000 2/16 Sch. 52 Forms/C2118/16

FEB. 1919.

Instructions regarding War Diaries and Intelligence Summaries are contained in F. S. Regs., Part II. and the Staff Manual respectively. Title pages will be prepared in manuscript.

**WAR DIARY** *or* **INTELLIGENCE SUMMARY.** *(Erase heading not required.)*

ANSON BATT 63rd (R.N.) DIV.

Army Form C. 2118.

| Place | Date | Hour | Summary of Events and Information | Remarks and references to Appendices |
|---|---|---|---|---|
| WASMES | 14th | | Battalion march to DOUR and in conjunction with 4 other Battalions of the Division were presented with H.M's Colours by General Sir HENRY HORNE commanding 1st ARMY. The colours were duly consecrated and handed over to the Battalion after which the Battalion marched past and then returned to WASMES. | |
| | 15th | | Educational classes & Games. Sub Lieut Claret RNVR to UK draft conducting. Ration Strength Officers 27 O Ranks. 242 | |
| | 16th | | Usual Church Parade Services. Lieut Comdr J. Cotte MC RNVR and Lieut FG Jenkins (Adjutant) M.C. R.N.V.R. to BRUSSELS on leave. Sub-Lieut Tovey RNVR assume duties of Adjutant. | |
| | 17th | | Training as arranged and lecture. | |
| | 18th | | Educational classes and lecture. Ration strength [illegible] 27 ranks. 228 | |
| | 19th | | Training as arranged and lecture. Sub-Lieut Nowell RNVR from leave U.K. | |
| | 20th | | Training as arranged and lecture [illegible] on "Bolshevism" | |

D. D. & L., London, E.C. (A10266) Wt W5300/P713 750,000 2/18 Sch. 52 Forms/C2118/16

EB 1919

Instructions regarding War Diaries and Intelligence Summaries are contained in F. S. Regs., Part II. and the Staff Manual respectively. Title pages will be prepared in manuscript.

# WAR DIARY
*or*
# INTELLIGENCE SUMMARY.

*(Erase heading not required.)*

ANSON BATT
63rd (RN) DIV

Army Form C. 2118.

| Place | Date | Hour | Summary of Events and Information | Remarks and references to Appendices |
|---|---|---|---|---|
| VAISNES | [illegible] | | [illegible] Strength Officers 23 O.Ranks 226 [illegible] RNVR to UK (draft conducting) | |
| do | [illegible] | | [illegible] (Brig RNVR to UK (draft conducting)) [illegible] to UK [illegible] RNVR to UK on leave. [illegible] to UK (draft conducting) [illegible] 17 [illegible] 200. | |
| do | [illegible] | | [illegible] arrangement. | |
| do | 26th | | Training [illegible] | |
| do | 27th | | Battalion [illegible] at Mons [illegible] 17 [illegible] 127 | |
| do | [illegible] | | [illegible] lecture. | |

A W Buckle
Commander RNVR
Commanding Anson Battn.

D. D. & L., London, E.C.
(A10266) Wt W5300/P713 750,000 2/18 Sch. 52 Forms/C2118/16

ANSON BATTALION,
63RD
(R.N.) DIVISION.
No. P35/17.
Date 1.4.19.

12

O i/c Records,
63rd (R.N.) Divn
A.G.'s Office at Base.

Herewith War Diary of this Unit for Mch. 19.

[illegible]
Lieut [illegible]
for O.C. Anson Bn

MARCH 1919.

Instructions regarding War Diaries and Intelligence Summaries are contained in F. S. Regs., Part II. and the Staff Manual respectively. Title pages will be prepared in manuscript.

# WAR DIARY
*or*
~~INTELLIGENCE SUMMARY.~~
*(Erase heading not required.)*

ANSON BATTN. 63rd (R.N.) DIV.

Army Form C. 2118.

| Place | Date | Hour | Summary of Events and Information | Remarks and references to Appendices |
|---|---|---|---|---|
| WASMES | 1st. | | Inspection parade. Ration strength:- Officers 16 O.Ranks 181. | |
| | | | Church parade service | |
| do | 2nd | | Inspection parade. Sub Lieut. Edwards RNVR. from U.K. (draft conducting) | |
| do | 3rd | | do do Ration strength. Officers 17 O.Ranks 169. | |
| do | 4th | | do do. Bathing under Company arrangements. | |
| do | 5th | | Sub Lieut. Cummington rejoin from leave to U.K. | |
| | | | Inspection parade. | |
| do | 6th | | do Sub Lieuts. Clarke RNVR and Whitley RNVR from UK [illegible] | |
| [illegible] | 7th | | ~~[illegible] RNVR [illegible]~~ BRUSSELS Ration Strength Officers 20 ORs 126. | |
| do | 8th | | Inspection parade. Sub Lieut Jackson RNVR to BASE (draft conducting). | |
| | | | [illegible] RNVR and [illegible] RNVR from U.K. (draft conducting) | |
| do | 9th | | C[illegible] Sub Lieut [illegible] RNVR [illegible] U.K. (draft conducting) | |
| do | 10th | | [illegible] Ration Strength 24 Officers 126 O.Ranks. | |
| | | | Lieut C.S. Barker RNVR [illegible] | |
| | | | [illegible] RNVR to U.K. on leave. | |
| | | | [illegible] | |

D. D. & L., London, E.C.
(A10:66) Wt W5300/P713 750,000 2/18 Sch. 52 Forms/C2118/16

MAR 1919

Instructions regarding War Diaries and Intelligence Summaries are contained in F. S. Regs., Part II. and the Staff Manual respectively. Title pages will be prepared in manuscript.

**WAR DIARY**
*or*
~~INTELLIGENCE SUMMARY.~~
*(Erase heading not required.)*

ANSON BATTn
63rd (RN) DIV.

Army Form C. 2118.

| Place | Date | Hour | Summary of Events and Information | Remarks and references to Appendices |
|---|---|---|---|---|
| WASMES | 13th | | Inspection parade. Ration Strength. 23 Officers 119 O. Ranks. Rev. T. Gowdie to U.K. for demobilization. | |
| do | 14th | | Inspection parade. Lieut C H Barker return from leave to Brussels. | |
| do | 15th | | Inspection parade. Sub. Lieut N D Phillips RNVR to U.K. (draft conducting). | |
| do | 16th | | Ration Strength. Officers 24. O Ranks 118. | |
| do | 17th | | Inspection parade. Sub Lieut E. Spencer RNVR. to U.K for demobilization. | |
| do | 18th | | do O/Capt E.C. Martin (S. Staff) from UK (draft conducting). | |
| do | 19th | | do Ration Strength. Officers 24. O Ranks 113 | |
| do | 20th | | do Sub Lieuts. T.E Rowe RNVR & S L Arlotte RNVR to UK for demobilz. Sub Lieut J ? Tovey R.N.V.R. from UK. (draft conducting). | |
| do | 21st. | | Inspection parade. Lieut A W Aula R.N.V.R. and Sub Lieut ? to U.K. for demobilization. | |
| do | 22nd | | Inspection parade. Ration Strength Officers 21. O Ranks 116. Sub Lieut Turner RNVR. return from leave to U.K. | |
| do | 23rd | | Comdr A W Buckle DSO. RNVR to U.K on leave. Lieut Comdr J Coote MC RNVR assumes command of Battn | |
| do | 24th | | Inspection parade. Sub Lieut Lee RNVR return from Course | |
| do | 25th | | do Ration Strength. Officers 21 O Ranks 95. | |

D. D. & L., London, E.C.
(A10266) Wt W5300/P713 750,000 2/18 Sch. 52 Forms/C2118/16

MAR 1919

# WAR DIARY
or
~~INTELLIGENCE SUMMARY.~~
*(Erase heading not required.)*

ANSON BATTN
63rd (R.N.) Div

Army Form C. 2118.

Instructions regarding War Diaries and Intelligence Summaries are contained in F. S. Regs., Part II. and the Staff Manual respectively. Title pages will be prepared in manuscript.

| Place | Date | Hour | Summary of Events and Information | Remarks and references to Appendices |
|---|---|---|---|---|
| WASMES | 26 | | Inspection parade | |
| do | 27th | | do | |
| do | 28th | | do Lieut Comdr J. Cook MC RNVR to UK for demobilization. Surgeon Lieut R K Shaw RN to 150th Field Ambulance. Ration Strength Officers 20 O Ranks 93 | |
| do | 29th | | Inspection parade Sub Lieut Howel RNVR to UK on leave | |
| do | 30th | | Sub Lieuts Huckelbridge & Torey to UK for demobilization | |
| do | 31st | | Inspection parade Ration strength Officers 18 O Ranks 87 | |

[illegible signature]
for Commander RNVR
Commanding Anson Bn

D. D. & L., London, E.C.
(A10286) Wt W5300/P713 750,000 2/18 Sch. 52 Forms/C2118/16

(8) Wt. W6092/P1773. 11/18 120M pads (20) D.St.

Army Form C348
(Pads of 100 in duplicate)

8

# MEMORANDUM.

| From O. i/c Records, 63rd (R.N.) Divn., G.H.Q., 3rd Echelon | To D.A.A.G. 1. G.H.Q., 3rd Echelon. |
|---|---|
| Date 9. 5. 1919 | |

Herewith is forwarded War Diary of Anson Battn. for April 1919.

Please acknowledge receipt.

G. G. Mault [signature]

Captain. R.M.

O. i/c RND Section

APRIL 1919

Instructions regarding War Diaries and Intelligence Summaries are contained in F. S. Regs., Part II. and the Staff Manual respectively. Title pages will be prepared in manuscript.

# WAR DIARY
*or*
~~INTELLIGENCE SUMMARY.~~
*(Erase heading not required.)*

ANSON BATT
63rd (RN) DIV.

63.

Army Form C. 2118.

Vol 35

| Place | Date | Hour | Summary of Events and Information | Remarks and references to Appendices |
|---|---|---|---|---|
| WASMES | 1st. | | Inspection parade. Ration Strength. Officers 17 O Ranks 98. | |
| do | 2nd. | | do | |
| do | 3rd. | | do. | |
| do | 4th. | | do Ration strength. Officers 13 O Ranks 95. | |
| | | | Sub Lieuts - Jackson, Gaghard, Lee + Whelley to UK for demobilization. | |
| | | | Re. Martin, C.F. rejoin from leave to U.K. | |
| do | 5th | | Inspection parade Sub. Lt. J.J. Connington. R.G. Burgess. Capt. C.E. Martin to Brussels. leave. | |
| do | 6th | | R.C. Church service Voluntary. Ration Strength. officers 6. OR. 68. Sub. Lts. S. Holland. | |
| | | | J.M. Law. J.E.C. Edwards. Lt. T.I. Williams to U.K. for Demobilization. | |
| do | 7th | | Inspection parade. Sub. Lts. J.J. Connington. R.G. Burgess Capt. C.E. Martin from | |
| | | | Brussels leave. | |
| do. | 8. | | Inspection Parade | |
| do | 9 | | " " Ration Strength. Officers. 8. O.Rs 64. Sub. Lt. J.J. Connington to U.K. demobilization | |
| do | 10. | | " " Sub. Lt. H.D. Phillips from U.K. Conducting. | |
| do | 11. | | " " Rev. C.W. Martyn. C.F. to army occupation. | |
| do | 12. | | " " Ration Strength officers. 9. O.Rs. 64. Sub. Lt. A. Heslop. from U.K conducting. | |
| do. | 13. | | Church Service R.C. (Voluntary) Comdr. A.W. Buckle. D.S.O. RNVR. from U.K. leave. | |

D. D. & L., London, E.C.
(A10250) Wt W5300/P713 750,000 2/18 Sch. 52 Forms/C/2118/16

APRIL. 1919

Instructions regarding War Diaries and Intelligence Summaries are contained in F. S. Regs., Part II. and the Staff Manual respectively. Title pages will be prepared in manuscript.

# WAR DIARY
*or*
~~INTELLIGENCE SUMMARY.~~
*(Erase heading not required.)*

ANSON BATT
63rd (RN) DIV.

Army Form C. 2118.

| Place | Date | Hour | Summary of Events and Information | Remarks and references to Appendices |
|---|---|---|---|---|
| WASMES | 14 | | Inspection Parade Comdr. A.W. Buckle D.S.O. R.N.V.R. assumes command Anson Bttn. | |
| | 15 | | do. Ration Strength officers 11. OR. 62. | |
| | 16 | | do. | |
| | 17 | | do. | |
| | 18 | | do. Ration strength. officers 11. ORs. 64. | |
| | 19 | | do. | |
| | 20 | | R.C. Voluntary Church Service. | |
| | 21 | | Inspection Parade. Ration strength. officers. 11. OR. 63. | |
| | 22 | | do. A/Lt. C.H. Barker RNVR. reverts to rank of Sub Lt. RNVR. on ceasing to command a Company. Sub. Lt. R.G. Burgess. RNVR. is appointed Brigade claims officer. | |
| | 23 | | Inspection Parade. Ration strength officers 11 OR. 64 | |
| | 24 | | do Sub Lt T.S. O'Brien to UK for Repatriation | |
| | 25 | | do | |
| | 26 | | do Ration strength officers 11 OR. 64. | |
| | 27 | | Church Service (Voluntary) | |
| | 28 | | do | |
| | 29 | | do Ration strength officers 11 OR. 64 | |
| | 30 | | do | |

A.W. Buckle

D. D. & L., L. (A10266) Wt W3300/P713 750,00[illegible] C2118/16

www.ingramcontent.com/pod-product-compliance
Lightning Source LLC
Chambersburg PA
CBHW080900230426
43663CB00013B/2591
* 9 7 8 1 4 7 4 5 3 3 9 7 3 *